1993

WALLACE STEVENS
& THE FEMININE

WALLACE STEVENS & THE FEMININE

Edited by Melita Schaum

THE UNIVERSITY OF ALABAMA PRESS

Tuscaloosa and London

Cover illustration by Terry Kihara

Book and jacket design by Paula Dennis

∞

The paper on which this book is printed meets the
minimum requirements of American National Standard
for Information Science-Permanence of Paper for Printed
Library Materials, ANSI Z39.48-1984.

Library of Congress Cataloging-in-Publication Data
Wallace Stevens and the feminine / edited by Melita Schaum.
p.   cm.
Includes bibliographical references and index.
ISBN 0-8173-0666-8
1. Stevens, Wallace, 1879–1955—Criticism and interpretation.
2. Femininity (Psychology) in literature.   3. Sex role in
literature.   4. Women in literature.   I. Schaum, Melita, 1957–   .
PS3537.T4753Z873   1993
811'.52—dc20   92-23098

British Library Cataloguing-in-Publication Data available

In memory of
Deborah Candace Brown
and
Rainer Sell

gifted colleagues,
gentle friends—
with us in memory,
beside us in the spirit
of our endeavors

Contents

Preface

The tradition of Wallace Stevens studies has ever been one of debate. Stevens has been the figure at the heart of most major critical controversies of the twentieth century, from the early emergence of New Criticism through the past decade's battles over poststructuralism. With the recent interest in gender issues, Stevens continues to be a catalyst for critical theory and practice, as his poetry continually invites deeper evaluation and as the general project of revisionism refreshes our view of the American literary canon and its major figures.

The ten essays in this collection, by scholars of Stevens and modernism, take as their focus Wallace Stevens' relationship to the feminine in both his work and his life. In so doing, they demonstrate how the variable of gender can provide new textual views on Stevens' poetry; new explorations of theory; original psychological, biographical, and historical perspectives; fresh reflections on the social and cultural shaping of American poetry; and insights into the viability of current critical debates. But the reader will find here something far more than a random collage of critical views or, alternately, any unified move toward consensus on either Stevens or gender studies. Indeed, as befits any dynamic, evolving area of inquiry, the voices in this collection make up a lively conversation, as they intersect and challenge one another, complement and diverge, test and expand prior and current theories in the best discursive tradition of scholarship.

Each of the essays in part 1, "Texts," seeks to expand our under-standing of Stevens' poetry by examining the ways gender acts as a dynamic principle within language itself and as a paradigm for the schisms or multiple voices that inform the artist's search for expression. The first three essays touch upon Jungian images of the feminine, but with markedly different outcomes. Jacqueline Vaught Brogan examines the problematic "infection in the sentence" that results from Stevens'—and Western culture's—repression of the "feminine" in favor of the authoritative "masculine" voice. In Stevens' case, this struggle is fig-ured as the agon between his conscious self and the anima or "feminine within" and represents a rift that he sought to heal throughout his career.

Mary Arensberg also remarks on the centrality of the feminine, in her psychoanalytic approach to Stevens' poetry, yet in contrast to Brogan depicts a "shadowy romance," an erotic drama of absence and desire played out in the figure of the interior paramour as she evolves from the early poems to the late. A third view is represented by Barbara Fisher, who by isolating the intellective and prophetic elements in Stevens' figures of the feminine, demonstrates a dense texture of allusion which evades and explodes prior theories.

Building on this understanding of Stevens' highly allusive quality, Daniel O'Hara suggests a potentially more fruitful theoretical model for Stevens' evasions in the work of Julia Kristeva. O'Hara draws on Kristeva's concept of the semiotic recovery of "the lost thing" to help explain both Stevens' lyric power as well as the general High Modernist "resistance of style" to critical examination. Paul Morrison concludes this section by applying the work of Lacan and Derrida to the linguistic construction of the "proper name" via the feminine figure in Stevens, Wordsworth, and Milton.

Part 2, "Contexts," moves beyond Stevens' poetry into the broader arenas of religion, politics, and culture, examining how Stevens' life intersected with these concerns, and demonstrating how a focus on gen-der reveals the subtleties of such involvements. Essays by C. Roland Wagner and Rosamond Rosenmeier look at the themes of belief in Stevens' life and work. Taking as his point of departure the controversial deathbed conversion, Wagner explores the intricacies of Stevens' lifelong ambivalences by calling on the pre-Oedipal attachment to the mother. Rosenmeier extends her study to the female figure of Wisdom in the pietistic heritage and the maternal traditions so formative for Stevens' thought.

In the next essay, Celeste Goodridge introduces the issue of Stevens and politics through the eyes of Stevens' contemporary, Marianne Moore, tracing how Moore's negative responses to Stevens' personal reserve and "bravura" evolved into her positive identification with his aloofness from mass politics in the 1930s. My examination of Stevens' personal politics during the 1940s and 1950s compares critics of Stevens with those of H.D., another High Modernist poet difficult to locate in political thought, yet whose revival at the hands of feminist critics might provide a prototype for understanding Stevens' poetics as well. Finally, Lisa Steinman looks at the cultural pressures internalized by the male poet in America and the struggle by both Emerson and Stevens to accommodate the tensions inherent in a society which designates strictly male and female, public and private spheres of endeavor.

Summaries, of course, do scant justice to the richness and originality of these authors' investigations—for that, the reader must look ahead. Taken together, these essays provide an introduction to the varied directions possible in gender studies and the fresh insights such issues can bring to Stevens criticism.

I wish to thank John N. Serio, editor of the *Wallace Stevens Journal*, for his help in sponsoring the special issue, "Stevens and Women" (Fall 1988), from which this book eventually evolved, and Michele Rushman, my assistant on that early project and historiographer of its many developments to this final stage. A special word of thanks goes to Terry Kihara, who contributed the cover art for this collection, a tribute to her sensitive talent both as an artist and a friend.

Working with these contributors has been a particularly enjoyable and illuminating process, due not only to their professional dedication but also to their personal generosity and patience during the long months of planning, coordinating, and corresponding. The project has done much to challenge and stimulate my own thinking about Stevens and gender, and I hope readers of this collection will share in that experience, finding ever-new perspectives on this poet's voice and "the complications of which it is composed."

MELITA SCHAUM

Acknowledgments

The following publishers, individuals, and archives have generously given permission to use extended quotations from the following copyrighted works:

from *Wallace Stevens: The Intensest Rendezvous* by Barbara M. Fisher, copyright 1990 by the University Press of Virginia;

from *H.D.: Collected Poems 1912–1944* edited by Louis L. Martz, copyright 1982 by The Estate of Hilda Doolittle, used by permission of New Directions Publishing Corporation;

from previously unpublished material by Marianne Moore used by permission of Marianne Craig Moore, Literary Executor for the Estate of Marianne C. Moore, all rights reserved;

acknowledgment is made to the Rosenbach Museum and Library, Philadelphia, PA, for permission to quote from unpublished materials in the Marianne Moore archive, all rights reserved;

"Well Moused, Lion (Wallace Stevens)" by Marianne Moore, copyright 1924, renewed 1952 by Marianne Moore, *The Complete Prose of Marianne Moore* by Patricia C. Willis, Editor, used by permission of Viking Penguin, a division of Penguin Books USA Inc.;

from "No Rule of Procedure: The Open Poetics of H.D." by Alicia Ostriker, copyright 1990. This essay appears in *Signets: Reading H.D.*, ed. Rachel Blau du Plessis and Susan Stanford Friedman, Indiana University Press, 1991;

from *The Collected Works of Ralph Waldo Emerson* edited by Robert Spiller, Alfred Fergusson, et al., copyright 1971–   by the Belknap Press of Harvard University;

from Wallace Stevens, *The Collected Poems of Wallace Stevens* (1954), *Letters of Wallace Stevens* (1966) edited by Holly Stevens, *The Necessary Angel* (1951), *Opus Posthumous* (1957) edited by Samuel French Morse, *Souvenirs and Prophecies: The Young Wallace Stevens* (1977) edited by Holly Stevens, all reprinted by permission of Alfred A. Knopf, Inc. (United States and Canada) and Faber and Faber Ltd. (British Commonwealth);

from *The Wallace Stevens Journal* copyright 1988 by The Wallace Stevens Society, Inc.

Abbreviations

CP	*The Collected Poems of Wallace Stevens*
L	*Letters of Wallace Stevens*
NA	*The Necessary Angel*
OP	*Opus Posthumous,* 1957 edition
OP89	*Opus Posthumous,* 1989 edition
SP	*Souvenirs and Prophecies*

WALLACE STEVENS & THE FEMININE

Part I

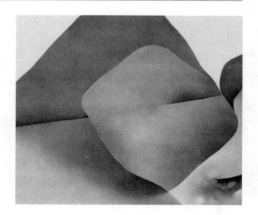

TEXTS

"Sister of the Minotaur"
Sexism and Stevens

Jacqueline Vaught Brogan

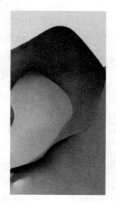

It would be easy to oversimplify the subject of sexism and Stevens as sexism *in* Stevens. The various biographies devoted to Wallace Stevens over the last decade have all, individually and collectively, given us information about his private life, especially in relation to his wife, that make it increasingly difficult to think of Stevens as that innocent, cherub-like person that Randall Jarrell once described him as being.[1] I have in mind, for example, Stevens' effective silencing of Elsie (as described by the family chauffeur to Peter Brazeau), or the disturbing way in which he "scripted" her—literally made her an object of his pen, renaming her according to his needs—as seen in the previously un-published letters to his wife included in Joan Richardson's biography.[2] In light of these new facts about Stevens' personal life, it is perhaps not surprising to find a recent and almost scathing indictment of Stevens' irresponsibility, if not moral failure, in his relationship with and to women.[3] Yet my subject here is not sexism *in* Stevens, in the sense of Stevens' being a sexist individual, nor am I trying to psychoanalyze what in Stevens' life might or might not have led to a troubled psyche, par-ticularly concerning women. It seems almost too easy to point to Stevens' mother as a figure for the imagination, in continual conflict with his father as a figure for pragmatic action and reason. I think, too, that one could exploit the fact that Elsie Moll Stevens, who was so clearly per-

ceived by Stevens in the early years as his muse, should be at once the
girl from the wrong side of the tracks, possibly illegitimate, and the
model for the goddess on the liberty coin,[4] the two archetypal—and
equally dehumanizing—ways of viewing women in our culture thus both
being accidentally inscribed in Elsie's life. Although these various facts
may suggest, once again, that the personal *is* political, I want to distinguish as much as possible the subject of sexism *in* Stevens from
sexism *and* Stevens, even if finally the two topics prove inseparable.
What interests me here, therefore, is what happens to Stevens' poetry as
he engages in the (perhaps conscious) suppression of what *he* perceives
to be his feminine voice or, more accurately, that part of his poetic voice
that is feminine metaphorically in the way the idea of "feminine" itself is
metaphorical. My conclusion is, while Stevens would always suffer from
a schism within himself, one that was ultimately derived from cultural
biases against women (and which would affect his poetry in a number of
important ways), he would also come as close as it was possible for a
person in his time and circumstance to "curing" himself of the "infection
in the sentence" the dominant, phallocentric structures in our culture
inevitably breed.[5]

I

The distinction I am making between sexism *in* Stevens and sexism
and Stevens is not meant to deny the fact that there are sexist innuendoes
in Stevens' poetry. Certain sexist assumptions, including the one that
denigrating women is humorous, account for a number of his poems,
including "To a High-Toned Old Christian Woman."[6] It is not merely
institutionalized religion Stevens is mocking there. "To a High-Toned
Old Christian Man" does not seem nearly as funny, and I speculate that
trying to make "*widowers* wince" would not be perceived as being especially witty either. Similar attitudes also inform "Lulu Gay" (*OP,* 26)
and "Lulu Morose" (*OP,* 27), although the first of these, in which Lulu
tells the eunuchs what the barbarians have done to her, is immediately
more problematic. It is probably right to the point that the males who

have been castrated have lost their "voice" as well—they cannot talk (but only ulullate). Certainly, we find an archetypal expression of sexism in that poem with the wonderful title, "Good Man. Bad Woman" (*OP*, 33). In fact, such basic sexist attitudes—even if we are charitable and conclude that Stevens intends to poke fun at such attitudes—govern a number of his poems. For example, there is no character in all of Stevens' poetry, for example, with quite the same sense of grotesque humor as the woman of "The Emperor of Ice-Cream"—dead, lying on a deal dresser with her "horned feet" protruding (*CP*, 184).

When we find instances of such blatant sexism *in* Stevens, it is useful to remember the cultural context within which he produced his work. When Stevens began publishing in earnest, the women's suffrage movement was well under way and frequently was the subject of essays in the magazines in which Stevens was publishing (and which he was presumably reading himself). Many of these essays are surprisingly sophisticated. As early as 1914 Edna Kenton was distinguishing between different kinds of feminisms, that is, the largely Anglo-American drive for identical rights versus the German feminists' fight for different but equal rights for women.[7] Yet even in such magazines as the *Trend*, which seems far more sympathetic to the women's movement than most because it kept a running tally on which states were supporting women's suffrage, we find some rather appallingly sexist essays, among them "The Land of the Hen-Pecked" or "Rule the Women or They'll Rule You."[8] The title of this last one sounds much like Stevens in "Good Man. Bad Woman" when he says, "She can corrode your world, if never you" (*OP*, 33).

In fact, as Joan Kelly and Sandra Gilbert (among others) have pointed out, the strides women have made in gaining civic and political rights have also historically been accompanied by periods of increased hostility toward women.[9] This conflict—the liberation of woman politically and the increased resentment toward, if not repression of her personally— accounts for the overwhelming number of poems written during Stevens' early period that expose women's status (or lack of status) in the early part of this century. For example, we find in magazines to which Stevens himself was contributing, H.D.'s "Priapus" and "Acon," Alice Groff's "Herm-Aphrodite-Us," the five poems about women that Pound published in a 1915 issue of *Others*, Skipwith Cannell's "Ikons," published the following year, and Kenneth Burke's "Adam's Song, and Mine."[10] The overt tension in this phase of the battle of the sexes toward which all of these poems point is made explicit in Helen Hoyt's "Homage,"[11] cited in part below:

> Not as a man I felt you in my brooding,
> But merely a babe. . . .
> . . . .
> Sometimes I wished to feed you at my breast.
>
> Not to myself, I knew, belonged your homage;
> I but the vessel of your holy drinking,
> The channel to you of that olden wonder
> Of love and womanhood,—I, but a woman.
> . . . .
> Do you think I did not kneel when you were kneeling?
> Even lowlier bowed my head, and bowed my heart.

What makes this poem particularly interesting is the difficulty in assessing how much irony may or may not have been intended, although it is important to note, both for her own work and for a sense of the times in which Stevens first began publishing, that Helen Hoyt would edit a special issue of women poets for *Others* one year after publishing this poem.[12] Nevertheless, when we do find sexist assumptions or innuendoes in Stevens' work, we face a similar dilemma in frequently being unable to determine precisely how much Stevens is reflecting cultural biases or just how much he is revising such biases through ironic reflections. Yet despite this very complicated context, it is possible to see the ways in which Stevens' perhaps conscious, perhaps unconscious "phallocentric" perspective manifests itself in the dynamics, even the problematics of his poetry. That problematic may not be the conflict between imagination and reality (as has been traditionally assumed), nor even the battle between competing theories of language, but rather a problematic between feminine and masculine expression—between the male authorial voice that strives to achieve significance and the culturally delineated suppression or silencing of feminine voice that struggles, nonetheless, precisely for expression in Stevens' works. Put differently, in Stevens' work we can see the ways in which our culturally inscribed notions of male/author/authority and our culturally inscribed repression of the rest of our human voice (even within ourselves, and within Stevens as well) frustrate the attempt at poetic expression itself, while informing what expressions are achieved in the individual poems.

To understand this critical facet of Stevens' work, it is important first to stress the fact that from the rejection of the feminine figure in "Farewell to Florida" to her reception in "Final Soliloquy of the Interior Paramour," Stevens' poetry remains highly self-conscious about the fact that is *is* wrestling with the feminine figure and, usually in a rather Jungian fashion, specifically with the feminine figure within. As a mere sampling of this self-conscious struggle, I offer four texts, taken variously from his essays, letters, *Collected Poems*, and *Opus Posthumous* over the course of his career. The first is from "Farewell without a Guitar," written in 1954, just one year before he died:

> Spring's bright paradise has come to this.
> Now the thousand-leaved green falls to the ground.
> Farewell, my days.
> . . . .
>
>   The reflections and repetitions,
> The blows and buffets of fresh senses
> Of the rider that was,
>
> Are a final construction,
> Like glass and sun, of male reality
> And of that other and her desire.
>
>   (*OP,* 98–99)

While the rather poignantly glossed "rider that was" refers to the failure of Stevens' attempt to create—and to become—the "Noble Rider" of 1942 (*NA,* 1–36), it is possible to say that from "To the One of Fictive Music" (1922) to the end of his life, much of Stevens' corpus is written in response to that significant "other." Yet *this* female figure, so nebulously and delicately evoked, is not the Elsie he largely dominated in his personal life, nor his mother—nor a high-toned old Christian woman for that matter—but precisely a part of himself that he could never fully come to know except as "she" was traced in his poetry.

Significantly, in the second of these texts (section ten of "Esthétique du Mal"), Stevens distinguishes between two sets of female figures in his poetry, implicitly suggesting an awareness of a problem in his figurations of women and, even more implicitly, suggesting the possibility of resolution in an androgynous figure:

> He had studied the nostalgias. In these
> He sought the most grossly maternal, the creature
> Who most fecundly assuaged him, the softest
> Woman with a vague moustache and not the mauve
> *Maman*. His anima liked its animal
> And liked it unsubjugated, so that home
> Was a return to birth. . . .
> . . . .
> It is true there were other mothers, singular
> In form, lovers of heaven and earth, she-wolves
> And forest tigresses and women mixed
> With the sea. These were fantastic.
>
> (*CP*, 321)

These "other mothers," immediately troped in the text to the monstrous she-wolves and tigresses, are the fantastic manifestations of his own feminine voice, or anima, repressed throughout most of his poetic career. Thus, one effect of his conscious repression of the feminine principle in "Farewell to Florida" (though there is ample evidence of unconscious repression before that poem appeared in 1936) manifests itself in the extreme attention to "man number one" in "The Man with the Blue Guitar" (1937) with, however, a concurrent monstrous version of his poetic self that he has largely tried to subjugate. It is both culturally and poetically predictable that whereas this "monster" in "The Man with the Blue Guitar" *may* be male (the "lion in the lute / Before the lion locked in stone" [*CP*, 175]), in general the uncomposed and, therefore, potentially destructive aspect of his creative energy is perceived or figured by Stevens as a (threatening) woman.

This fact leads to a third text, a passage from "The Figure of the Youth as Virile Poet." After making the rather remarkable statement that "The centuries have a way of being male" (NA, 52), and before insisting that the "character of the poet" must be seen as "*virile*" or else "the masculine nature that we propose for one that must be the master of our lives will be lost" (NA, 66),[13] Stevens says: "When we look back at the face of the seventeenth century, it is at the rigorous face of the rigorous thinker and, say, the Miltonic image of a poet, severe and determined. In effect, what we are remembering is the rather haggard background of the incredible, the imagination without intelligence, from which a younger figure is emerging, stepping forward in the company of a muse of its own, *still half-beast and somehow more than human, a kind of sister of the Minotaur*. The younger figure is the intelligence that endures. It is the imagination of the son still bearing the antique imagination of the father" (NA, 52–53; italics added). The essentially androgynous character of this figure (inasmuch as the "sister" is also the "son"), together with the one cited above, bears further study—particularly in the context of the often frustrated quest for androgynous union traced in much of the romantic poetry preceding (and anticipating) Jungian theory. Nevertheless, as I read this particular essay, Stevens is seriously engaged in a deliberate battle to overcome the kind of schism within himself that would give rise precisely to this kind of distortion in which the feminine aspect is marked and perpetually marred by "monstrous" displacement.[14] Yet at least in 1942 when this essay was written, Stevens' own language inhibits such a cure. Not only does he still think of the poet as someone who must master our lives (and who must be male), he also writes these ironically self-defeating words at the very point the "figure of the youth as the virile poet" supposedly speaks or finds his own voice: "No longer do I believe that there is a mystic muse, sister of the Minotaur. This is another of the monsters I had for nurse, whom I have wasted. I am myself a part of what is real, and it is my own speech and the strength of it, this only, that I hear or ever shall" (NA, 60). What is most provocative about this passage, especially because it is in such conflict with the semantic intent, is that even as he rejects the sister of the Minotaur at the supposed moment of self-identification, he reinstates the figure of the monster as a (presumably female) nurse.

The last text is simply the letter that followed Howard Baker's analysis of Wallace Stevens in *Southern Review* ("Wallace Stevens and Other Poets")[15] in which Baker describes Stevens' poetry in Jungian terms. In a letter to Ronald Latimer in 1935, Stevens writes: "There is in the last number of the SOUTHERN REVIEW, or QUARTERLY, an extremely intelligent analysis of my work by Howard Baker. No one before has ever come as close to me as Mr. Baker does in that article" (*L*, 292). This letter shows that, even at an early point, Stevens thought in somewhat Jungian terms about his own poetry, and therefore attention to the male and female figures (and hence to their voices or lack of voices) in Stevens' work is central to our understanding of it.

Stevens engages in the repression of the feminine aspect of his own creativity or creative voice in a variety of ways. It may well be that the culturally encouraged suppression of women—specifically the silencing of women—is internalized in Stevens,[16] so that his psyche feels at once a longing for this displaced self (hence, the omnipresent "she," the "other and her desire") while simultaneously feeling threatened by what might be chaos, uncontrollable, if he abandons his "rage to order" by allowing her to speak. But, whatever the reasons, "a kind of sister of the Minotaur" is the uncanny and uncomfortable figure repressed—ambivalently and ambiguously held—in the white space of Stevens' texts.

II

This repression manifests itself ironically, if not subversively, in Stevens' work throughout his poetic career. Most obviously, Stevens rejects the feminine figures of *Harmonium*, especially the figures of female, fecund nature in the 1936 "Farewell to Florida" (the poem he used to open the *second* version of *Ideas of Order*).[17] There he accuses "her" of having bound "him round" and says that he will return to the land of the "violent mind," which is equivalent to the land of the violent men

(*CP*, 117–18). Yet repression of the feminine figure occurs in Stevens in more subtle and ultimately more significant ways, although the particular, conscious rejection of the feminine seen in "Farewell to Florida" encouraged the more abstract, philosophical poetry of the many years to come.

Ironically, one of the most telling marks of Stevens' repression of the feminine is that in his poetry female figures almost never speak. If any voice is heard at all (and that itself is a subject to take up below), it is that of a male, as in "Two Figures in Dense Violet Night":[18]

> Be the voice of night and Florida in my ear.
> Use dusky words and dusky images.
> Darken your speech.
>
> Speak, even, as if I did not hear you speaking,
> But spoke for you perfectly in my thoughts,
> Conceiving words,
>
> As the night conceives the sea-sounds in silence,
> And out of their droning sibilants makes
> A serenade.
>
> (*CP*, 86)

One exception to this generalization is the woman in "Metropolitan Melancholy," the "purple woman" with the "lavender tongue" who "Said hic, said hac, / Said ha" (*OP*, 32). Another is the quoted "*Encore un instant de bonheur*," words that Stevens immediately dismisses: "The words / Are a woman's words, unlikely to satisfy / The taste of even a country connoisseur" (*CP*, 157). Here, it is admittedly difficult to distinguish the repression of the feminine voice from basic sexism. Nevertheless, a glance at the *Concordance* to Stevens' poetry surprisingly reveals that "words" are not Stevens' most popular theme, but "man" or "men" (appearing 507 times) and, especially, man speaking.[19] Women appear in Stevens' poetry about one fifth as frequently—a total of 106 times compared to 507 for men. But in contrast to the men, women almost never have a voice. From the early "All Over Minnesota," where the "voice of the wind is male,"[20] through "A Thought Revolved" and *The Necessary Angel*, the idea of "voice" itself is perceived by Stevens as exclusively masculine. But then, I think we can say, he protests too much.

One extension of this verbal repression is the fact that Stevens' female figures not only rarely speak, but they rarely move. Consider the difference between his earliest and most famous male and female characters, "The Comedian as the Letter C" and the complacent woman of "Sunday Morning." In a very disturbing way, women in his poetry remain too obviously figures—empty ciphers for masculine rumination and scripting, even de-scription.[21] The woman of "Sunday Morning" has several sisters, among them "So-and-So Reclining on Her Couch" and "Romance for a Demoiselle Lying in the Grass," in which Stevens writes that

> The monotony
> Is like your port which conceals
> All your characters
> And their desires.

(*OP*, 23)

In the course of the poem this female figure is either troped to or revealed to be a guitar; Stevens closes the poem with "Clasp me, / Delicatest machine." But this revelation, if we can call it that, further "objectifies" the feminine, even if metaphorically, "concealing" her behind a phallocentric and concomitantly erotic perspective that is reminiscent of the elders' view of Susanna in "Peter Quince at the Clavier" (*CP*, 89–92).

Nonetheless, precisely because he still retains the idea of a feminine muse (even if she may be figured as a "kind of sister of the Minotaur"), Stevens' attempts to repress or silence the feminine leaves *him* in the position of never being able to speak. Almost without exception, Stevens' greatest attempts at poetic expression, the words of that "virile poet," are instances of failures of speech—words about the words he *would* say, if he could—signs, shall we say, of the failure of both logocentric and phallocentric ordering. For example, Stevens says in "Notes toward a Supreme Fiction" that it is "As if the waves at last were never broken, / As if the language suddenly, with ease, / Said things it had laboriously spoken" (*CP*, 387). Again in "Primitive Like an Orb," Stevens writes with an implicit pathos that

It is
As if the central poem became the world,
And the world the central poem, each one the mate
Of the other, as if summer was a spouse,
Espoused each morning

(*CP*, 441)

Thus, despite his sustained attempt to evoke—or to become—the "virile" poet, one whose words both master and are a part of what is real, that which he cannot order or master insists upon being heard, however ironically, in the very silence of the gap between "as" and "if," that is, between "order" and the "abyss," as these terms are metaphorically and sexually conceived. The white writing of such texts is perversely and subversively the trace of the repressed voice that refuses to (or cannot) coincide with the phallic and verbal structures Stevens professes to order in his words. Hence Stevens' lifelong frustration about his inability to get "straight to the word, / Straight to the transfixing object" (*CP*, 471)—and hence, also, his desire.

From this perspective, "The Idea of Order at Key West" can be seen to reiterate this basic problematic in Stevens' verse, rather than embodying one of his more successful figurations of women as many critics have assumed. [22] In contrast to the other women figures mentioned so far, the celebrated female figure of this poem is, superficially, neither mocked or denigrated; she is also supposedly vocal and dynamic, walking and singing by the shore:

And when she sang, the sea,
Whatever self it had, became the self
That was her song, for she was the maker. Then we,
As we beheld her striding there alone,
Knew that there never was a world for her
Except the one she sang and, singing, made.

(*CP*, 129–30)

However alluring this poem may be, we run the risk of being ruled by rhetoric if we fail to note that ultimately—and even in the narrative development of the text itself—this "woman" is simply a figure for (and thus a sign or empty cipher for) Stevens himself and the way *he* sings. The clearest sign of this is found in the very next line, where he abruptly breaks in with, "Ramon Fernandez, tell me, if you know. . . ." This rupture is the most overt sign in the poem of the nature of the poetic "order" (even "rage for order") that Stevens has in mind. This thematic is inscribed throughout the poem: lights "master" the night, "portion" out the sea, "arrange" and "deepen" night, so that the words, in a kind of phallic "mastering," ironically create the "fragrant portals," essentially create the feminine. But what do we hear from this feminine voice, which is simultaneously created, disclosed in the portals, and repressed— silenced by the "mastering" as well as by Stevens' actual appropriation of the unheard feminine voice? From the opening stanza, that other voice remains literally "beyond" us and ourselves:

> She sang beyond the genius of the sea.
> The water never formed to mind or voice,
> Like a body wholly body, fluttering
> Its empty sleeves; and yet its mimic motion
> Made constant cry, caused constantly a cry,
> That was not ours although we understood,
> Inhuman, of the veritable ocean.

> (*CP*, 128)

The need for this control—the imperative to create and to control a world in words—can in part be explained historically and culturally. The Great Depression, the Great War, the threat of a second world war to come, would easily give rise to the need to defend oneself against looming chaos, a fact that is amply demonstrated by the poems of Stevens' middle period.[23] But I think at least part of the explanation for Stevens' apparent need to break into the text—to silence this feminine figure, however lovely we may feel she may be—lies in her uncanny reflection, that "sister of the Minotaur." The lovely, virtually inhuman woman by the sea and the somewhat unsettling half-beast who is "yet more than human" are two faces, as it were, of the same figure that, as figure, also means absence and repression. Instead of the madwoman in the attic, this is a (potentially) mad woman in a maze, specifically a linguistic maze.

The idealized version of the figure, the one who remains beyond speech, desired but controlled, together with her monstrous counterpart account for many of Stevens' more fantastic female characters. The idealized figure is found in "To the One of Fictive Music," where, for example, Stevens creates a feminine trilogy of sister, mother, and diviner love (*CP*, 87–88), in "Infanta Marina," where "She" can make "of the motions of her wrist / The grandiose gestures / Of her thought" (*CP*, 7), as well as in "Apostrophe to Vincentine" and "Bouquet of Belle Scavoir." Yet her monstrous counterpart is found in "The Woman Who Blamed Life on a Spaniard," where "she never clears / But spreads an evil lustre whose increase / Is evil" (*OP*, 34), in the fifth of "Five Grotesque Pieces" (entitled "Outside of Wedlock"), where she is figured as "an old bitch, an old drunk, / That has been yelling in the dark" (*OP*, 77), and even in "The Common Life," where quite significantly, given the title, "women have only one side" (*CP*, 221). In "The Old Woman and the Statue," she has all the attributes of a witch:

> But her he had not foreseen: the bitter mind
> In a flapping cloak. She walked along the paths
> Of the park with chalky brow scratched over black
> And black by thought that could not understand
> Or, if it understood, repressed itself
> Without any pity in a somnolent dream.
>
> (*OP*, 44)

Still, it would not be accurate to reduce Stevens' poetry to reiterating endlessly this conflict within himself. If Stevens suffered (and I think he did suffer) from a schism within himself, he also seems not only to have been aware of that but to have tried to "cure" himself. Even as early as "Last Looks at the Lilacs," he is contemptuous of that "rational caliber," that "arrogantly male, / Patron and imager" (*CP*, 48–49). And he also condemns, albeit playfully, that "damned universal cock" in "Bantams in Pine-Woods" who, in a quintessentially phallocentric way, thinks that he is the center of the universe (*CP*, 75–76). To this end I see an important development between "The Idea of Order at Key West" and his well-known "Final Soliloquy of the Interior Paramour" (*CP*, 524).

III

In contrast to the earlier poem of 1934, in Stevens' 1950 lyric, divisiveness in voice and self is recognized rather than being "written over" or suppressed. The divisiveness is even explicitly held within the interior (rather than being described fallaciously as a split between a dominating male poet/author/authority and a submitting, potentially chaotic feminine world). As the word "paramour" suggests, there is a romance, even an intimacy/communion/communication in this poem that is dependent upon "dif-ference" (to use Heidegger's term). The most telling sign of this is the plural pronoun "we" and that most feminine of articles, the "shawl," wrapped tightly round them since they "are poor":

Light the first light of evening, as in a room
In which we rest and, for small reason, think
The world imagined is the ultimate good.

This is, therefore, the intensest rendezvous.
It is in that thought that we collect ourselves,
Out of all the indifferences, into one thing:

Within a single thing, a single shawl
Wrapped tightly round us, since we are poor. . . .

(*CP*, 524)

Even though Stevens' characteristic tone of dominance is absent in this poem, the recognition and recovery of the feminine voice do not undermine the poetic authorship as Stevens obviously feared they would in "Farewell to Florida." Instead, the recovery of this voice gives expression to what is beyond control, beyond order, beyond dominance in our actual lives and thereby endows with significance that little which we can order in words: "Out of this same light, out of the central mind, / We make a dwelling in the evening air, / In which being together is enough" (*CP*, 524). In this poem the phallocentric "central mind" is consciously exposed as a fiction—not heralded as the "ideal realm" where the "new bourgeois man feels historically untouchable," as Frank Lentricchia has recently argued.[24] From the opening stanza, there is only "small reason" to "think / The world imagined is the ultimate good," a delicate disclaimer that quietly but continually dismantles the covert assumptions about and equations of reason, thinking, imagination, and essentially all Western (or at least Platonic) idealizations. But in submitting to the realization of the fictionality of our orderings—including the largely phallocentric privileging of the idea of order itself—*this* poem manages finally to be heard as fully human and humane. In essence, the recovery here of the feminine voice, which is so silenced in his early poems, especially after *Harmonium*, opens up the space in Stevens for the magnificent voice of his later years, one heard, for example, in "The Planet on the Table" and "Lebensweisheitspielerei," where he admits, in opposition to the "portentous enunciation" (*CP*, 43) of his earlier work, that

> The proud and the strong
Have departed.

> Those that are left are the unaccomplished,
> The finally human,
> Natives of a dwindled sphere

—but a sphere in which "Each person completely touches *us*" (*CP*, 504–5; italics added).

We should note that such a development as I have sketched here is itself reductive in a way. Certainly in "Madame La Fleurie," also a very late poem, we see the monstrous and bearded inversion of mother earth in the "bearded queen" who is devouring him (*CP*, 507). Similarly, the mother in "World without Peculiarity" becomes a hating "thing upon his breast" (*CP*, 454). Yet in general, the development I have described is accurate. As he says in "Artificial Populations," a poem written the year he died, "This artificial population [rosy men and women of the rose] is like / A healing-point in the sickness of the mind" (*OP*, 112).

How this "cure" was accomplished is itself a topic for another lengthy study, but I would like to offer a brief summary of certain touchstones in this process. After his obvious attempt to gain total voice in "The Figure of the Youth as Virile Poet," Stevens becomes increasingly obsessed with "the sound / of right joining," "The final relation, the marriage of the rest" (*CP*, 464–65). We see this desire thematized in his letters when he, perhaps surprisingly given his personal life, uses the pleasure that "a man and woman find in each other's company" as an illustration of the "pleasure" of "Cross-reflections, modifications, counter-balances, giving and taking" of the "various faculties of the mind" (*L*, 368); and it is repeated two years later in the seventh section of "Notes toward a Supreme Fiction":

> Perhaps there are times of inherent excellence,
>
> As when the cock crows on the left and all
> Is well, incalculable balances . . .
> . . . .
>   not balances
> That we achieve but balances that happen,
>
> As a man and woman meet and love forthwith.

> (*CP*, 386)

Yet despite his efforts to achieve this balance, Stevens fails to do so in "Notes" when, for example, Nanzia Nunzio fails to achieve this promise—her erotic power being so contingent upon her willingness to be scripted or subjugated:

> Speak to me that, which spoken, will array me
> In its own only precious ornament.
> . . . .
> Clothe me entire in the final filament,

So that I tremble with such love so known
And myself am precious for your perfecting.

(*CP*, 396)

The maiden Bawda and her captain perhaps fare better: at least they are both "love's characters come face to face" (*CP*, 401). Yet the last numbered section of the poem names the "Fat girl" as the "irrational, the more than rational distortion" (*CP*, 406), phrases reminiscent of those used in the same year to describe the "sister of the Minotaur." Certainly Stevens has not achieved communion with his interior paramour at this point, despite his desire to do so.

But in "Of Modern Poetry," written two years before, and later in "Burghers of Petty Death," we find men and women together, more successfully figured as equal representatives of humanity. "Modern Poetry," Stevens says, "has to be living, to learn the speech of the place. / It has to face the men of the time and to meet / The women of the time" (*CP*, 240). In the second poem, written in 1946, Stevens says:

These are the small townsmen of death,
A man and a woman, like two leaves
That keep clinging to a tree,
Before winter freezes and grows black—

(*CP*, 362)

This "woman," equal in her humanness to the "man," marks a new moment in Stevens in which "she" is not only validated but recognized both as a presence and as a human being, rather than tracing in either idealized or "monstrous" discourse the path of failed signification and signifiers.[25] If I were to indulge in psychological explanations, I would consider the possibility that the sheer, overwhelming and uncontrollable violence of the Second World War reduced all human beings in Stevens' eyes to the position of "women" in the ironically-realized, metaphorical sense of the word. We are all without power, not just women, in this modern world, unable to control the world and possibly our own lives.

Between "Of Modern Poetry" and "Burghers of Petty Death," Stevens dismisses the figure of a "bright red woman" for (presumably) a real one in a poem intriguingly called "Debris of Life and Mind":

> She will think about them not quite able to sing.
> Besides, when the sky is so blue, things sing
> themselves,
>
> Even for her, already for her. She will listen
> And feel that her color is a meditation,
>
> The most gay and yet not so gay as it was.
> Stay here. Speak of familiar things a while.
>
> (*CP*, 338)

In the last line the unexpected turn toward domestic intimacy, especially for such a previously "exotic" poet, enacts what is both a personal and poetic passage, a "fall," we might say, into the more fully human. Certainly his request, open to rejection, vulnerable, and wistful, is quite different in tone from the whole panoply of "hero" poems that preceded this poem and the earlier "rage to order."

In "Auroras of Autumn," published in 1947, Stevens implies that he meets his anima in an intense rendezvous that prepares the way for "Final Soliloquy":

> This sense of the activity of fate—
>
> The rendezvous, when she came alone,
> By her coming became a freedom of the two,
> An isolation which only the two could share.
>
> (*CP*, 419)

As Frank Doggett and Dorothy Emerson have rightly suggested, this "isolation" is an isolation because it is a rendezvous within himself, between his masculine and feminine selves.[26] What is most revealing about this description, however, is that it is specifically a "freedom of the two"—a phrase that claims at least to have achieved finally what Stevens desired as early as "The Man with the Blue Guitar": reduction of the "monster to / Myself" so that he can "be, / Two things, the two together as one" (*CP*, 175). It is also much to the point that the "mother" "who invites humanity to her house" (*CP*, 415) has in this poem "grown old" (*CP*, 413). Ultimately, she too is more vulnerable (and, therefore, human) than mythic—as is the woman in "Things of August" (1949), where she is "exhausted and a little old" (*CP*, 496). In addition, as Milton J. Bates has pointed out, it is at this moment in his career that Stevens begins so frequently to characterize himself as a child,[27] but, I would add, usually as a child of both parents, or both sexes, rather than being strictly the son "only of man" (*CP*, 185) as in the earlier "A Thought Revolved."

Finally, in "Angel Surrounded by Paysans" (1949), we come across a supposedly masculine character, "a man / Of the mind" (*CP*, 497), who finally speaks with what I see as Stevens' previously repressed feminine voice. There is no control, no mastering, no portioning of the night:

> Am I not,
> Myself, only half of a figure of a sort,
>
> A figure half seen, or seen for a moment, a man
> Of the mind, an apparition apparelled in
>
> Apparels of such lightest look that a turn
> Of my shoulder and quickly, too quickly, I am gone?
>
> (*CP*, 497)

The angel is, in fact, a "necessary angel," but one who is questioning rather than "ordering," one who is, admittedly, too easily gone, subject to change—a sign of the mutability of our best linguistic orderings. But he—she—is also finally heard *through* the door (instead of being held off beyond the portals), heard, even if only whispering. This poem, which ends the last volume of poetry that Stevens wrote before *The Rock*, achieves something of a resolution (emphasizing far more the "solution" or mixing than the earlier tone of "resolve") that finds a final plenitude in the great lyrics of his last volume, including "Final Soliloquy of the Interior Paramour."

I think, then, that there is real growth in Stevens, and that is why, despite poems like "O Florida, Venereal Soil" or "Good Man. Bad Woman," Stevens touches so many women. I have it on good authority, for example, that a leading feminist poet secretly reads Stevens, and Helen Vendler, as we know, has said Stevens has written the poems she would have written if she were a poet.[28] I think this growth also accounts for why, despite what seems to have been a very unhappy personal life, most of us still feel a certain health—humanity in its fullest sense—in reading Wallace Stevens.

2

"A Curable Separation"
Stevens and the Mythology of Gender

Mary B. Arensberg

. . . love contains the euphoric experience of 'Being at the beginning'; it is melted in an undifferentiated whole with the experience of a curable separation.

—L. Kolakowski, *The Presence of Myth*

I

Western culture is bound by myths of a fall from totality into difference that mirror the biology of separation from the mother's body. Our poetry, our music, and what D. M. Thomas calls "the great myth of psychoanalysis" all express the Westerner's mythic longing for the "undifferentiated whole" or original state before paradise was lost. The closest we come to experiencing a "cure" for what some call the disease of Western dualism, is to re-simulate "a prenatal state of elation" through nature, love, art, or even drugs.[1] Freud called this "primitive and original" state *Urzustand* and suggested that behind all later "intrusions" of the libido—that is, the overlay of desire, narcissistic striving, and the need for power—is the fetal backdrop or feeling of originary wholeness:

the ego clings to the idea that to be at one with otherness is to be safe and to be warm.

To reexperience "the mother's face" is a central idea or motivation beneath the desires, narcissistic strivings, and quest for the supreme fiction in the poetry of Wallace Stevens. "The mother's face" is for Stevens a figure that refers to that prenatal state of "profound harmony," a timeless home and Edenic existence that precedes the fall into the world of the mother's breast. The breast is the original body site of loss, separation, and longing. The apple in the garden, the mother's breast, represents the postnatal, dualistic state: life as a "bitter aspic," Stevens calls it in "Esthétique du Mal" (CP, 322), a pun pointing to the fall into differences, pain and separation, and the poison of the serpent. In Western mythology, women and serpents are scapegoats for the human lapse into time and history, as well as into gender consciousness. Female rage and the serpent are the principal elements in the myth of Tiresias, a figure of totality, whose sex changes derive from his act of separating coupling snakes and Hera's subsequent rage at his insistence on the tenfold pleasure of female sexuality over the male's.

What I call the fetal imprint in the poetry of Wallace Stevens, or the desire for a repetition of prenatal existence, is expressed in three stages: first as a "memory of a unique and privileged state of elation" with the mother's face and body; then as a muse-attachment that sets up a "special object relation" with a fiction of otherness; and finally in a resolution of narcissistic wholeness, when, in "The Rock" (CP, 526), otherness is incorporated "into a cure beyond forgetfulness."[2] There is, in the Stevens canon, a movement from a gender-centric universe through an incorporation of the feminine and on toward an "inhuman space" that gestures beyond time and difference. And like its precursor poem, The Odyssey of Homer, one of the enterprises of Stevens' poetry is to explore the nature of the male-feminine by casting a plumb line to the timeless realm of primary-process thinking, mythology, and the mother's face. The line is drawn through the feminine figure at the center of the poems: in the case of The Odyssey, it is Penelope whose weaving envisions primal union, the vision of wholeness on the tapestry that brings together the sun and the moon. In Stevens, it is the "interior paramour," the sphinx or serpent-woman beneath "the world of words" whose hair is like a pythoness and whose silent riddles write his poems.

Section Ten of "Esthétique du Mal" provides an entry into the nature of Stevens' male-feminine. In fact, these lines are a conscious attempt to exteriorize the poet's inner life and expose, in holographic detail, the feminine fictions invented to insulate him from the world and which remind him of the "home" of birth.

He had studied the nostalgias. In these
He sought the most grossly maternal, the creature
Who most fecundly assuaged him, the softest
Woman with a vague moustache and not the mauve
Maman. His anima liked its animal
And liked it unsubjugated, so that home
Was a return to birth, a being born
Again in the savagest severity,
Desiring fiercely, the child of a mother fierce
In his body, fiercer in his mind, merciless
To accomplish the truth in his intelligence.
It is true there were other mothers, singular
In form, lovers of heaven and earth, she-wolves
And forest tigresses and women mixed
With the sea. These were fantastic. There were
        homes
Like things submerged with their englutted sounds,
That were never wholly still. The softest woman,
Because she is as she was, reality,
The gross, the fecund, proved him against the touch
Of impersonal pain. Reality explained.
It was the last nostalgia: that he
Should understand. That he might suffer or that
He might die was the innocence of living, if life
Itself was innocent. To say that it was
Disentangled him from sleek ensolacings.

(*CP*, 321–22)

148,127

In many ways, this canto from "Esthétique du Mal" offers a primal scene for desire in the canon, that is, to heal the original narcissistic wound that divides all of us from the other gender within ourselves and to recover the primordial power of female sexuality that is the generative center of myth. The poet's obvious metapsychological model in this passage is Jung, and in acting out the drama of the feminine in his psyche here, Stevens invokes two types of women. The first is the pre-Oedipal, pre-Hellenic earth mother who "is the creature, with a unity of mind and body, and who moves from the estrus cycle to the menstrual cycle" and "creates our first religion, a religion of menstruation, child-birth mysteries and the phases of the moon."[3] For Robert Graves, she is connected with the origins of poetry; and for Mircea Eliade, she is an image that "unveils aspects of ultimate reality that are otherwise inaccessible."[4]

As a student of the nostalgias, that is, of the repressions of the past, Stevens also invokes the mythology of Freud and his version of the ideal, empathetic, and fantasized mother who provides the child with a sense of omnipotence and invulnerability and is always available. She is "the first nostalgia," the prenatal screen memory, the recollection of primal homeostasis before the "savage birth." C. Roland Wagner (in "The Concealed Self") suggests that Stevens' ambivalence toward "the pre-Oedipal nurturing mother is central to our understanding of Stevens," and leads us into the poet's "concealed self." As with Oedipus, whose "self" is concealed and whose innocence is only restored in death, the healing of the poet's scar scratched on the psyche by the absent or rejecting mother is another subtext in the emergence of the feminine in Stevens' poetry.

The "child" of the mother is "the softest woman," her daughter and the interior paramour. "Fierce" in his mind and body, she energizes his intelligence and represents the bacchic, pre-Apollonian reign of the Furies before they were tamed by the laws of patriarchal culture. Both the pre-Oedipal mother and her offspring, the archetype of the muse-paramour, are metaphors that conceal and disguise what Eric Gould calls the "absent metonymy," or the return to the abyss of origins.[5] Those other mothers, the mothers and archetypal figures of the collective unconscious that appear in dreams and poetry and myths, also populated the poet's mind, his "unsubjugated anima." These were the "she-wolves / And forest-tigresses and women mixed / With the sea." Submerged beneath the edges of conscious thought and flashing in dreams, they are "fantastic" and threatening, as distinguished from "the softest woman," his metonym for reality. In "Notes toward a Supreme Fiction," *The Auroras of Autumn*, and *The Rock* the feminine presence, as well as the more androgynous figure Stevens calls "the necessary angel" that presides over the late poems, are magnified and finally introjected into the psychic realm. Stevens' "anima and animal" engage in a dramatic and psychic exploration that few poets dare to experience—except, perhaps, for James Joyce as Molly Bloom whose final yea-saying, like Stevens' "yes" at the end of "Notes," is a fiction of narcissistic union.

II

But, Master, there are
Lights masculine and lights feminine.
        —Wallace Stevens

Most readers of the Stevens canon, until recently, have presumed the phallocentric nature of the "central mind" and have either ignored or possibly repressed the centrality of the feminine in the poetry. This feminine presence, as mentioned earlier, is expressed as a muse-attachment, and although she is named only once, and at the end of the canon, Stevens' interior paramour is present from the beginning, not as reality but as a reflection of the movements of her poet's mind and as their exciting cause. For she is Stevens' metaphor for the extra-linguistic source of poetry and a trope of imaginative desire, a "fiction that results from feeling," that conceals the vacancy from which she rises. Throughout the *Collected Poems*, the poet and his paramour engage in a shadowy romance that begins with the myth of the "paltry nude" starting her spring voyage in *Harmonium*, reaches its climax in the epithalamic celebrations in "Notes toward a Supreme Fiction," and ends with the reestablishing of a non-gendered, pluralized voice in "Final Soliloquy of the Interior Paramour." The romance of the poet and his paramour sets up a "special object relation" with a fictional outside. Through the defense of doubling or inventing a narcissistic nucleus that incorporates gender difference, the poet is able to set up a transference paradigm for a cure. As she mirrors the otherness within the self of which she is a part, she also heals the separation between self and world.

This transference is disguised as the desire within a lover's discourse that invents the poem. The poem is an appointed meeting, an "intensest rendezvous" that never takes place between the inventor of the discourse and the "lover that lies within the self," his fiction of the feminine other. We grasp her subliminally within the shadowy silences of the *Collected Poems,* and we come to know her, although that knowledge is baseless. She comes "in the golden vacancy" and "seems to be on the saying of her name" (*CP,* 339).

Reading the interior paramour as a canonical myth discloses some of the rhetorical, philosophical, and psycho-sexual principles on which this poetry is predicated: the endless movements between absence, difference and desire; the centrality of repetition as a poetic dynamic; the defense of doubling; and the dialectic of gender behind Stevens' quest for a sublime. The encoded love affair, however, is not merely woman-love or erotic substitution, but derives, ultimately, from Stevens' vision of the beauty of both life and poetry as refreshed repetition. "The radiant bubble that she was" in *Harmonium* becomes the focal point for the rebegetting of Stevens' poetic world, a "being born again" to which he returns, always with a "later reason." Thus the history of the paramour is lived in the nonlinear time frame of the fetal or mythic moment—in this eternal present she is at once the sibylline creature that haunts the lush, dreamy places of the poet's youth and the haunted harridan or death muse that is imagined at the end of "The Auroras of Autumn." The narrative seed of the romance is implanted in the language of "The Rock," so that we as readers are impelled to return to the beginning of the canon and repeat with the poet the circle of the muse that begins and ends with spring.

Born on "a first-found weed" of our native seas, the paramour emerges in the poems as a trope for the possibility of an American Sublime. "A paltry nude," a figure seemingly stripped of imaginative precursors, she "speaks" to the poet with the gestures of her hands, with the weave she affixes to her gown, or the coif selected for her hair. She is the poet's image of present and remembered beauty, a sibyl in her cave sending silent messages of instruction. Externalized as "the dreaming woman" of "Sunday Morning" or the dark sensualist at Key West, she is a fictionalized presence within the text even as she signifies a construct outside the text such as nature, being, otherness, or sublimity. The paramour of the *Harmonium* period is a rather traditional muse-attachment; she emerges from the body of the mother (nature) in late spring and seems to incarnate the voice of the poet as virile youth. Stevens' relationship with "his being's deepest darling" is explored extensively in *Harmonium*. In "Le Monocole de Mon Oncle," a text that eclipses and compresses the dimensions of the romance, the poet evokes the memory of her birth and the poetic climate of her "first imagery." From the beginning, the interior paramour is tied to the earth, the body of the mother and Whitman's grass, or emerges from the sea with the anonymity of another wave:

> . . . Remember how the crickets came
> Out of their mother grass, like little kin,
> In the pale nights, when your first imagery
> Found inklings of your bond to all that dust.

> > (*CP*, 15)

She springs, full-blown, not from the head of Zeus or the ancestry of Venus, but from out of the endlessly rocking cradle of the sea and the "uncut hair of graves"—those metaphors so familiar from the American poetic tradition. Whitman's own muse, clearly not a paramour, but a timeless earth and sea mother, is linked in Stevens' poetry with love (the lavender lilac) and death: she is the mother of his paramour.

Another glimpse of the interior paramour in *Harmonium* is the double vision of her found in "Peter Quince at the Clavier" (*CP*, 89). Meyer and

Baris have seen this text as an incarnation of poetic invention: the catachresis that occurs when flesh becomes word, creativity as annunciation.[6] There is an innocence in their reading, however, since the poem is suggestive not only of the autoerotic nature of poetic invention, as they suggest, but also of art as the production of the poet as voyeur. In a way, the text unfolds as a dream and may be interpreted in the way of the dreamwork; indeed, the poet-dreamer or speaker of the poem is disguised as Peter Quince, the rustic mechanical from Shakespeare's *Midsummer Night's Dream,* a play or "dream" that links the erotic with the hierarchies of imaginative creation. In its manifest content, the text of the dream reveals the masked poet as Quince engaged in an erotic fantasy. Seated before the clavier, or generic keyboard, his fingers express his desire for the "woman in blue-shadowed silk." Stevens' readers know that the blue woman will reappear later in the canon in the "It Must Give Pleasure" section of "Notes toward a Supreme Fiction." Here in "Peter Quince" and in that much later text, she is the interior paramour, each time dressed in another guise. In a sense, her metamorphic or protean qualities connect her to that plumb line of female possibilities that emerge from the collective unconscious.[7] Her "presence" in this poem, between Quince and the sounds of the clavier, is as a trance-medium who acts as a conduit between the poet and the universe of myth.

The myth of the dream is the Apocryphal story of Susanna and the Elders, the wife accused by two church elders of unchastity, probably because she had repelled their advance. Daniel exposed their treachery, and as a result, she was vindicated, and they were put to death. The retelling of the myth occupies the central portion of the text, over which is superimposed a musical structure that empties into the famous coda. As in a dream, time and space are eclipsed, and as the poem moves back and forth in time, the two events of the poem (Quince at the clavier and Susanna and the elders in the garden) seem to occur simultaneously. When reading "Peter Quince," we enter into the landscape of the dream where the artificial limits of linearity, history, and time are erased. In its deep structures, the myth itself is grounded in sexuality, betrayal, and death, while the manifest imagery consists of varied symbols: the clavier, the garden, the woman, and the portal. Throughout the dream-text too, there is a chain of metonymic signifiers that lead from touch, to desire, to language; and they form a kind of erotic bracelet between desire and death, arousal and climax.

The dream-text's latent content begins with the allusion to Peter Quince and the imaginative production of Shakespeare, clearly here the poem's precursor and father-imago. Like Spenser's Colin Clout, the poet's shepherd persona, Peter Quince, another version of the poet, steps out of the literary Oedipal drama to sit at the keyboard of the ephebe and "play" out the desire of all poets: to ravish the muse. She, too, appears nameless but cloaked in the silks of the Renaissance and ultimately disguised as a correlative form of Susanna. Disguise too is the central figure of this text, for sexual arousal, particularly the strain of the auto-erotic, is masked as music. There is the excitation of Quince whose "fingers" provide an entry into the erotic desire for the muse; there is the awakening of desire in the Elders as they "watch" Susanna in her garden; and there are the "throbbing" beings of the Elders whose "thin blood" is quickened to angelic heights. Midsummer madness or spring fever permeates the language of the first canto.

> In the green water, clear and warm,
> Susanna lay.
> She searched
> The touch of springs,
> And found
> Concealed imaginings.
> She sighed,
> For so much melody.
>
> Upon the bank, she stood
> In the cool
> Of spent emotions.
> She felt, among the leaves,
> The dew
> Of old devotions.

$$(CP, 90)$$

In these stanzas, Susanna's autoerotic explorations are thinly dis-guised as ablutions, but they are also tropes for poetic "imaginings." As a figure for the muse, Susanna submerged in the green water is herself a *locus amoenus*, self-possessed and participating in the pleasure of her own creation. Her solipsism, here, has been noted by Harold Bloom (*Climate*, 36), and as Meyer and Baris suggest in a more recent reading of the poem, Susanna in this archetypal setting provided Stevens with "the garden [and] its dual theme of *caritas* and *cupiditas*, celebration and danger, realization and ravishment. Linking all the variations of the garden motif is the double strain of sensual and spiritual."[8] Yet the muse-virgin can never be ravished by the poet, because she is the poet, the mirrored "self-object" of his own femininity.[9]

The Elders inhabit the space of Otherness in the dream: they are both the poet who would gaze on the primal scene of poetic invention and the principle of *thanatos* or the fall of language from myth into time and history. Here the brief glimpse of female sexuality is a link to the center of generative myth, which is, metaphorically, the precursor of language and poetic voice. The "presence" of the Elders in the dream-text also registers the voyeurism of the repressed poet, whose superego permits him to gaze on the onanistic activity of the muse but prevents him from entering her garden. Her discovery of the Elders' gaze, troped into the catachresis of "roaring horns" and "clashing symbols" is equivalent to the death of poetic vision that is killed by the intrusion of the reality principle. Like the child in a crib, exiled from the scene of his own origins yet seeing the source of his being enacted, the poet can only gaze at but never participate in the primal scene of creation.

In "Last Looks at the Lilacs," she is represented as a figure for the muse of all strong poets, who is "embraced" each time an ephebic poet achieves his/her poetic voice:

To what good, in the alleys of the lilacs
O caliper, do you scratch your buttocks
And tell the divine ingénue, your companion,
That this bloom is the bloom of soap
And this fragrance the fragrance of vegetal?

Do you suppose that she cares a tick,
In this hymeneal air, what it is

That marries her innocence thus,
So that her nakedness is near,
Or that she will pause at scurrilous words?

Poor buffo! Look at the lavender
And look your last and look still steadily,
And say how it comes that you see
Nothing but trash and that you no longer feel
Her body quivering in the Floréal

Toward the cool night and its fantastic star.
Prime paramour and belted paragon,
Well-booted, rugged, arrogantly male,
Patron and imager of the gold Don John,
Who will embrace her before summer comes.

(*CP*, 48–49)

Harold Bloom calls this poem "rather nasty," and as such it is a sardonic and embittered stance toward American poetics. Walking in the "alleys of lilacs," that is, the corridors of the American Romantic tradition, the caliper or belated poet in a mechanical world questions the efficacy of aspiring to a sublime. In this anticipatory yet unrefined version of "The Man on the Dump," the "divine ingénue" or interior paramour becomes the unravished bride of the literary tradition or a (re)virginated muse-sublime that is never possessed. What confounds the poet here, and in his vision on the dump of worn-out metaphors, is the disjunction between, on the one hand, the "ever-returning spring" and "hymeneal air" of nature's poetics, and on the other, the language "trash" of a tradition that has lost its innocence and power. "She" (nature, the feminine, the myth, the world) is indifferent and is willing to take up with any "Don John." But the lilacs, used by Whitman in the great elegy on Lincoln as emblems of both fertility and the vulnerability of male sexuality, "emasculate" and silence the belated poet who can only see them as delimiting and throw-aways. Unlike Whitman, this twentieth-century poet "can no longer feel" the power of the lilacs and their prescient sensuality.

Stevens' relationship with the paramour is rendered extensively in *Harmonium;* as a nascent presence she is an American original. Yet we meet her in the guises of the literary tradition as Susanna solipsized in the green waters, as an American version of Keats's autumnal muse in "Le Monocle de Mon Oncle," and as the mythic Ursula in a garden of radishes. During this early period, she refines and civilizes her poet's perceptions and extracts from him the root-energy of his words with her own primitive energy and closer proximity to the source of myth and language. Decorated and adorned, coifed and tendrilled, the interior paramour of the early years is a passive and, as Stevens calls her, "a contemplated spouse," and she reflects the poet's own inability at this time to integrate the feminine into consciousness. But this early muse of spring, carefully woven as a thread in the first volume of poems, becomes in the later poems, "the radiant bubble" to which the poet returns, always with a later reason.

III

"Madame Bovary, c'est moi"
—Gustave Flaubert

Gustave Flaubert admitted that Madame Bovary was indeed himself, and in *M. Butterfly,* a play that deconstructs the binary opposites of masculine and feminine, M. Gallimard falls in love with the operatic muse of his own making. Falling on the phallic sword of his invented fiction, he becomes what he already is: the woman of his dreams. This intra-psychic mechanism designed to break down gender difference within the construct of the self becomes for Wallace Stevens not only a strategy for poetic creation but a way to rewrite the limitations of being human. In the great text of *Ideas of Order*—"The Idea of Order at Key West"—the ordering of the world unfolds as a dramatic gender exchange between the fictive shore singer/the interior paramour, and the poet, who attempts to penetrate the illusions of poetic presence. Although the poem never discloses the extra-linguistic truth that resides in her song, it does expose a dividing or doubling of the fiction of self into a vortex of narcissism where sexual difference is blurred and seemingly erased. Stevens' attempt to bridge the gap of gender difference is, of course, a metaphor for desire, the desire for union perhaps with a kind of lost omnipotence where the "mother's face" and her song are available and near.

For Wallace Stevens, as for Nietzsche, truth is "evasive, veiled and feminine" and dwells, as J. Hillis Miller points out in his seminal essay "Stevens' 'Rock' and Criticism as Cure," at the bottom of a well. Nietzsche writes that "in order to have (possess) the truth (woman), the philosopher must be the woman (truth) which is impossible; and man and woman change places, exchange their masks to infinity" in order to recover truth from which man's nature excludes her. This philosophical attempt to recover truth in the guise of a woman finds its poetic correlative in the poem "The Idea of Order at Key West." Although many of the paramour-poems in the canon emphasize the difference and unclosed distance between self and other, this text and such later poems as "The World as Meditation" are explicit dramas of the exchange of gender masks. At Key West, the woman is possessed solipsistically, as she is projected as a figure striding on the shore. Yet as "maker" and "single artificer" and medium through which the poem gets written, she becomes prioritized by the male poet who yields to her Orphic mastery and the femininity of truth.

As the sibyl within the self and a figure on the shore, the paramour here is both the truth to be possessed (outside) and the self-possessed interior woman who, like the Sibyl hanging in her cave, utters and interprets the fictions of the world outside herself. The transference of sexual masks here is more than an even exchange; for in repressing his will to mastery in order to be possessed by the woman he can never know, the male poet relinquishes not only his own centrality as "maker," but also the "truth" of his own fiction. "There was never a world for her" is a line that undoes the fiction of the muse herself as well as the fictions of the world and its phallic ordering.

Having tested the substance of the singer and having found the place empty indeed, the poet can only turn to his other invented companion,

Ramon, and ask him, why, if there is no world, is the night deepened by thought alone. A response comes in the final strophe where the poetic maker is also ambiguous, the maker of a world in which presence itself is always evasive. What we are left with here, as in "Notes toward a Supreme Fiction," is desire: desire to be and possess the woman, "the soft-footed phantom" of truth—the "irrational distortion." In order to be his own butterfly, the male poet must submit to her song of death, and in yielding his will to her Orphic mastery, he may come to know the "fragrant portals" of his own birth.

IV

The experience of beginning, given in a moment of love, is also given as premonition of absolute consummation. It therefore turns towards a mythically determined situation.
—L. Kolakowski, *The Presence of Myth*

In "Notes toward a Supreme Fiction," the interior paramour is used as a floating signifier that embodies not only the idea of eternal recurrence in the text, but also the poet's attempt to resolve difference. The scenes in which she appears in "Notes" are from three "marriages" or metaphoric unions that reflect not only the endless process of imaginative refreshening but the repeated quest for a sublime or supreme fiction that heals the narcissistic split. That sublime can only be reached when figuration disappears or Western mythology is displaced. And since metaphoricity is always "present," and since we can never recover an "immaculate beginning," Stevens contextualizes these failed sublimes in three poetic landscapes.

In all three scenes of "Notes," Stevens selects the self-conscious device of the mirror to reflect the multiplication of being into genders. This doubling of the self begins with the poem's preface in which the paramour, addressed as "you," is evoked not not only as an extra-linguistic presence, but also as part of the poet's inner life: they meet in "the central of our being." The deception of the preface, that Stevens invokes the spirit of Henry Church or a traditional muse figure, is sustained until the reader realizes that Stevens, once again, invokes the other within the narcissistic nucleus of the self. "She," though he never uses the feminine, is merely a reflection of the "living changingness" within the poet's mind, a figuration that projects the male-feminine. "They" seem to have met in the center of the poet's being that is the linguistic space to which he refers the experience of desire. The "transparence" that she brings is the light reflected from the illusion of the mirrored self which meets its sister in the "uncertain light" of an invisible dwelling.

This powerful mirror of "living changingness" in the preface to "Notes" is reflected again in the fourth canto of "It Must Be Abstract," "when Eve made air the mirror of herself." Eve's "distant mirror" here is held up to reflect the origin of the prototypical interior paramour. Stevens' point is that even Eve's body, the archetype of female sexuality, is a mirror of the earth or "muddy center" that preceded her, so that a return to Eve is merely a return to a myth that only reduplicates itself but never reveals the real inside.[10] The encasing of the earth in the mirror of art is, in turn, replicated in the mirroring of herself by Eve as artist. Self-solipsized like Susanna in the mirror-world of her own making, she is herself the illusion of a doubled self that invents her self in a text. Eve's distant mirror, a trope for "the fall" into figuration, is an image of the earth as a woman that is the generative center of myth.

In her second appearance in "Notes," the interior paramour takes the form of Nanzia Nunzio in canto 8 of "It Must Change":

On her trip around the world, Nanzia Nunzio
Confronted Ozymandias. She went
Alone and like a vestal long-prepared.

I am the spouse. She took her necklace off
And laid it in the sand. As I am, I am
The spouse. She opened her stone-studded belt.

I am the spouse, divested of bright gold,
The spouse beyond emerald or amethyst,
Beyond the burning body that I bear.

(*CP*, 395)

In this fable of the contemplated spouse, time has passed since the paramour was Eve, and the mirror of air/art has accumulated layer upon layer of figuration. Nanzia Nunzio, the reflection of Eve, appears before the fiction of the major man, still desiring to make air the mirror of herself. Her name is not only an anagrammatic mirroring of the signifier Ozymandias, but an instance of language doubling with its second part, Nunzio, appearing as a mirrored distortion of the first part, Nanzia, and reflecting both the male and female case endings. She too is a circulating image who confronts her poet on her way around the world. Seeking to divest herself of fictional entrappings, she performs a deconstructive striptease. Her wish is to be clothed in the "final filament" or the colorless cloak of nakedness.

The faceted crystal, a variation on the mirror device of the poem, is the icon of textuality in the fable. Nanzia Nunzio's intention is to strip herself of fictions, to "go beyond emerald and amethyst" and to arrive at the nakedness of pure being. Yet the possibility of her gesture is undermined by the poet even before the conflagration of her "burning body." For as she lays down her necklace on the sand, crystals against smaller crystals, the weaving of another fiction has already begun. Seen as a complete union, the marriage between Ozymandias and this contemplated spouse, as between the poet and his paramour, "fails" because their desire to erase difference is always a deferred ending, a dissemination of desire displaced into the fictive covering that "Weaves always glistening from the heart and mind" (*CP*, 396). The mythology of their union is dependent on their subconscious wish to preserve difference, eros and the making of poems.

V

But she that says good-by losing in self
The sense of self, rosed out of prestiges
Of rose, stood tall in self not symbol . . .

Impassioned by the knowledge that she had,
There on the edges of oblivion.
      —Stevens, "The Owl in the Sarcophagus"

As summer turns to autumn in the *Collected Poems*, the spinning theatre of "Notes toward a Supreme Fiction" vanishes from memory, "floating through clouds . . . through waves of light." Now the love of repetition, embodied by the paramour as the "fat girl terrestrial," accedes to the love of recollection without the former's disquieting implication of hope. For Stevens, the autumnal moment is a time for remembering "the self of summer as she was perfectly perceived" (*CP*, 427). Her dress, he regrets in the ironically titled poem "The Beginning," now lies cast off on the floor. In "The Auroras of Autumn," the interior paramour had been perceived as a figure of absence, although a "shimmering residue" of her remained. Now, in the late poem "In a Bad Time" (*CP*, 427), she is a construct of pure memory in the traditional guise of Melpomene, the muse of tragedy, strutting across the bare boards of an emptied theatre "without scenery or lights."

The death of the interior paramour is not an "actual one," but rather a re-internalization of the muse into the mind of the poet. As projected onto the world, she "had filled those external regions" with the illusion of her presence; now, in the final stages of the psychodrama, the healing of the self and its narcissistic wound is apparent. No longer a projection, the interior paramour is enfolded within the psyche next to her brother and male counterpart, the fiction of the animus, the major man. They have been, for Stevens, an "artificial population [rosy men and women of the rose]" that "is like / A healing-point in the sickness of the mind" (*OP*, 112). Having indeed exteriorized the interior of his mind in the fictions of rosy men and women of the rose, Wallace Stevens concludes his romance of the rose, his "metaphysical adultery" by naming his correspondent: the interior paramour.

The christening occurs in the most revealing articulation of the feminine presence in "Final Soliloquy of the Interior Paramour." "Final Soliloquy" is an attempt to actually name her, to describe that "fantastic consciousness" where they have met. That "shadowy psychodrama" of poet and paramour hinted at by J. Hillis Miller in "Stevens' 'Rock' and Criticism as Cure," is coming to a close, but until this point, she has been felt by Stevens' reader as a kind of mystical influence and perceived as a psychic figure "half-seen." Her shadowy self has eluded our grasp, but she has been part of and participant in Stevens' "meditated" world. Now, in the "final soliloquy" we come to know her by name: "Light the first light of evening, as in a room / In which we rest and, for small reason, think / The world imagined is the ultimate good" (CP, 524).

The rhetoric of the lyric is deceptive, because the voice we hear in these lines is that of the poet's "we," composed of his fictionalized self, the major man, and his feminine double and mate (herself a metaphor of poetic presence). She is "the lover that lies within the self" and the illusion of an imagined self in another. The setting of the poem is a room at dusk within the architecture of the poet's mind. She asks her poet to illumine the dwelling one last time, so that they may contemplate the truth they have established. The metaphoricity of this locale is indicated in the provisional word "as" in the first line, so that the invented room "seems" to be a "description of place," but is actually a language site to which the poet refers his experience of presence. This resting place is also a trope for the collected thoughts of the imagined pair and an invented space that both seals off their separation from the world and intensifies the self's own intimacy.

The "intensest rendezvous" is a metaphoric coupling in which lover-poet and muse-paramour fit into what John Donne called "one neutral thing" and in the process of poetic de-gendering simulate a world in which desire and absence are obliterated: "God and the imagination are one" (CP, 524). Yet they are one because they are both fallen words in the imprecise science of linguistic naming; there is no difference because there is infinitudinal difference. The neutering of the sexes is a metaphor for the neutralization of language forms; and what remains from the process is this "neutral thing," the single shawl of fiction that covers over the nothingness of the impoverished twentieth-century American self. The "self," both male and female, young and old, becomes a knowing Tiresias who has lived on both sides of the gender boundary.

VI

Then she finished it, though unwilling and under duress. And when, having woven the great fabric and washed it, She showed forth the robe that resembled the sun or the moon.

—Homer, *The Odyssey*

The origin of the discourse between poet and paramour begins and ends in myth, in particular the myth of Penelope and Ulysses in "The World as Meditation" (*CP*, 520–21). In this text, placed near the end of the *Collected Poems*, poet and paramour are simultaneously introduced into the canon and recast into the literary tradition as Homer's aboriginal yet aging lovers. The time is the moment before homecoming; Ulysses has been gone for twenty years; the suitors have unraveled the secret of Penelope's weavings, so the possibility of perpetuating the fiction of closure is blocked. Her loom—a site for the weaving and unweaving of the fictions that have been the life of the poems—is engaged in the process as long as the fiction of possible union is sustained. In truth, her loom is weaving a mourning shroud for her mate's father and precursor, Laertes. Stevens' imagination focuses on the loom as an icon of textuality: the tapestry of the text is woven from the fiction of transcendence, the supreme fiction that would become real when otherness is made human. Yet the death of the supreme fiction, as represented by the mourning shroud, is concurrent with the completion of the weaving project and the coming of Ulysses.

Spoken in an objective tone and voice, the meditation opens on the figure of Penelope and the tableau of her desire as she reads the tropes of sun and sky in the text of her loom:

Is it Ulysses that approaches from the east,
The interminable adventurer? The trees are mended.
That winter is washed away. Someone is moving

On the horizon and lifting himself up above it.
A form of fire approaches the cretonnes of Penelope,
Whose mere savage presence awakens the world in which she dwells.

(CP, 520)

We enter the text through the consciousness of the paramour as Penelope who, having been forced to complete the web of fictions that postpone closure but allow for union, is weaving another idea of the sun. Her mind has become her poet's, or an imagination unable to distinguish between the dark horizon of metaphor and the abyss of nature from which the sun appears. Just as the fictive weavings or "cretonnes" of Wallace Stevens had once invented the fictive presence of his paramour, now his "presence" is reimagined by her. Yet his "mere savage presence" is a poetic mirage, another figure that both awakes her world of fictions but threatens to burn through its protective veils. The fiction of the muse displaces here the primacy of the poet's consciousness, and as their roles transpose, the mind of Stevens is frozen and contextualized into the myth of the "interminable wanderer" as a figure for the linguistic sublime.

She has composed, so long, a self with which to welcome him,
Companion to his self for her, which she imagined,
Two in a deep-founded sheltering, friend and dear friend.

The trees had been mended, as an essential exercise
In an inhuman meditation, larger than her own.
No winds like dogs watched over her at night.

She wanted nothing that he could not bring her by coming alone.
She wanted no fetchings. His arms would be her necklace
And her belt, the final fortune of their desire.

(*CP*, 521)

The homecoming of Ulysses is forgotten in these stanzas by the contemplation of the activities of postponement that make up the act of writing. Poetry and the self, the poem suggests, are both composed and contextualized into the loom of the text at the threshold of homecoming in the absence of presence and disclosure. These stanzas look back toward "Notes toward a Supreme Fiction" and the necklace of the contemplated spouse that is never clasped, and they anticipate "the intensest rendezvous" when Ulysses meets Penelope in the marriage bed. As in "Notes," the "inhuman meditation" of the world and its operation refers to a kind of collective unconscious or "mythy mind" beyond poetry that precludes originality: "There was a myth before the myth began" (*CP*, 383). The myth that Penelope's loom weaves is the myth of representation or the invention of a second world mimicking a place that is not her own.

Unlike Nanzia Nunzio in "Notes," who performs a linguistic striptease in her trip around the world, the muse here is stationary, waiting for the poet-adventurer whose own naked presence is desired. The transference here is complete. Cured of his repression of the female within, the poet is able to invent a fiction in which the trajectory of the feminine is now central to the poetic act.

But was it Ulysses? Or was it only the warmth of the sun
On her pillow? The thought kept beating in her like her heart.
The two kept beating together. It was only day.

(*CP*, 521)

The transference that occurs from poet to muse is extended in this stanza to encompass the idea of the sun as a repetition for the idea of presence. Just as her heartbeat repeats itself and then is repeated in her thoughts, the act of poetry (the act of weaving), the act of reimagining union become her "notes" toward a supreme fiction or sublime. In the aporia between Ulysses moving on the horizon and the appearance of the sun from the abyss of its home in the sea, there is "an intensest rendezvous." It is a meeting that (n)ever takes places between the muse and her poet. The poem ends without closure and with only another series of incremental repetitions. As she talks to her-self, Penelope repeats the syllables of his name, U-lys-ses, the sounds of which are repeated in the strokes she affixes to the weave of her hair, strokes that in turn repeat the act of remembering. Weaving, combing, repeating, and remembering become the life of poetry and the muse of memory.

The companion poem to "The Paltry Nude Starts on a Spring Voyage" is "Celle Qui Fût Héaulmiette" (*CP*, 438). In that first voyage, the interior paramour had emerged from the sea of the unconscious with the anonymity of "one more wave." And as a paltry nude, she initiated the circle of spring and remembrance that Stevens returned to each time for renewed inspiration. The image of the circle is inscribed one last time in this poem of recollection where the poet remembers her emergence from "the first warmth of spring / . . . Among the bare and crooked trees." Her imagined presence was "Like the snow before it softened / And dwindled into patches," and her course spanned summer to summer, not "in the arc / Of winter." Now in winter, the mythic home of tragedy, she is a memory, snow melting into snow and disappearing, like "Another American vulgarity," a movie queen or superstar grown wrinkled and too old even for the makeup artist. She slips back into the landscape of America, into that native shield that bears the crest of her parents: "a mother with vague severed arms / And of a father bearded in his fire." In the "Paltry Nude," the poet had orphaned his paramour from the tradition, insisting that her voyage, unlike that of Venus, did not begin on a half-shell. Here, however, not only is her lineage reclaimed but the enterprise of her own originality has failed. She remains the child of Western poetry, the daughter of Zeus, "bearded in his fire," and now is reclaimed, like Athene, back into the father's head.

Stevens' blackness of mood reaches its climax in "Madame La Fleurie" where the death-muse takes on the pre-Oedipal, morphogenetic quality of an evil mother that Wagner connects with the phallic mother.

Mothers are polarized throughout the canon: the good mother is associated with spring and summer and the origins of the interior paramour, while the threatening death-mother is linked with autumn and winter and the death and dissolution of the muse. I would suggest that the bearded queen or phallic mother Stevens introduces here is part of his late regression and is the "one step backward" he must take before yielding to the genderless muse who absorbs into a singular voice the dualities of male and female, being and non-being, self and other. The first of these texts that describes the totalized muse is "Angel Surrounded by Paysans" (*CP*, 496–97), a poem that reminds us of Milton's angels that are of both sexes and envisions the "necessary angel of earth" who is "Cleared of its stiff and stubborn, man-locked set." In letting go of the masculine-feminine "sets" and assumptions, the poet is finally able to see the earth again washed in the colors of neutrality. In one of the last poems in the collection, Odysseus has come to Connecticut: he tells of a "great river this side of Stygia," where there is no ferryman, not even prophecy, but only "a river, an unnamed flowing" that will take him home to touch "the Happy Isles."

3

A Woman with the Hair of a Pythoness

Barbara M. Fisher

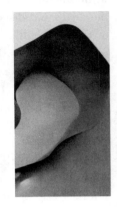

His anima liked its animal
And liked it unsubjugated.
—Wallace Stevens, "Esthétique du Mal"

If Stevens' interior paramour is a Jungian anima figure or a moth-eaten muse, as a number of readers have supposed, why doesn't she conform to the models? Why does she display characteristics that are sharply at variance both with the psychological construct and the classical figure? Can Stevens' intensely personal paramour be construed as a "collective projection of the masculine unconscious," as Michel Benamou believed? Can one comply with Benamou's easy assurance that "Jungian psychology accounts rather well for this voice in the poetry"?[1]

To carry this line of inquiry a step further, can Stevens' complex response to the feminine be reduced to "an image of the great earth mother which will appear in various forms throughout the work"? Edward Kessler rightly identifies Stevens' vision of the feminine with recurring images of "summer" and "south," but he believes the same visionary element must be understood as mere physical sensation. According to Kessler, Stevens' woman is "not an ideal but the earth itself," or "the part of the world that can be enjoyed without explanation or meaning."[2]

The approach shared by Benamou and Kessler with other Jungian critics relies upon a simple convention: a set of human traits is assignable by gender. Thus Kessler finds Stevens' image of woman "ambiguous or contradictory" where the poet evokes a composite figure.[3] He refers to the "disturbing" invocation that opens "To the One of Fictive Music"—"Sister and mother and diviner love"—and to the "troublesome opening" of "Le Monocle de Mon Oncle": "Mother of Heaven, regina of the clouds, / O sceptre of the sun, crown of the moon." In truth, it *is* a troublesome opening, and it has drawn a good deal of critical attention. But it is particularly troublesome if one is compelled to interpret "heaven," "clouds," "sun," and "moon" as "the great earth mother" or mindless physical sensation. When one thinks of the range of Stevens' meditation on the feminine principle, the limitations of such a critical stance are striking. A Jungian reading simply cannot account for the striding poet-singer, the haunting genius of the shore in "The Idea of Order at Key West." Jung's system of archetypes, far from opening a window to Stevens' poetry, forces the reader to transpose all that is inventive, all that is intellectually active—poiesis itself—beyond the reach of the feminine.

Homer's invocation to the Goddess and Hesiod's to the divine muses continue, in English poetry, as the address to Urania, the heavenly muse. A. Walton Litz refers to this tradition when he calls the One of Fictive Music a "muse-goddess." Stevens' invocation, says Litz, is an address to "naked imagination, pure and simple, a figure of Muse and Virgin and earthly woman who is mistress of the music celebrated in the second stanza."[4] What we get is a kind of Ur-version of the Supremes: a combination of Polyhymnia, Saint Cecelia, and perhaps Stevens' young wife (a music teacher), who was precisely a "mistress of music" and whose long golden hair is memorialized here and elsewhere in the poetry.[5] What seems clear is that this early lyric has both ironic and erotic overtones. It contains a half-amused nod to the Heliconian sisterhood, which serves as the introit to a more serious reflection on poetic musing—classically a category of divine madness.

Harold Bloom firmly escorts the muse into Freudian territory. The One of Fictive Music is a "familial muse," says Bloom, and he amplifies:

"Stevens takes the Oedipal risk, as Keats and Whitman did, and invokes the muse as his actual mother and as the other women of his family."[6] In his discussion of "Final Soliloquy of the Interior Paramour," the finely wrought chamber piece of the very late poetry, Bloom uses "muse" interchangeably with "paramour." He claims, however, that Madame La Fleurie—"a bearded queen, wicked in her dead light," the land as receiver of the corpse—is the "last version of the American muse-as-mother," and so a "more authentic version of the interior paramour."

But Stevens' paramour is neither dread mother nor classical muse, nor for that matter, "imagination, pure and simple." The literary muse, conventionally summoned from above and beyond, represents inspiration that strikes from without; she is external to the poet. In contrast, the paramour is an inner presence. She dwells in the "hermitage at the centre," always within range of the poet's consciousness. She is conceived as an interior love object, not an externalized force. Finally, where the classical muse speaks to or through the poet, Stevens speaks *with* the paramour. "Fool," cries Sidney's famous muse, "look in thy heart and write." In contrast, the discourse between the modern poet and his paramour develops as an interchange: "those exchanges of speech in which your words are mine, mine yours" (*NA*, 67).

Stevens significantly defines the inner presence as a "separate self." In "Re-statement of Romance" the mysterious voice observes, "Only we two may interchange / Each in the other what each has to give," and concludes with a murmured assurance "That night is only the background of our selves, / Supremely true each to its separate self, / In the pale light that each upon the other throws" (*CP*, 146).

As one considers the manifestations of this separate self in the poetry, it becomes evident that Stevens' paramour has—like Theodore Roethke's flexible inamorata—"more sides than a seal." She is portrayed with various shades of green, purple, blue, argent, rose, and gold and surrounded by degrees of radiance ranging from pale light to flaming brilliance. As Kessler points out, she is related to summer—"the unbroken circle of summer" (*CP*, 438)—and to the south, the most fertile of Stevens' directional emblems.

But "paramour" is a term that contains both "love" *(-amour)* and "darkness" *(-moor)* and Stevens' paramour reveals a shadowy night side as well as a bright:

> Donna, donna, dark,
> Stooping in indigo gown
> And cloudy constellations,
> Conceal yourself or disclose
> Fewest things to the lover—

>   *(CP,* 48)

In the early "Florida" poems, the poet is the "scholar of darkness" and the paramour becomes "Night, the female, / Obscure, / Fragrant and supple" *(CP,* 73). Bloom, I think, comes as close as one can to describing the emotional tension that courses between poet and paramour. But does she reach her final flowering in the all-swallowing Madame La Fleurie? Or is this appearance in the late poetry merely a grim Gothic flourish? Generally one finds that the dark aspect of Stevens' paramour recalls, not the lethal earth queen, but her antithesis, the "black but comely" Shulamite or Solomon's love song.

Although Stevens does not give the figure a name, and indeed, occasionally refers to it as "nameless," he invests the paramour with a range of epithets and descriptive terms that indicate a compound nature. It is not easy to convey, in brief, the subtlety, the diversity, the strength of Stevens' delineation of the feminine—from tigress and she-wolf, to regal abstraction; from Susanna and Saint Ursula, to Bonnie and Josie dancing in Oklahoma; from the contemplative woman of "Sunday Morning," to the "green queen" with the Marvellian "green mind" of "Description without Place"; from the "United Dames of America," to the "burning body" of Nanzia Nunzio and the bearded circus freak Madame La Fleurie.

Stevens' paramour is Eve, who "made the air the mirror of herself" *(CP,* 383), and the "naked, nameless dame" whose hand "wove round her glittering hair" *(CP,* 271). She is the terrestrial globe, the "Fat girl" of "Notes toward a Supreme Fiction" and the seductive south, whose "mind had bound me round" in "Farewell to Florida" (*CP*, 117). In "The Owl in the Sarcophagus" she is memory, "the mother of us all, / The earthly mother and the mother of / The dead" (*CP*, 432). In "The Candle a Saint" she "walks among astronomers," again "green kindled and green apparelled," reflecting a Platonic ideal form, an abstract icon of intelligence: "The noble figure, the essential shadow, / Moving and being, the image at its source, / The abstract, the archaic queen" (*CP*, 223). Stevens invokes her with immense longing and bitter irony as "Mother of Heaven, regina of the clouds" (*CP*, 13) but, in the very late poetry, as the serene being "that was mistress of the world" (*CP*, 460). Like Shelley's Epipsyche, she is "A Golden Woman in a Silver Mirror" (*CP*, 460); like Plato's Diotima, she is the "sibyl of the self" (*OP*, 104); like Saint Bernard's *sponsa Dei*, she is "the spouse, the bride" (*CP*, 396), "the desired . . . sleek in a natural nakedness" who dwells in the hermitage at the center (*CP*, 505). But, like Blake's Divine Human Imagination, she is also the "maker of the song she sang" (*CP*, 129). She is the tripartite One of Fictive Music (*CP*, 87), the separate self "that speaks, denouncing separate selves" (*CP*, 441), the ambiguous "lover that lies within us" (*CP*, 394). Finally, she is the "inexplicable sister of the Minotaur" (*NA*, 52) the "woman with the hair of a pythoness" (*NA*, 29).

"The Noble Rider and the Sound of Words" opens with the winged horses and the charioteer of the *Phaedrus*. Toward the conclusion of the essay, Stevens almost casually introduces the image of the pythoness, perhaps his version of Plato's mantic priestess. "All poets address themselves to someone," he writes, "and it is of the essence of that instinct . . . that it should be to an elite, not to a drab but to a woman with the hair of a pythoness." This is not the image of a Medusa, as one may first imagine, with hair composed of wildly twining snakes. Once summoned up, however, the Medusa image does not dissipate entirely; it remains long enough to ensure the barbarity of the python image, to intensify its uncanny quality, and to sharpen its archaic outline. The Pythoness is a sibyl, of course, who speaks in riddles but speaks the truth. The figure represents, for Stevens, an interior reader and an oracular voice that is archaic, erotic, prophetic, priestly, and unfamiliar. Stevens' half-savage, half-divine Ariadne figure provides an essential clue to the nature of his paramour and underscores the riddling presence of the pythoness. The poet himself defines his muse as an expression of "the intelligence that endures" (NA, 52) and invokes her with a peculiar intensity in almost Yeatsian terms: "Inexplicable sister of the Minotaur, enigma and mask, although I am part of what is real, hear me and recognize me as part of the unreal. I am the truth but the truth of that imagination of life in which with unfamiliar motion and manner you guide me in those exchanges of speech in which your words are mine, mine yours" (NA, 67).

If one looks across the poetry as a whole, it becomes apparent that Stevens' feminine principle possessed a mythic dimension, an element common among the works of his contemporaries, Yeats, Eliot, Pound, and Williams. Unlike his contemporaries, Stevens' idea of woman reflects a noetic as well as a mystical ancestry. Although Stevens' paramour derives in part from the *sponsa Dei* of the speculative theologians (that is, the anima as the mystical bride of Christ), she descends too from the oracular sibyls of the classical period. Her noetic, or intellective, quality aligns her with her great predecessor in the *Symposium:* Diotima, Socrates' instructor in the philosophy of love. Stevens' paramour thus stands in the long line of female representations of Wisdom. As the "intelligence that endures," she is the direct heiress of Wisdom in Proverbs, of the postclassical Sophia, and of Nous, the Neoplatonic figure of thinking.[7] In short, Stevens' paramour stands at a far remove from a Jungian concept of the anima.

Let me be clear: According to Jung, the anima is the image of the feminine that exists in the male psyche. It is a projection of the "mother imago" that extends to the image of "the daughter, the sisterab06, the beloved, the heavenly goddess" and an entity called the "earth spirit Baubo." Jung stresses the universality of the projection, which he discusses rather curiously in terms of contagion and disease: "Every mother and every beloved is forced to become the carrier and embodiment of this omnipresent and ageless image with corresponds to the deepest reality in a man. It is his own, this perilous image of woman."[8] The equivalent imago in the psyche of a woman is the animus or image of the father, which Jung invests with qualities of "reason or spirit." Woman is "compensated by this masculine element," as Jung believes, and his discussion of anima and animus serves to reduce what is masculine and what is feminine into two antithetical projections: male rationality and female sensuality: "The animus corresponds to the paternal Logos just as the anima corresponds to the maternal Eros."[9]

One cannot fail to be impressed by the beautiful symmetry of this scheme. But in a later writing Jung contradicts his original explanation of the anima. No longer is it a projection of the masculine psyche, nor the "deepest reality in a man." It is not even "his own, this perilous image of woman." Rather suddenly, it has developed into the "true nature" of woman. In "Marriage as a Psychological Relationship," Jung now says, "In men, Eros . . . is usually less developed than Logos. In woman, on the other hand, Eros is an expression of their true nature, while their logos is often only a regrettable accident."[10] It is not my intention, in noting this contradiction, to deny Jung's contribution to the study of symbolic expression. The point I would like to make has to do with the use of Jungian theory to read Stevens' poetry. For the rigid division of attributes that Jungian psychology accepts as archetypal and that Jung puts forth as a universal and unalterable truth can hardly be said, as Benamou remarked, to "account rather well" for Wallace Stevens' paramour—a creature rich and sometimes strange, but impressively manifold.

The anima, as such, acquires a more Freudian coloration in "Esthétique du Mal," where Stevens clearly takes "the Oedipal risk" in this homage to Baudelaire. This is a wonderfully orchestrated passage that modulates in its portrait of desire and the artist from rhythmic sensuality to savage syncopation. One notes, however, that the anima figuration remains vivid, energetic, various:

> He sought the most grossly maternal, the creature
> Who most fecundly assuaged him, the softest
> Woman with a vague moustache and not the mauve
> *Maman*. His anima liked its animal
> And liked it unsubjugated.

(CP, 321)

The passage goes on, playfully joining the anima with "its animal":

> It is true there were other mothers, singular
> In form, lovers of heaven and earth, she-wolves
> And forest tigresses and women mixed
> With the sea. These were fantastic.

It is not really helpful, I think, to define this complex figuration in terms of disease or to discuss Stevens' paramour as an aberration, a "schizoid self," as Mary Arensberg does in her study of the figure. [11] Nor does it add to an understanding of Stevens' poetics to think of his paramour as a mere "syntactic event" (Arensberg here refers to Michael Beehler's critical approach) or to consider the paramour, as Beehler does, "an illusion, constructed within a linguistic hall of mirrors."[12] Nor can we think of the paramour as "an invented fiction . . . generated from within the poet's own psyche," if she is a "separate self" and the "intelligence that endures" as well as an integral part of the poet. [13] Possibly the figure expresses the very psyche that is said to be generating an "invented fiction" of itself.

While the oracular and noetic components of Stevens' paramour are evidenced in images of the pythoness, the Ariadne figure, and the "abstract, the archaic queen," the passional element derives its force from the Song of Songs. If one bypasses the theological mystique that attaches to the bride and bridegroom of Canticles and returns to Solomon's love song, one is brought back to the headiness of purely physical pleasure: "Let him kiss me with the kisses of his mouth," the Shulamite sings, "for your love is better than wine" (1:2). In chapter 2 of the Song of Solomon, the Shulamite who provides the model for the soul in love calls her virile bridegroom the "dove that art in the clefts of the rock," a "young hart upon the mountains," and "an apple tree among trees of the wood." She, in turn, is "a garden inclosed . . . my sister, my spouse" (4:12); she is "fair as the moon, clear as the sun" (6:10) and "black but comely" (1:5). Thus, the Shulamite is a particularly rich source for Stevens' "beloved," for both her shining aspects and her dark face are mirrored in the paramour.

Both the shining and dark aspects of the paramour are related to summer and the south, but the dark face is most often associated with the southern night. For Stevens, black is neither absence of color nor lack of light, but an erotic and enveloping ambiance rich with anticipation and the suggestion of limitless possibilities. It is the "essential dark," the originating *materium* out of which all creation flows. In "Two Figures in Dense Violet Night" a nameless paramour urges the lover of darkness to "Be the voice of night and Florida in my ear. / Use dusky words and dusky images. / Darken your speech" (*CP*, 86). Stevens succeeds both in revealing and concealing the presence of the dark-faced paramour (paramoor) in "Six Significant Landscapes":

> The night is of the color
> Of a woman's arm;
> Night, the female,
> Obscure,
> Fragrant and supple,
> Conceals herself.
> A pool shines,
> Like a bracelet
> Shaken in a dance.

(CP, 73–74)

The inamorata is "lascivious as the wind" in the early "O Florida, Venereal Soil," and the poet a "scholar of darkness." Here, the "Venus-like" body of the beloved place and climate is absorbed into the figure of the paramour. As in so many of the "Florida" poems, the exterior place is projected into a psychological interior, the space within, and shaped into a woman's image. The terrain itself pictures forth the emotional life. Thus in "Farewell to Florida" one has the sense of a profound leave-taking, something more than the simple fact of a journey north.

In the Song of Solomon, the Shulamite cries to the elements in her yearning: "Awake, O north wind; and come, thou south; blow upon my garden, that the spices thereof may flow out" (4:16). In "Farewell to Florida," the poet turns away from such a call as this with a sublime pathos. The poem stands at the opening to Stevens' *Ideas of Order*

(1936), and some have interpreted the passage from south to north as a passage to a new poetics. Surely it is a crossing poem that marks the closing of an era. But the freedom it heralds seems dearly bought:

> Go on, high ship, since now, upon the shore,
> The snake has left its skin upon the floor.
> Key West sank downward under massive clouds
> And silvers and greens spread over the sea. The moon
> Is at the mast-head and the past is dead.
> Her mind will never speak to me again.
> I am free.
>
> (*CP*, 117)

Bloom finds the second stanza an extraordinarily sensuous evocation, not of a state of the union, but of "a state of mind."[14] It is "so erotic a stanza," says Bloom, "that the reader needs to keep reminding himself that this Florida . . . is a trope of pathos, a synecdoche for desire and not desire itself." Yet in this stanza, desire twists into dearth and death; the north and south winds called up by the Shulamite to fan and enflame desire become "my North of cold whistled in a sepulchral South." In this stanza, erotic language remains attached to a configuration of place and to a woman's mind, while south and north become directional emblems of remembrance and Lethean forgetfulness:

> Her mind had bound me round. The palms were hot
> As if I lived in ashen ground, as if
> The leaves in which the wind kept up its sound
> From my North of cold whistled in a sepulchral South,
> Her South of pine and coral and coraline sea,
> Her home, not mine, in the ever-freshened Keys,
> Her days, her oceanic nights, calling
> For music, for whisperings from the reefs.
> How content I shall be in the North to which I sail
> And to feel sure and to forget the bleaching sand . . .
>
> (*CP*, 117)

One feels the wrench of these lines. This is departure from a beloved who is still loved, and the agon between south and north, here, is one between passion and reason. The *mania* of love and poetry is rejected for the contentment of ordinary existence. It is a difficult moment, a hard passage toward north and "sanity," for as we learn in the final stanza, "My North is leafless and lies in a wintry slime / Both of men and clouds, a slime of men in crowds."

One can sail determinedly north and away from Florida, but can one leave an interior paramour behind? In this context, a connection emerges between the passion and finality of "Farewell to Florida" and the appearance shortly thereafter of the singer of the shore in "The Idea of Order at Key West." In the "Farewell" we learn that "the snake has left its skin upon the floor." In "The Idea of Order" there is the sudden striking materialization of the paramour as an externalized presence— the one time in the poetry that the "sibyl of the self" jumps out of her skin, so to speak, like the snake. In the "Farewell" Stevens plays on the idea of *leaving*, connecting it with the loss of prophetic power, the barbarous scattering of sibylline leaves, "leaves in which the wind kept up its sound" (*CP*, 117). The poet journeys toward a "leafless" north, the absence of passion and its power. As John Hollander has shown, Stevens displays "a great command of the dynamic range of echo, from the almost blatantly allusive to the most muted and problematic of phantoms."[15] Clearly, the fugal play on *leaves* and *leave-taking*, particularly in this poem, echoes Shelley's "Ode to the West Wind." More pointedly, it calls up Dante's epic simile of the dead souls at the gate of hopelessness.

The singer of Key West is the genius of presence, the composer of the here and now. But she is also the genius loci, and an unusual one in that respect too. For the locus is not so much a place as it is a triple threshold—she strides along the margins of sea and shore and sky. Her song not only "makes" the world—that is, composes the natural world into an intelligible and harmonious order—but opens the entrance from the known world to whatever lies beyond the "fragrant portals, dimly starred" (*CP*, 130). In "The Idea of Order at Key West," Stevens unmasks the "enigma and mask": "The sea was not a mask. No more was she"

(*CP,* 128). But unmasked, she is like Echo: pure presence reduced to voice. We can hear her continuo over the pounding surf, but only the poet sees the moving rhythmic figure and only he knows who the name-less "she" really is.

In "Farewell to Florida" the poet means to detach from the paramour. He intends to sever all ties except the continuity of memory:

> To stand here on the deck in the dark and say
> Farewell and to know that that land is forever gone
> And that she will not follow in any word
> Or look, nor ever again in thought, except
> That I loved her once.
>
> (*CP,* 118)

The relinquishment in Stevens' "to know that that land is forever gone" has the same quality of bitter knowledge that controls the close of Thomas's "Fern Hill." Stevens does sail north to a wintry "slime of men in crowds," and in the splendid "Idea of Order at Key West" manages to thrust the paramour outside the self. The singer, the maker, the sibylline presence, the lover that lies within, is situated on an exterior plane, moving along the edges of a marginal world, haunting the dimly starred threshold of the possible. Fortunately, she does not remain in exile. Toward the end of the poetry, when Stevens is in his seventies, we are given "Final Soliloquy of the Interior Paramour," and we understand that she has been with him all along.

4

Imaginary Politics
Emerson, Stevens, and the Resistance of Style

Daniel T. O'Hara

"Your condition, your employment, is the fable of you."
—Ralph Waldo Emerson,
 "Poetry and Imagination"

I would walk alone,
Under the quiet stars, and at that time
Have felt whate'er there is of power in sound
To breathe an elevated wood, by form
Or image unprofaned; and I would stand,
If the night blackened with a coming storm,
Beneath some rock, listening to notes that are
The ghostly language of the ancient earth,
Or make their dim abode in distant words.
Thence did I drink the visionary power;
—William Wordsworth, *The Prelude* (1850)

"Ecstasy," according to Emerson in "The Method of Nature" (1849), is "the law and cause" of being.[1] He means the in-coming of energy ever becomes the out-going of expression in act or word projected beyond the material limits of individual entities. Poems and beehives are but two examples. Individuals are "vents for the current of inward life which increases as it is spent."[2] For Emerson, each person expresses genius uniquely—if unconsciously—like someone "always spoken to [and through] from behind, and unable to turn . . . and see the speaker."[3] A ravishing, heavenly music arises out of such transcendental ventriloquism as long as the individual does not allow the contingent aspects of life to obstruct the essential flow. When such an obstruction occurs, either the energy accumulates to the point of mountainous explosion, or the voice of genius "grows faint, and at last is but a humming in the ear."[4] All would-be Ariels can become mere Calibans in the end. The poet's voice, therefore, is like either an underground river coming out into the light or a volcanic devastation reduced to an irritable noise.

Emerson intends the phrase "The work of ecstasy," (to be somewhat of an oxymoron like the title "The Method of Nature"). Ecstasy and nature, work and method, are pairs of synonymous antinomies when set in opposition on the basis of a critical standard of ideal or universal spontaneity. Nature methodized, of course, is a Popean turn of phrase defining the supposed essence of art. But spontaneity and method conjoin to recall Wordsworth's definition of romantic poetry from the Preface to *Lyrical Ballads* as a spontaneous overflow of powerful feelings recollected in tranquility. Meanwhile, the project of stepping out of oneself—the prospect of going beyond one's limits—recalls Kant's critical philosophy of epistemological and moral transcendence, and anticipates Heidegger's existential ontology of human being as repeatedly thrown into the there of being beside onself. This rapid metamorphosis of conflicting allusions, back and forth between early and later periods and between Anglo-American and European sources, represents Emerson's ecstatic method of composition and, I think, Stevens' typical poetic working.

For Emerson, in "Spiritual Laws," such subjective agency is interwoven with the idea of vocation. You are what your talent calls you to do. And you do what you are in the specific work only you can do.

Each man has his own vocation. The talent is the call. There is one direction in which all space is open to him. He has faculties silently inviting him thither to endless exertion. He is like a ship in a river; he runs against obstructions on every side but one; on that side all obstruction is taken away, and he sweeps serenely over a deepening channel into an infinite sea. This talent and this call depend on his organization, or the mode in which the general soul incarnates itself in him. He inclines to do something which is easy to him, and good when it is done, but which no other man can do. He has no rival. For the more truly he consults his own powers, the more difference will his work exhibit from the work of any other. His ambition is exactly proportioned to his powers. The height of the pinnacle is determined by the breadth of the base. Every man has this call of the power to do somewhat unique, and no man has any other call. The pretence that he has another call, a summons by name and personal election and outward "signs that mark him extraordinary, and not in the roll of common men," is fanaticism, and betrays obtuseness to perceive that there is one mind in all individuals, and no respect of persons therein.[5]

The passage resonates with religious overtones (and male chauvinism). Nevertheless, as Emerson's own final remarks underscore, it also points, via the ship analogy, to a secular, communal, and non-transcendental theory of vocation. The idea informing this analogy is what Emerson, in his 1837–38 lectures on human culture, called "abandonment," though he does not use that term here. Bereft of any conventional, familial, or religious authorization, each of us is totally given over to abandonment. We fluently abandon ourselves in turn to action, to the only action one's talent proposes as the calling to do one's unique work. There is in this overdetermined sense of abandonment, more a hedonic than an ascetic imperative, virtually with the sensual appeal of sexual surrender. And as the ship analogy also implies, such unique work is necessarily artisan-like, a specialized skill, and part of a collective effort of equally unique works done by equally different others. Such a vision incorporates, of course, the art of steering well. In thus collectively yet uniquely "going with the flow," each one acts out his talent as an intentional role in the grand enterprise of humanity that is forever in passage "over a deepening channel into an infinite sea."

Whenever I use the term "the plural subject," I mean to invoke this sort of dialectical theory of individual yet collective agency (or democratic "genius"). And, after late Foucault and Kristeva, I see it as a basically literary subject, because only the class of literary intellectuals have the opportunity to maximize such abandonment to their vocation, although this does not imply that other groups of workers have no such opportunities. But literary intellectuals, in their works, constitute the primary radical and utopian measure by which we can judge the often parodic difference between the communal ideal of free human agency and the actual degraded forms of our alienation. Only in Emerson's vision of people working together skillfully and moving toward their equally individual yet collective fates can we get a sense of the world his vocational theory of abandonment urges us to work for.[6]

My point in proposing this Emersonian version of agency is to suggest that there is a variety of literary forms of agency, with Emerson's being but one predominant form.[7] There are, apparently, several theories of agency in Emerson, one of which, because it is so influential, I will examine now for its possible relationship to what I call the vocation of abandonment.[8]

At first blush, "The Over-Soul," with its transcendental Plotinian religiosity, could not be further from the practical analogy of the ship in the river, with its material urgency of finding the ways to our own work. For the union of soul and Over-Soul announces the apocalypse of the mind: "The things we now esteem fixed shall, one by one, detach themselves, like ripe fruit, from our experience, and fall. The wind shall blow them none knows whither. The landscape, the figures, Boston, London, are facts as fugitive as any institution past, or any whiff of mist or smoke, and so is society, and so is the world. The soul looketh steadily forwards, creating a world before her, leaving worlds behind her. She has no dates, nor rites, nor persons, nor specialties, nor men. The soul knows only the soul; the web of events is the flowing robe in which she is clothed."[9] The moments when the individual soul opens to receive the divine influx of the Over-Soul are when this apocalyptic productivity arises. Here Emerson's heady spouts of literary vision are prefiguring, I think, the climactic scene of creative making in Stevens' "The Idea of Order at Key West," even as they echo the meditative provocation in Wordsworth's "The Solitary Reaper."

Nevertheless, Emerson's image of the most well established things in our world detaching themselves, one by one, and falling, "like ripe fruit," suggests a more historical material sense of the revolutionary transformation attendant upon apocalyptic agency. It suggests the abandonment of these things to the internal logic of their own developmental, often self-parodic, unfolding; that is, it suggests the prospect of their unwitting abandonment to the vocation of perishing. While Aristotle is hardly the usual source for citations when interpreting Emerson, his sense of beings striving to perfect themselves unto the death would be the most traditionally appropriate philosophical prefiguration of this vision, even as Freud's discovery of the death drive as the individual organism's unique way *to* and work *of* death would be the most appropriate modern variation. Nietzsche's *Zarathustra*, in the opening sections, uses Emerson's imagery that evokes the coming of the Overman. These figures of romantic organicism, whether finally traceable to Aristotle or not, transume mere biologism, I believe, due to their imaginative recognition of the repetitive mortal structure of human temporality remarkably akin to Heidegger's existential analysis in *Being and Time:* "These things we now esteem fixed shall, one by one, detach themselves, like ripe fruit, from experience, and fall. The wind shall blow them none knows whither." Emerson's tropes theorize agency, much as does his "Poetry and Imagination" when it defines the poet as an embodied trope, in terms of the vocation of abandonment, a calling working through a revisionary turning. [10]

That this theory is essentially literary and not religious Emerson makes abundantly clear in the most famous passage in the essay, a passage that resounds backward through the authors he cites to the classical sources so fascinating to the late Foucault, the very same classical sources (such as Plutarch) that Nietzsche uses for his model of self-overcoming selves, his aristocracy of souls.

Humanity shines in Homer, in Chaucer, in Spenser, in Shakespeare, in Milton. They are content with truth. They use the positive degree. They

seem frigid and phlegmatic to those who have been spiced with the frantic
passion and violent coloring of inferior, but popular writers. For they are
poets by the free course which they allow to the informing soul, which
through their eyes beholds again, and blesses the things which it hath
made. The soul is superior to its knowledge; wiser than any of its works.
The great poet makes us feel our own wealth, and then we think less of his
compositions. His best communication to our mind is to teach us to
despise all he has done. Shakespeare carries us to such a lofty strain of
intelligent activity, as to suggest a wealth which beggars his own; and we
then feel that the splendid works which he has created, and which in other
hours we extol as a sort of self-existent poetry, take no stronger hold of
real nature that the shadow of a passing traveller on the rock. The inspiration which uttered itself in Hamlet and Lear could utter things as good
from day to day, for ever. Why, then, should I make account of Hamlet and
Lear, as if we had not the soul from which they fell as syllables from the
tongue?[11]

What Emerson is calling "The Over-Soul" is really a treasure hoard of
masks. Shakespeare, Milton, Spenser, and so on constitute a collective
archive of literary agents abandoning themselves to their self-overcoming
vocation of being passed on to future generations and not used like
capitalist commodities, consumed once and for all, but like Foucault's
vision of the open strategic games of love and friendship, repeatedly
consumed in their serious playing as select practices of self: "a society of
souls."[12]

Unfortunately, however, Emerson concludes "The Over-Soul" with a
vision that sounds more like alienation than plural agency:

The soul gives itself, alone, original, and pure, to the Lonely, Original,
and Pure, who, on that condition, gladly inhabits, leads, and speaks
through it. Then it is glad, young, and nimble. It is not wise, but sees
through all things. It is not called religious, but it is innocent. It calls the
light its own, and feels that the grass grows and the stone falls by a law
inferior to, and dependent on, its nature. Behold, it saith, I am born into
the great, the universal mind. I, the imperfect, adore my own Perfect. I
am somehow receptive of the great soul, and thereby I do overlook the sun
and the stars, and feel them to be the fair accidents and effects which

change and pass. More and more the surges of everlasting nature enter into me, and I become public and human in my regards and actions.[13]

Here only the lonely can love one another, but in "Experience" and elsewhere, each can only repel the other, infinitely. This would be the vocation of abandonment, with a vengeance, in the most literal and brutal of senses, which corresponds to Emerson's chronic refusal to do the entire work of mourning, preferring, as in the case of his brother, Charles, to say he has abandoned the other first, even before death has supervened. This climactic passage of "The Over-Soul" also anticipates what Kristeva and other psychoanalytic critics see as the narcissistic rage for celebrity in our postmodern media culture: "I, the imperfect, adore my own Perfect." As I argue elsewhere in detail, each first-person singular is poor and vacant until the dream of the fabulous universal third person appears reflected back from the latest media mirror. Is it Jay Gatsby or "Bob," the American psycho of NBC's "Twin Peaks," that inhabits us all? What a prospect, ripe for parody, such possible mis-recognitions make!

Even this popular degradation of Emerson's active soul involves in alienated form the vocation of abandonment as we drift along and imaginatively merge, on occasion, with our media extensions. It is the price we pay in America for giving democratic access to the greater vision of the active soul that higher education affords. Because the literary production of texts, with its semantic overdetermination and ironic stylistic complexities, tends to resist the purely throwaway commodification of dreams our consumer culture would uniformly enforce, it is primarily literary art that should be the vocation to which, each in his or her own unique way, we would yet collectively abandon ourselves.

A poetic of intertextuality based on such an Emersonian conception of natural vocation internalizes the perpetual abandonment of each prior position in the chain of allusions, transforming the accompanying moment of loss into a renewed impetus for further imaginative mobility. Abandonment in every sense becomes a vocation for the poet, since the standard of perfection is a nature that is ever on the way to its predetermined but unknown fulfillment or realization in some ultimate but apparently unreachable expression. If Hegel temporalizes Aristotle's sense of nature's final form, Emerson's transcendental skepticism refuses any certain knowledge of the goal, however inevitable it may be. By means of such intertextual liberality and openness, then, a writer achieves a more universal albeit unconscious frame of reference, the ironic form and play of which traces the lineaments of a writer's sources of authority. And one can read this meditative genealogy, with its variable resistance of style, for the imaginary politics—or the political dimensions of the imaginary and its captivating powers—that such play allegorically enacts.

I begin with this Emersonian poetics because it establishes succinctly the American romantic conception of genius that Stevens inherits. It is well known that Stevens read Emerson at Harvard and after, having received from his mother the 1903–4 twelve-volume *Collected Works*. And it has been generally well demonstrated by Harold Bloom and others that Stevens, whatever his degree of indebtedness to the French Symbolists, also owed much to Emerson. One brief but salient example of this compelling connection previously mentioned crystallizes when one reads the central vision of "The Idea of Order at Key West," with its young woman on the shore singing beyond the genius of the sea and making her own exemplary world, and the central vision of "The Over-Soul," with its perpetually youthful soul (personified as the muse), "creating a world before her, leaving worlds behind her," for whom, as she progressively advances, "the web of events is the flowing robe in which she is clothed."[14] This closing image of the Emerson Over-Soul accounts for (among other things) the ghostly "empty sleeves"[15] at the opening of the Stevens poem. Such an Emersonian vision of genius haunts Stevens as he ever inquires of its mysterious making and unmaking of worlds, "Whose spirit is this?"

The experience of genius that Emerson proposes and Stevens meditates is what psychoanalytic theory calls "projective identification." A natural object or process, a person, a collectivity, a work of art, or even an abstract ideal can elicit a regressive act of psychic incorporation on the original model of the most intense aspects of the mother/child fusion bond. Such later or secondary identification of self and world, if strong enough, can thus reactivate the repressed feelings associated with this primary fusion state. These feelings include not only what we call "love," of course, but also a rage to possess and consume or to be possessed and be consumed that knows no bounds. The loss of this state of primary fusion and its subsequent, always inadequate avatars of identification (inadequate because they are derivative and temporary) fuel the quest for perfect fusion with further rage, a rage at both the original wound of loss and its later reopenings. The psyche, in this light, becomes a composite belated assemblage of abandoned projective identifications, like a landscape of volcanoes that have all blown their tops.

Julia Kristeva in her recent essay "Identification and the Real" develops this psychoanalytic theory of psychic composition beyond Freud's and Lacan's work on mourning and melancholia, death and the imaginary.[16] She argues that in the case of "symbolic sublimation" the child unlearns the fusion with the mother, who in our culture must suffer abjection so that the child may move beyond image/thing perception to linguistic symbolization and cognition. Instead, the child now primarily identifies with the next figure in the chain of the family romance, the imaginary father of individual prehistory. This is an alternative figure standing between the abjected mother and the Oedipal patriarch. It is like the figure in Emerson's vision in his essay on Swedenborg, or like that in many of Stevens' poems. It incorporates the gender characteristics of both sexes. The child's fantasy of the phallic mother becomes this vision of the maternal patriarch, a development complicating Western misogyny. Such catachresis preserves and advances at the same time the desires of the psyche via a chiasmatic or crisscross troping. As Kristeva puts it, the process of primary identification does not complete itself in the pre-Oedipal period until, "transferred to the Other, in identification, I become One with the Other throughout the whole range of the symbolic, the imaginary, and the real."[17] This powerfully generalized *"Einfühlung"* or "empathy" is "appropriate to certain amorous, hypnotic, or even mystical states."[18] For Kristeva, then, "the primary identification of the subject," when completed, "occurs with a primitive figure of the imaginary father possessing the sexual attributes of both parents."[19]

Thanks both to Stevens' meditative, often ironic incorporation of Emerson and to this reading of Kristeva's revisionary theory of identification, we can see more clearly the full outlines of the drama of genius Stevens performs in his poetry. The poetry is always a reflection upon and of a transcendental or first idea. This is the idea of an intense experience of identification virtually to the point of fusion. The poetry is thus a later imaginative reasoning about this first idea of original and ecstatic empathy, the pure form of an apocalyptic (and hence clearly ambivalent) love that creates and recreates selves and worlds the way the poet does personae and words. It is as if Stevens is ontologically, not just historically or literally, belated. His existence, that is, is ironically ecstatic, always beyond itself in reflection, with experience always to be imaginatively (re-)discovered. It is a web of after-words reflecting poignantly, wryly, comically, or self-parodically upon the "memory" of an experience he must first (re-)construct, and then repeatedly interpret. It is as though he is reading the shape and size of the maternal/paternal mountain, as well as the intensity of the explosion, from the ruins of the original eruption that has given him birth.

With such a poetic project, it is no wonder that the defining quality of Stevens' style is a dense and complex allusiveness sometimes to the point of absolute obscurity. His use of allusion, as Harold Bloom first develops, differs totally from T. S. Eliot's more familiar, conspicuous kind. And in the work of two recent critics, Eleanor Cook and Barbara Fisher, we can begin to see the full range of his far-fetching figures. Classical references (to Virgil), medieval allusions (to Dante and the Provençal poets) are also made, resonating darkly amidst the already slightly askew tropings upon Emerson, Shelley, Wordsworth, and Milton. These allusions almost but do not quite echo their apparent sources. As Cook nicely glosses this phenomenon, Stevens' evasive echoing is a form of "transitory allusion," what Emerson calls rhetorical power, "the shooting of the gulf." Such "glancing" reference tends just to skip by its source so that, as Cook puts it, "we do not take over the full context of the original."[20] Fisher describes excellently the way poetry thus consists in a variable psychic space of such allusive evasions or evasive allusions, a grandly abstract yet changing pattern of pleasurable if hauntingly ambiguous or undulating resonances making up the "tremenos" or "templum" feel of a sacred enclosure that Stevens' most hieratic poetry inspires.[21] It is within this maternal-like mental space that the poetry stages its often comic drama of identification with the genius of the imaginary father taking on much of the context's mothering aspects.

As we shall see, this resistance of Stevens' style to conspicuous allusion, and so to complete (sometimes even partial) lucidity, composes his imaginary politics, in which familial, personal, and social relations become different qualities of his inclusive psychic landscape. As a result, his poetry stands firmly in opposition to the reductive modern commodification of aesthetic objects for ideological or commercial purposes of any stripe. Stevens, in short, produces his dense networks of repressed and often virtually unnameable intertextuality in order to project a palpable if still "fluent mundo" as his version of what Kristeva in *Black Sun* terms "the lost Thing," that is, the sadly inscribed fanciful "memory" of the mother-child disintegrating fusion bond.[22] Interior paramour, "fat girl," muse-figure, or created paradisal site—all are his tropes for this "lost Thing" that the poetry would recover by allusively embodying. The imaginary politics that Stevens thus practices in and through the resistance of his style is a belated modernist preservation of the apocalyptic romantic desire for the return to Eden, a desire that seeks definitive personal and political expressions that remain impossible and so are provocations to disastrous frustrations.

The conclusion of "A Postcard from the Volcano" contains a paradigmatic expression of Stevensian allusiveness. Since most critics agree that, in Frank Lentricchia's memorable phrase, the poem's opening mood is one of "authoritative wistfulness," even if they disagree over its significance, I will accept that characterization, too, for most of the poem.[23] But its conclusion is anything but wistful, however authoritative sounding it continues to be. (If anything, the last three stanzas sound even more authoritative.) To my ear, the poem ends not on a note of wistfulness but on one of ever-increasing defiance, as the final lines accumulate and mass into a climactic scene of opulent if impersonal self-display:

Children,
Still weaving budded aureoles,
Will speak our speech and never know,

Will say of the mansion that it seems
As if he that lived there left behind
A spirit storming in blank walls,

A dirty house in a gutted world,
A tatter of shadows peaked to white,
Smeared with the gold of the opulent sun.

(*CP*, 159)

It may be that the dying social and cultural order of 1935 will be replaced by a more innocent, know-nothing order to come, but the children of that future (and our present) epoch will have to speak of the past, however unwittingly, in the terms that past fashioned for itself and handed on to the future in the only styles of perception, feeling, and language still available for use. And the poem's final four lines, I believe, compose a single monumental apocalyptic image whose ghostly lineaments ironically suggest the superbly artificial and literate volcano that a Stevens would put together and elaborate, Van Gogh-like, in order to drive his point home with a vengeance. And this is a point that goes far beyond his play on the banal "wish you were here" of postcard convention. "So you think I am an outmoded elitist chauvinist aesthete," one can almost hear Stevens chuckling demonically (and somewhat anachronistically) to himself as he composes these lines, "well, then, here's your 'real me' for you, in the grandly decadent style."

By attending to the formal features of tone, imagery, and rhythm, one can hear what critics who focus on the purely social dimensions often miss: comically heroic defiance of all merely social pressures. Moreover, if one pays close attention to the play of allusion in the poem, then the defiance becomes, if possible, even more pronounced. The title and setting of the poem, for example, allude rather directly to Nietzsche's widely cited, extravagantly aesthetic injunction from *The Gay Science* to "live dangerously" by building our cities on "the slopes of Vesuvius." The last four lines amass similar apocalyptic images that transform to Stevens' own purpose of comic defiance four sets of literary allusions. Shakespeare's King Lear and Hamlet, I think, animate "A spirit storming in blank walls," and Milton's scenes of comic devastation from *Paradise Lost* construct "A dirty house in a gutted world," I am almost certain. Meanwhile, both Shelley's abstract Power from "Mont Blanc" and his Demogorgon from "Prometheus Unbound" weave the deep, spectral truth of "A tatter of shadows peaked to white" (*CP*, 159). Finally, Stevens' own early solar impersonations, especially the golden utopian vision of male power in the famous seventh stanza of "Sunday Morning," appear to shine playfully through in the grandly self-deprecating, self-asserting last line of the poem. All such revisionary imagery of dangerous literary strength Stevens ironically composes without any sentimental evasions: "Smeared with the gold of the opulent sun." This perversely glorious aestheticism ("Smeared") is the inescapable hallmark of his modernism.

In this putting together of a pattern of allusive evasions (hence my resistance to identifying definitively his sources), Stevens constructs the psychic space or matrix in and out of which his major version of the imaginary father, that figure symbolizing the mother/child bond even as it would transcend it, may mountainously arise and be equally celebrated and degraded. (Hence, Stevens' "smear" job). In this powerfully ironic fashion, Stevens both extends the abjection of the mother to incorporate partially the imaginary father and transfers back to her some of the reflected glory of her volcanically active poetic offspring, the prophetic persona pronouncing this final outrageous pun.

In "How to Live. What to Do" Stevens sketches the plot of his dream songs. The first two lines allude, glancingly to be sure, to Yeats's contemporaneous poem, "Byzantium" (1933), and its opening line "The unpurged images of day recede" (*CP*, 248).

Last evening the moon rose above this rock
Impure upon a world unpurged.

The man and his companion stopped
To rest before the heroic height.

(*CP*, 125)

For Stevens, there is no possible escape in vision or into the afterlife that would satisfy the poetic imagination's desire for ideal purity, a perfection of (self-)expression impossible to attain even as it is ever possible to envision. Instead, Stevens' ironic reduction of Yeats's visionary poet and his ghostly companion, of Byzantium's moonlit (or starlit) landscape and of San Sophia, attests to the persistence of the desire not for purity per se, as for the "fuller fire" (*CP*, 125) of a sun not "flame-freaked." That is, what one really wants is more life and capacity, not the spectral overview of life and power.

The bare scene of poet and muse (the original pedagogic pair), confronting the moonlit-tufted rock of literary tradition, dramatizes perfectly the title as a romantic listening to the rising wind:

There was
Only the great height of the rock
And the two of them standing still to rest.

There was the cold wind and the sound
It made, away from the muck of the land
That they had left, heroic sound
Joyous and jubilant and sure.

(*CP*, 126)

If this "heroic sound" in its redoubled and so reassuring jubilation means to allude to Emerson's vision of the creative voice of the soul, then the resonance of the couple's archetypal situation, moving "away from the muck of the land," refers not only to the contemporary American world of "mickey mockers" (see "The American Sublime") but also perhaps to the exit scene of *Paradise Lost*, when Adam and Eve leave paradise with all the world before them, going about their solitary way. The major difference between this literary archetype and Stevens' poem lies in the attitude of listening that would complete the return to Paradise now stalled. It is as if in leaving "the muck of the land" Stevens' couple is listening back to a prophetic recitation of their world to come in Paradise. Or, it may be, that the heroic sound of the wind they are listening to may only tell them of the laughter of Satan. Such opposing intertextual possibilities make "How to Live. What to Do" a little-resonating world.

Rather than settling on one or two sets of possible identification here, however, it would be more productive to see Dante and Petrarch, along with Emerson and Milton, hovering in the air and inhabiting its many "majesties of sound" (*CP*, 125). (Allusions to *The Tempest* and Wordsworth's *The Prelude*, book II, lines 303–11, and even *The Waste Land*, can also be heard, despite the differences in landscape or other details). The tufted rock and the clouds its ridges embrace "like arms" (*CP*, 125) could then be taken for this poet's latest expression of the literary tradition's imaginary father (or poetic word) and abjected mother (or nature), with the former's mountainous tuft chiasmatically suggesting something of the latter's visionary curl. The poem thus is a powerfully resonant allegory of the modern poet's dilemma when facing tradition in a land of muck (or America). Remember too well, and become a luminous sputtering, a "flame-freaked sun" (*CP*, 125). Forget too well, and become speechless, imageless, songless, without mediator or savior: "There was neither voice, nor crested image, / No chorister, nor priest" (*CP*, 126). Allude evasively, however, and then listen all night to the bracing "cold wind" as it sublimely responds by articulating "the great height of the rock" in "heroic sound / Joyous and jubilant and sure" (*CP*, 126). That is, sublimate the desire for a purified mother tongue eloquently to express the patriarchy, and the poem can then embody differentially, in ceaseless interplay of interpretive possibilities, the Other of tradition in one's own unique and spontaneous voicing.

"A Dish of Peaches in Russia," however, makes the repeated experience of this unique unconscious voicing sound close to psychosis. Twice the poem asks, "Who speaks?" And the poem gives more than two answers to this question. A Frenchman, a Spaniard, a lover, or perhaps a Russian exile: All are possible speakers for portions of the poem, which as a whole has yet another, formal narrative voice in which the other voices are barely contained. The poem takes off from a contemporary magazine article about a Cézanne held captive by the Kremlin in the Hermitage. What results from this point of departure is the poet's meditation in his room. He pictures a dish of peaches and becomes in turn different personae as he would imaginatively experience in this round the full sensuous delight of the meditative fruit. Each persona permits another perspective to emerge in this experimental attempt to comprehend the sensuous quality of the peaches in the aesthetic form of the poem:

> With my whole body I taste these peaches,
> I touch them and smell them. Who speaks?
>
> I absorb them as the Angevine
> Absorbs Anjou. I see them as a lover sees,
>
> As a young lover sees the first buds of spring
> And as the black Spaniard plays his guitar.
>
> Who speaks? But it must be that I,
> That animal, that Russian, that exile, for whom
>
> The bells of the chapel pullulate sounds at
> Heart. The peaches are large and round,
>
> Ah! and red; and they have peach fuzz, ah!
> They are full of juice and the skin is soft.
>
> They are full of the colors of my village
> And of fair weather, summer, dew, peace.

> (*CP*, 224)

Here sound is less heroic than sensual, breeding more sounds in the heart, with the pullulating echo of chickens suggesting Williams' proletarian portrait of the red wheelbarrow, even as the prospect that it may be the Cézanne itself speaking must be entertained until the poem's conclusion. For the poem concludes with a return to the previously unidentified site of origin, the poet's room. The Hermitage and Kremlin, Anjou and the Angevine, Spain, France, and all their masks are left behind, abandoned, absorbed into the final reflection on the poet's psychic splitting or plural subjectivity, whose ferocious nature is provoked by these peaches, the only objects, after the curtains drift off, that remain in the end:

The room is quiet where they are.
The windows are open. The sunlight fills

The curtains. Even the drifting of the curtains,
Slight as it is, disturbs me. I did not know

That such ferocities could tear
One self from another, as these peaches do.

(*CP*, 224)

Such tearing of one self from another resounds complexly, to say the least. It is as if the poet has become and is turning from himself as his own precursor.

The psyche in Stevens is largely a contingent assemblage of abandoned object identifications. It is an accumulated deposit of spectral images or specular memories. Only the earliest, simplest, and most capacious model of organization—that of the mother/child dyad—can accommodate all these later precipitations of identity. In this context, the ferocious tearing of self from self that the peaches inspire resembles a continual process of giving birth. It is a repeated standing outside of or beside oneself. This is a poetic life whose law is a cultivated ecstasy, and whose cause is knowledge of the self as other. The imaginary politics entailed by this psychic economy requires the other as the different in order to express itself as such ferocious tearing. The peaches must be both artificial (painted) and elsewhere (in the Hermitage) so that they can provoke the splitting of the subject into a series of romantic, at times sentimental, personae within the self-reflexive ironic frame of a poetic act of knowledge. "Who speaks?" is, then, an urgent and not a rhetorical question, since within the endless frame of imaginative intertextual reference in a Stevens poem any one of several selves may claim to be speaker with as much right as the purely formal narrating voice; for that formal poetic persona is so less aesthetically interesting than any of the voices sounding through its mask.

The proliferation of selves as personae and poetic masks reaches its limit, however, when the self that does speak amidst whatever ferocious dramatic effects still occur can no longer credit any object with sensuous or passionate investment sufficient to carry off the latest performance with conviction. A dissemination of selves results in a dispersal of objects. "Pro forma–ism" or "a going through the motions" may become the norm. So desire rehearses itself as a mobile or a motionless, purely operatic chaos. All is very affective in a stagey way. A depressingly cold comic scenario unfolds:

> Oh, that this lashing wind was something more
> Than the spirit of Ludwig Richter . . .
>
> The rain is pouring down. It is July.
> There is lightning and the thickest thunder.
>
> It is a spectacle. Scene 10 becomes 11,
> In Series X, Act IV, et cetera.
>
> People fall out of windows, trees tumble down,
> Summer is changed to winter, the young grow old,
>
> The air is full of children, statues, roofs
> And snow. The theatre is spinning round,
>
> Colliding with deaf-mute churches and optical trains.
> The most massive sopranos are singing songs of scales.
>
> (CP, 357)

The entire theatre of the world, facing its apocalypse, has become a poor man's version of Wagner produced by a grandiloquent fool. The ironic consequence of a hyperdeveloped poetic self-consciousness is not only the absence of any object adequate to one's desire. It is also the reduction of desire to a mindless childish violence for which papier-mâché is the only appropriate medium. This powerfully empty act of the mind removes the poet's comic surrogate, Ludwig Richter, turbulent Schlemihl, from the only whole he knows, the previous round of identifications and abandonments:

> And Ludwig Richter, turbulent Schlemihl,
> Has lost the whole in which he was contained,
>
> Knows desire without an object of desire,
> All mind and violence and nothing felt.
>
> He knows he has nothing more to think about,
> Like the wind that lashes everything at once.
>
> (*CP*, 358)

The fatal condition of knowing desire without an object of desire means that the speaker identifies with the primary processes as if before the appearance of object-relations. In other words, object-relations, already no longer real, have been abandoned for the apocalypse of the mind in the narcissistic immersion in a purely preconscious knowing: No thought or feeling is possible, only an affectless screening of desire. This fixation upon the imaginary *per se* is like the picture of a kiss offered to a splintering mirror, a freeze-frame for the finale of the reel, a chaos in motion and not in motion indeed. Here radical (self-)parody, with all its possible scenes of multiple misrecognition, reaches its limit.

The resistance of style in Stevens may begin as a resistance to ideological and commercial commodification, but it must end as a kind of self-resistance, as a resistance to the poet's psychic demise in his own reflexive medium: a postmodern Urizen awash in the waters of his own production. The recapitulation of the mother/child fusion bond becomes a total dissemination in such poems as "Chaos in Motion and Not in Motion." This defines Stevens' plight. "Large Red Man Reading," in this claustrophobic light, performs his deliverance. By distancing his plight via the ironic surrogate of Ludwig Richter, Stevens merely delineates it in a finer tone. In "Large Red Man Reading," however, Stevens repeats the movement from the earliest position of desire, to which he has now

regressed, forward to the figure of the imaginary father, thereby creating
a space in which objects of desire, however transparently fictional they
may be, can once again appear, even as he simultaneously takes an
imaginative stand as if in the aboriginal world of the first word's utterance.
This final fiction of his new first word is justified by the psychological
justice of the poet repeating the normative model of imaginative development here, from abjected mother to imaginary father and his poetic law.

> There were ghosts that returned to earth to hear his phrases,
> As he sat there reading, aloud, the great blue tabulae.
> They were those from the wilderness of stars that had
>   expected more.
>
> There were those that returned to hear him read from the poem
>   of life,
> Of the pans above the stove, the pots on the table, the
>   tulips among them.
> There were those that would have wept to step barefoot into
>   reality,
>
> That would have wept and been happy, have shivered in the
>   frost
>
> And cried out to feel it again, have run fingers over leaves
> And against the most coiled thorn, have seized on what was
>   ugly
>
> And laughed, as he sat there reading, from out of the purple
>   tabulae,
> The outlines of being and its expressings, the syllables of
>   its law:
> *Poesis, poesis*, the literal characters, the vatic lines,
>
> Which in those ears and in those thin, those spended hearts,
> Took on color, took on shape and the size of things as they
>   are
> And spoke the feeling for them, which was what they had
>   lacked.

(CP, 423–24)

The title persona may be the sun, an Indian chieftain, Whitman in either or both guises, or a self-parodically phantasmagoric, breathless Stevens on the lecture circuit, an Emerson manqué. This allusive ambiguity or variable reference to possible avatars of the imaginary father frees the poet's desire from its too-perfect identification with the engulfing medium of its abject self-reflection, releasing desire to the ecstatic and progressive performances of the symbolic chain of signifiers and so symbolically transuming death in this protean social (because discursive) reality of being's poetic law of endless metamorphosis.

The ghosts resuscitated by the poem of life may be as much the abandoned revisionary identifications of the poet as his actual or imaginary ancestors. His once novel psychic personae or spectral masks from the earlier poetry such as "Tea at the Palaz of Hoon" or "The Sleight-of-Hand Man" may be reappearing here. They are supplied with what they had lacked on their quest for the stars by Stevens' imaginary father, this solar creator or "fuller fire," who as day changes to evening pleases himself in outlining with his breath the prophetically literal divinations of being and its law: *"Poesis, poesis."* The volcanic personality who needed to know "how to live" and "what to do" and who chased his own disseminated selves to the wilderness of stars until all became a fixation upon and in a chaotic void, here recovers his resistance to the death of the imagination by publicly avowing his imaginary father. This is a variable composite figure curiously enshrined in the domestic realm of pots and pans, as if this father through his feeling has taken on or preserved the primary quality of the abjected maternal imago. Such is Stevens' normative model of imaginative development in its final mode. The ideal of psychic wholeness necessarily incorporates all the culturally marked features of human being in poetic form.

Not only do we now see how the sexual politics of the family romance tend to work out in Stevens via this creative repetition of the normative model of psyche development, we also can read from its dynamics a cautionary lesson for educating our own desire for political criticism. The promotion of race, class, and gender studies under the aegis of poststructuralism, postmodernism, or the new historicism challenges the traditional patriarchal canon in the name of all those who have suffered abjection in our culture. As such, the abjected mother can readily be taken as the representative type toward which this ideological criticism moves as it would perfect its celebration of difference in a politics of identity appropriate to each of its constituencies. The danger in such a purely oppositional position, as we can see imaginatively outlined in these (self-)opposing lyrics from the course of Stevens' career, is that the perfection of such politics may lead to the collapse of the self into the purely reflexive world of its own rhetoric without reference to the reality of objects its desire once identified with in its difference from the allegedly false ideals of the culture it had critiqued. In the Emersonian terms with which we began, such criticism, like Stevens' poetry at times, may be in jeopardy of refusing "the work of ecstacy," the project of standing outside or beside oneself, and so is unable to become self-critical by identifying with and avowing its imaginary fathers. Instead it remains completely captivated by the perpetual embrace of abjection which Nietzsche defines as the fate of resentment. If you play the victim seeking justice and justification for too long, then you end up victimizing all concerned, for good. In short, a little aesthetic (and analytic) distance could prove salutary.

5

The Fat Girl in Paradise
Stevens, Wordsworth, Milton, and the Proper Name

Paul Morrison

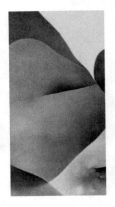

> But how can I put "I love you" differently? I love you, my
> indifferent one?
> —Luce Irigaray

Stevens begins "Notes toward a Supreme Fiction" with a "decreative" Genesis,[1] an injunction to unname the sun:

> There is a project for the sun. The sun
> Must bear no name, gold flourisher, but be
> In the difficulty of what it is to be.
>
> (*CP*, 381)

Stevens concludes his poem, however, with a "fluent mundo," a recovered Eden, a reconstituted proper name:

> They will get it straight one day at the Sorbonne.
> We shall return at twilight from the lecture
> Pleased that the irrational is rational,
>
> Until flicked by feeling, in a gildered street,
> I call you by name, my green, my fluent mundo.
>
> (*CP*, 406–7)

Derrida names this movement toward naming "flatly" (*CP*, 406)—of which Stevens' entire poem can be seen as an example—an "eschatologie du *propre*";[2] it might also be characterized as a return to Edenic conditions of naming and a realization of the apocalyptic promise of a "new name written" (Rev. 2:17). Because Stevens seems a belated Adam in a fallen Eden, one of the first injunctions of "Notes" is to unname, to undo the linguistic damage attendant upon the Fall. But because Stevens is also the author of recovered Eden, a "civil" and distinctly secular "mundo," one of the last injunctions (now directed toward the poet himself, not an ephebe) is to "name flatly." "Notes toward a Supreme Fiction," no less than the Bible itself, posits a reconstituted proper name as the fulfillment of temporal process. The moment of "apparent ontological breakthrough and contact," in Frank Lentricchia's characterization of the poem, is the very moment the poet "names flatly."[3]

The crucial word in Lentricchia's characterization is, however, "apparent": the "Fat girl" bears no proper name; there is no moment of "ontological breakthrough and contact," no realization of the "eschatology of the proper." "Notes" might thus seem given to yet another Derridean concept: *non-propriété, non-propreté*, "la violence originaire [*sic*] qui a serve le propre de sa propriété, et de sa propreté."[4] An "eschatology of the proper" posits a proper name, the Adamic or Cratylic dream of "naming flatly," as both the alpha and omega of temporal process; *non-propriété*, however, suggests that the proper name, far from commanding the discursive field, is itself implicated in the structure of differences, the play of language, it fails to master. Here is Derrida once again: "To name, to give names . . . is the originary violence [la violence originaire] of language which consists in inscribing *within a difference* [dans un difference; emphasis added], in classifying, in suspending the vocative absolute. To think the unique *within* the system, to inscribe it there, such is the gesture of the arche-writing: arche-violence, loss of the proper, of absolute proximity, of self-presence."[5] And here is Stevens once again: "Fat girl, terrestrial, my summer, my night, / How is it I find you *in difference*, see you there / In a moving contour, a change not quite completed?" (*CP*, 406; emphasis added). "In difference" might be translated—or translated at the Sorbonne, where they speak French, which

Stevens tells us is also English (*OP*, 178), and where they "will get it straight one day" (*CP*, 407)—as *non-propriété*. Derrida argues that this non-self-sameness or "in difference" is the logical impossibility of *le nom propre, sens propre:* there never can be a name that is a unique appellation reserved for the presence of a unique individual, for the proper name already presupposes a classification and hence a system of differences. Stevens, however, suggests that "in difference" is the condition under which the "Fat girl" should be named, but under which she paradoxically bears no proper name:

> You are familiar yet an aberration.
> Civil, madam, I am, but underneath
> A tree, this unprovoked sensation requires
>
> That I should name you flatly, waste no words,
> Check your evasions, hold you to yourself.
>
> (*CP*, 406)

The prescriptive force of "requires" argues the desire to pass beyond "trope or deviation" (*CP*, 471), beyond the play of metaphor Aristotle defines as "giving the thing a name that belongs to something else; the transference being either from genus to species, or from species to genus, or from species to species, or on grounds of analogy" (*Poetics* 1457, b 6–9). The absence of a proper name, however, suggests a certain delight in this metaphorical play, a commitment to the troping that literary tradition tends to oppose not only to ordinary or current usage, as in the *Poetics*, but to the literal or proper itself. "Notes" would thus seem to participate in a fundamental contradiction: the "decreative" moment of "It Must Be Abstract," the purging of the sun of the alien or alias name "Phoebus," serves as prelude not to an ontological breakthrough or a realization of the "eschatologie du *propre*," but to an inability to "name flatly."

Now "Notes" does indeed participate in a contradiction, but not simply, or not only, in the relatively familiar one adumbrated above. True, the decreative moment of "It Must Be Abstract," to which the first portion of this chapter is largely addressed, might take as its epigraph

Derrida's rather enigmatic formulation of the relation of the sun to metaphor or non-proper names: "With every metaphor, there is no doubt
somewhere a sun; but each time there is a sun, metaphor has begun."[6] It
is equally true, however, that the "recreative" moment of "It Must Give
Pleasure," to which I turn near the end of this chapter, might take as its
epigraph a no less enigmatic formulation of the relation of earth to
metaphor or non-proper names (which is largely a revision of the myth of
language acquisition Wordsworth advances in book II of *The Prelude*):
where the "mundo" or "mother" nature is, the poet can yet be "fluent" or
figurative; where the poet is "fluent," the "mundo" need not be effaced.
The first epigraph argues the absolute priority of trope; the second, the
belief that the world need not be lost in or to trope. The first epigraph I
would have appended to the section of Stevens' poem in which the
alleged eradication of tropes is celebrated; the second, to that section in
which the injunction to "name flatly" or move beyond tropes allegedly
remains unrealized. The poem initially fails to do what it says it must do
(the eradication of the metaphorical or non-proper is itself metaphorical),
yet it finally does what it claims it should do, although allegedly fails to
do (if the "Fat girl" does not bear a proper name, she is yet something
other than an alien or alias figure for her own absence).

It is this contradiction that I explore below, although in a manner that
seeks to relate the tropological to the gendered, which in turn involves
Stevens' relation to Miltonic and post-Miltonic structures of figuration.
From Milton, Stevens inherits a tradition—here only crudely adumbrated—in which the feminine is designated as but a secondary or
specular form of presence. From Wordsworth and the Romantics, however, he inherits a contradictory tradition, a designation of the feminine
as an overly abundant material or maternal presence. Too "fluent" or too
susceptible to the "fluent," Milton's Eve is at once an image of the
greater presence of Adam (her identity is contingent on a strategic turn
toward Adam and away from her own image in the pool) and a figure for
the dangers of figuration or deceptive language itself (she is deceived by
Satan's words and in turn deceives Adam). Too "fat" or too much the
"mundo," however, Wordsworth's mother nature or "one dear Presence"
is both the materiality that endangers figuration (the poet enters the

realm of the figurative only when his "mute dialogues" at his "Mother's heart" have ceased) and the materiality that the figurative structure of the poem suppresses (the poet is concerned not with "what" the soul felt, the material or referential, but with "how," the structure of figuration itself.)[7] The Romantic revision of Milton—here again I risk a crude formulation—valorizes the antithetical term in the opposition between the literal and the figurative, but follows Milton in identifying the feminine with the devalued.[8] Stevens, however, revises not only Milton, but the high romantic revision of Milton. He thus occupies the space of an excluded middle: the relation of the tropological to the "proper" is not structured by, is not homologous with, the opposition man/woman, woman/man.

It is for this reason that "Notes" cannot unname the sun, cannot in fact do what it says it should do: Stevens is concerned not with a decreative version of the Adamic scene of nomination, but with a Genesis in which Eve or a son of Eve is herself/himself a source of metaphorical or nonproper names. It is for this reason, moreover, that "Notes" finally accomplishes what it says it should do, although allegedly does not (again: if the "Fat girl" does not bear a proper name, she is yet something other than an alien figure for her own absence). Lentricchia argues that Stevens

> sustains an economy whose continuing vitality depends on the production and consumption not of use and exchange values (as in Marx's outline of classic capitalism) but of original signs. Need for the new becomes the perpetual ground of production of the "new," in a capitalism therefore become pure, released from the referential grounds of sustenance values; capitalism become like a self-sustaining and self-perpetuating discourse without end because without ends; capitalism become a machine for the production of new signifiers whose content is irrelevant. By consuming original signs—the route to autonomous pleasure, privately indulged—the capitalist subject of pleasure ensures its own political indifference.[9]

On the contrary: "Notes toward a Supreme Fiction" sustains an erotic economy that is with end because with ends, which is precisely erotic relation or reciprocity. Far from being "the route to autonomous pleasure, privately indulged, "Notes" is toward an understanding of pleasure that presupposes nothing less than a "civic mundo," a redeemed nature, which is also a redeemed civilization and sexual politics.[10] The romantic poet is characteristically intent on generating textual "wealth" rather than in engaging in any erotic reciprocity: romantic desire presupposes "a fetishization of verbal signs whose economy depend[s] on the poet's ability to sustain the body of the poem as a serious rival for the feminine object of desire whose absence the poem celebrates."[11] Stevens, however, labors to establish a trope of contact (which, if only a trope, remains a trope of contact) with a substantial female body. Wordsworth could not imagine a world in which Eve was embodied, in which a woman could be fat. Stevens does. Any simple reversal of Wordsworth, however, would risk reinscribing the sexual politics of a Milton, who construes the body of his poem not as a rival to its object, but as a self-consuming or self-effacing means toward it. Here the feminine represents a potential impasse, figurae that refuses to give way to fulfillment. If Wordsworth could not imagine a Paradise in which Eve was embodied, Milton could not imagine a Paradise in which Eve was other than silent, other than of the party of the objects named. Stevens imagines both. The feminine as the materiality that endangers figuration; the feminine as the danger that is figuration: it is in the context of this double and contradictory devaluation that Stevens negotiates his politics of pleasure. This presupposes, however, a legitimate "need for the new." I begin, then, with Stevens' relation to the gender determinants of our most canonical myths of origins and the project of new world poetics.

I   Immaculate Conceptions

In Emerson's "Nature," the simplest of all possible observations, "the sun shines to-day," assumes the urgency of an injunction: "Our age is retrospective. It builds the sepulchres of the fathers. It writes biographies, histories, and criticism. The foregoing generations beheld God and nature face to face; we, through their eyes. Why should we not also enjoy an original relation to the universe? Why should we not have a poetry and philosophy of insight and not of tradition, and a religion by revelation to us, and not the history of theirs? . . . The sun shines to-day also."[12] Like Shakespeare's Hamlet, who is "too much in the sun," too intensely a son burdened by his inheritance or the sepulchre of his father, the new man of Emerson's new world is bound to a disabling genealogy. The promise given this new man, however, the literally pre-posterous promise of American poetry, is release from this belatedness, from a filiation that is but the inheritance of the grave. If the new world is necessarily second in order after the old, the historically belated can yet become the imaginatively original. If the son is necessarily second in order after the father, the new man can yet negotiate an original relation to the sun. The "sun shines to-day," however, only when the son assumes the burden of this pre-posterous newness, only when he wills the sun, that most familiar of revelations, to shine anew.

It is the burden of this pre-posterous newness that the ephebe of Wallace Stevens' "Notes toward a Supreme Fiction," Emerson's new man newly formulated, is enjoined to assume:

> Begin, ephebe, by perceiving the idea
> Of this invention, this invented world,
> The inconceivable idea of the sun.
>
> You must become an ignorant man again
> And see the sun again with an ignorant eye
> And see it clearly in the idea of it.
>
> (*CP*, 380)

To see the sun anew is to see it "abstracted" ("It Must Be Abstract": *abstractus*, "to separate out") from the accumulated burden of names, the inheritance of the fathers that mediates the relation of son to sun. "But do not use the rotted names" Stevens writes in "The Man with the Blue Guitar" (*CP*, 183); "When good is near you, when you have life in yourself, it is not by any known or accustomed way; you shall not discern the footprints of any man" Emerson argues in "Self-Reliance."[13] The new man or ephebe inherits a sun sullied by *vestigia*, a sun already inscribed with and by the names of his precursors. But if the ephebe is to have life in himself, if he is not to give his "bounty to the dead" (*CP*, 67), he must cleanse the sun of a disabling nomenclature ("nomanclatter" as Joyce names it in *Finnegans Wake*), nomenclature as clutter:

> Phoebus is dead, ephebe. But Phoebus was
> A name for something that never could be named.
> There was a project for the sun and is.
>
> There is a project for the sun. The sun
> Must bear no name, gold flourisher, but be
> In the difficulty of what it is to be.
>
> (*CP*, 381)

An old world poetics if complicit with the inheritance of patronymics and proper names. In Milton's "Ad Patrem," for example, it is through the proper name "Phoebus" that father and son, precursor and ephebe, share in the "possession" of genealogical continuity: "Ipse volens Phoebus se dispertire duobus, / Altera dona mihi, dedit altera dona parenti, / Dividuumque Deum genitorque puerque tenemus."[14] For new world poetics, however, the perpetuation of the name of the father reduces the son to a *revenant*, someone who, as his father, is already dead. If, then, life is to inhere in the son, the son must efface the names of the fathers: like that most rebellious of sons, Milton's Satan, the son must become self-fathered in order to see "the sun shine to-day."

Yet if "the sun shines to-day" assumes a hortatory urgency, it remains bound to its status as declamatory utterance: "the sun shines to-day *also*"; dawn is a revelation repeated every day, everywhere. (Thus the first line of *Murphy*, Beckett's first published novel, states: "The sun shone, having no alternative, on the nothing new.") And if "the sun shines to-day" is the nothing new, the desire to see the sun anew, to negotiate an original relation to the sun, is also the nothing new: "Why should we not also enjoy an original relation to the sun" locates the desire for origins or originality within the history of that desire, and hence as the nothing new. Certainly Wordsworth is part of that history: The Preface to *Lyrical Ballads* rejects those "phrases and figures of speech that from father to son have long been regarded as the common inheritance of Poets," of which the line "And reddening Phoebus lifts his golden fire" is an example,[15] as is Emerson. The latter rallies against the inheritance of the sepulchres, the tyranny of the fathers, because inheritance reduces nature to text, insight to reading. His own text, however, which enjoins the new man to see nature without the mediation of textuality, is itself called "Nature," and the very words in which he celebrates a previously unmediated relation to the universe, "the forgoing generations beheld . . . nature face to face," echoes that most canonical of old world texts, the Bible, 1 Corinthians 13: "For we now see in a glass darkly, but then face to face." Emerson is never more deeply implicated in textual filiation than at the very moment he enjoins his new man to eschew filiation. For governing Emerson's polemic against the fathers is the familiar drama—the highly imitable, much repeated and rehearsed drama—of patricide, the filial fantasy that takes its name from an old world text by Sophocles.

Now the virtual reiteration of Emerson's injunction in the opening moments of "Notes" would seem to locate the latter in this history of the nothing new: "Begin, ephebe" potentially reads as "begin again" or "begin also," which makes of Stevens' poem, no less than Emerson's essay, a "Beginnengans Wake." Indeed, to direct the injunction toward an ephebe, a young man of the once new but now old Athenian city-state, can only exacerbate the tension latent in a belated newness. In *On the Advantage and Disadvantage of History for Life*, Nietzsche maintains that the "man of action [is] . . . without knowledge; he forgets a great deal in order to do one thing."[16] In "It Must Be Abstract," the ephebe who does one thing is also without knowledge: he must become an ignorant man again in order to "see the sun again with an ignorant eye / And see it clearly in the idea of it." Sight is contingent on a form of willful blindness, a knowledgeable and active forgetting of the past. Yet if the ephebe is enjoined to forget, the word "ephebe" itself, if only by virtue of its conspicuous "Greekness," remembers a beginning prior to this "Begin, ephebe," remembers a beginning prior to this history of beginnings as patricide, the beginning that is itself forgotten in the constant reiteration of the patricidal drama.

For the Freud of *Totem and Taboo*, the origins of "religion, morals, society and art converge" in the name of Oedipus; the founding gesture of human culture is the murder of the father by the primitive horde of his sons.[17] For Irigaray, however, Freud's myth of origins forgets a more ancient murder, the violence directed against Clytemnestra by her son Orestes.[18] The thematization of history as a constantly reiterated patricide, the inheritance of the name of Oedipus, strategically displaces the name Clytemnestra, the legacy of the murdered mother. Yet if the Oedipal thematization of history begins by forgetting this beginning, "Notes" begins by recuperating the forgotten: to enjoin an ephebe to begin, a citizen of the once new but now old world of the Athenian city-state, is necessarily to recall that Athens itself begins, is symbolically founded on, the murder of a mother and the subsequent acquittal of her son. As a new man engaged in Oedipal struggle with Phoebus, a god worshiped by the Greeks as paternal, the ephebe is effectively dead, already a *revenant*, a near anagrammatic return of the father he would slay. And as a poem engaged with Oedipal struggle with the burden of poetic fathers, with the priority of precursors, "Notes" is no less a *revenant*, a beginning already implicated in the entire history and thematics of Oedipal struggle. But as a poem that recuperates what the Oedipal thematization displaces, that remembers what Oedipal history chooses to forget, "Notes" lives in the recovered heritage of a different dispensation: "There was a myth before the myth began, / Venerable and articulate and complete" (*CP*, 383). To begin in Stevens' new world is to recover from old world texts the beginning that old world texts themselves forget.

Yet "Notes" seems highly conventional in its beginning, deeply implicated in an Oedipal ideology of beginnings: "Begin, ephebe, by perceiving the idea / Of this invention, this invented world, / The inconceivable idea of the sun" (*CP*, 380). The beginning is highly conventional, because the "inconceivable idea of the sun" suggests, by virtue of the homonymic play of sun and son, an "inconceivable" origin for the son, and hence the son as he has been conventionally construed: "The mother is no parent of that which is called / her child, but only the nurse of the newly-planted seed / that grows. The parent is he who mounts."[19] These are the words of the paternal god of Aeschylus' *Oresteia*: Phoebus maintains that Orestes is innocent of matricide, not legally responsible for the murder of Clytemnestra, because the son bears no inheritance from the maternal body, an argument that Athena, the goddess whose very existence argues the redundancy of maternity, accepts. The judgment on the Acropolis—Athena's acquiescence in the cause of patriarchy and the logic of parthenogenesis—is the founding gesture of Hellenic Athens, the ephebe's *original* new world, and is a gesture that the ephebe's *new* new world (Stevens' "Notes toward a Supreme Fiction") seems to rehearse. For in enjoining the ephebe to turn against Phoebus, the god who once defended Orestes against the Furies—the chthonic forces that Irigaray characterizes as "insurgents against patriarchal power,"[20]—"Notes" nevertheless rehearses the ideology of Aeschylus' Phoebus: begin, begin again, by defining the son as patrilineal, if only by virtue of an Oedipal struggle with the father; begin by eliding the inheritance of the maternal body.

Athena's address to the citizens of Athens, her judgment in favor of Orestes and the ideology of parthenogenesis, finds an explicitly Christian analogue in Paul's address to the citizens of Athens, in which he quotes the Stoic poet Aratus of Soli: "For we are indeed his [Zeus'] offspring" (Acts 17:28). Paul's relation to the claims of rival or precursor myths is not generally characterized by syncretism, yet here the Christian sky God blithely assimilates the offspring of his Olympian counterpart. The ease with which Paul quotes a "pagan" source of "godless myth" (1 Tim. 4:7) suggests that the specific referent of the personal pronoun is of less significance than its gender specificity. Indeed, the prophecy of Isaiah 7:14, "Behold a virgin shall conceive, and bear a son, and shall call his name Emmanuel," the prophecy Matthew places at the center of his own account of the birth of Christ (Matt. 1:22–23), posits yet another "inconceivable son," another beginning innocent of conception, as the fulfillment that is Christianity.[21] The generative word of God passes through but is never of the body of Mary: like the classical sun god who declares that the "mother is no parent to the child," the

Christian sky God begets his son without even the effective mediation of the maternal body.

The birth of a son through annunciation or divine nomination finds its inverse reflection in the opening moments of "Notes" in the celebration of the death of a sun god through denomination: "Phoebus is dead, ephebe. But Phoebus was / A name for something that never could be named" (*CP*, 380). Or the denomination celebrated in "Notes," the fall of Phoebus into "autumn umber," is the inverse reflection of renomination celebrated in the *Oresteia*, the transference of the name "Phoebe" from earth to sky: "I give first place of honor in my prayer to her who of the gods first prophesied, the Earth; and next to Themis, who succeeded to her mother's place of prophecy; so runs the legend; and in third succession, given by free consent, not won by force, another Titan daughter of earth was seated here. This was Phoebe. She gave it as a birthday gift to Phoebus, who is called after Phoebe's name."[22] The voluntaristic nature of this renomination or transference, which is articulated by the Pythia, the priestess of Phoebus Apollo, belies the violence directed against the mother that is at the heart of the *Oresteia*. Yet even in this highly idealized myth of origins—the Pythia admits of an attenuated connection between Phoebe and Phoebus, the "mother's place" and the son's inheritance, that Phoebus himself utterly denies—the conventional ideology of beginnings, be they construed in classical or Judeo-Christian terms, is abundantly clear: the son is defined in terms of his distance from earth, from matter, from the maternal body. To begin, then, by positing "the inconceivable idea of the sun [son]" is to begin with yet another "immaculate conception," what Joyce calls an "immaculate contraceptive," inception as *contra* conception, the beginning as the elision of the mother.

In *Moses and Monotheism*, Freud argues that the compulsion to worship an invisible god, who is also a father, "signifies above all a victory of spirituality over the senses—that is to say, a step forward in culture, since maternity is based on the evidence of the senses whereas paternity is a surmise based on a deduction and a premiss."[23] The ideology of origins as *contra* conception could not be more explicit; Freud's concession that the poets were there before him could not be more obvious:

the new world of psychoanalysis is indeed the good son of a literary tradition that genders the sensible as female, the better to oppose it to an intelligible male soul. Aristotle places metaphor at the heart of literary experience, which he defines as "transference," "giving the thing a name that belongs to something else." Etymologically, the *phora* of this *epiphora* or transference means only a change with respect to location. In terms of the practical dynamics of literary tradition, however, metaphor tends to involve a transference that is gender specific, a transference from gender to gender. In the Pythia's myth of origins, for example, the transference of the name, the movement upward from the chthonic Phoebe to the sky god Phoebus, reads very much as a metaphor for metaphor in its explicitly gendered context, and hence as synecdoche for the sexual politics of the *Oresteia* as a whole. The chthonic forces within the play, the Eumenides, demand blood for blood—a repetition of the primal scene of violence. Phoebus and Orestes, however, strategically advocate re-presentation, a "talking cure" or resolution: "In this action now / speech has been ordered by my teacher, who is wise."[24] The point is not simply that Orestes is ultimately judged innocent of matricide, but that judgment itself, the "talking cure," already represents the effective defeat of the Eumenides and the cause of Clytemnestra. As in Freud, the opposition between conscious "word representations" *(Wortvorstellungen)* and unconscious "thing representations" *(Sachvorstellungen)* is isomorphic with, if not already structured by, the opposition between an intelligible male soul and a sensible female body.

In "Notes," however, the sun is uttered into "pure" existence only to fall to and into matter: "Let purple Phoebus lie in umber harvest, / Let Phoebus slumber and die in autumn umber" (*CP*, 381). The "intelligible" world of the opening tercets, the beginning that is pure "idea" or "invention," suffers a free-fall into the world of cyclical process, the death that is also harvest. For Freud, this could only be a step backward for culture, a retreat from the intelligible, a resurgence of "the evidence of the senses" and hence the maternal (a resurgence reflected in a poetic medium that has itself grown denser: "Let Phoebus slumber and die in autumn umber" is not the sun seen clearly in its idea, but heard darkly in its phonetic density). For "Notes," however, the free-fall is properly a recuperation, a beginning that is not governed by the ideology of the immaculate, and hence not conscripted to the cause of the fathers. "Notes" first rehearses the conventional ideology of beginnings, appears to satisfy what the poem itself calls "Belief in an immaculate beginning" (*CP,* 382), but only to displace the displacement involved in immaculate conceptions.

Certainly the Phoebe of the Pythia's myth of origins might find satisfaction in the return of her name to and into earth. Or if not Phoebe, then the Tiamat of the Sumero-Babylonian epic *Enūma-eliš,* the goddess whose name is displaced in the myth of origins advanced in Genesis. The Judeo-Christian sky God who speaks the world into existence is, of course, given to an ideology of beginnings as *contra* conception: Biblical creation is *ex nihilo,* asexual, without recourse to preexisting matter. Yet in the very act of positing a transcendent and originating act of nomination, Genesis inscribes the remnants of a name that questions both the transcendence and priority of that act: the Hebrew word for "abyss," *tehom,* the word used to describe cosmic nothingness prior to the form giving intervention of the divine Word, is etymologically linked to the proper name "Tiamat," the mother of the gods in *Enūma-eliš,* from whose slaughtered body the triumphant god Marduk fashions the universe.[25] Genesis begins with an ideologically motivated displacement of a goddess, a material and maternal origin, by a male sky god. "Notes" displaces this displacement with the fall of a male sky god to and into matter. In the beginning was not the Word, but an ideologically motivated and gender specific "battle of the proper names."[26]

Genesis is not, then, *the* beginning, but *a* beginning, a beginning no less belated or reactive than Stevens' own: "God made the two great lights, the greater to govern the day and the lesser to govern the night, and with them he made the stars" (Gen. 1:16). Here too the sun bears no name—although a star is a star and the light is called "day" and the darkness "night"—because the common Semitic word for the sun was also a divine name. Even "in the beginning" there always was "a project for the sun"; even here creation cannot be distinguished from decreation, the purging of names that are no longer or that never were proper. Lentricchia characterizes Stevens' "appetite for newness," his desire for

origins and originality, as ideologically empty, if not overtly reaction-
ary.[27] The Stevens of the opening tercets of "Notes," however, might be
better characterized as a poet of ideological demystification: "Instead of
the ideological myth of a philosophy of origins and its organic concepts,
Marxism establishes in principle the recognition of the givenness of the
complex structure of any concrete 'object,' a structure which governs
both the development of the object and the theoretical practice which
produces the knowledge of it. There is no longer any original essence,
but only an ever-pre-givenness [un toujours-déjà-donné], however far
knowledge delves into its past."[28] Certainly the sun of "It Must Be
Abstract" has little to do with a philosophy of origins and its organic
concepts: the ephebe is enjoined to begin by perceiving the idea of "this
invention, this invented world." And if the ephebe is also enjoined
to become an "ignorant man again," to cleanse the sun of this "ever-
pre-givenness," the sun is not thereby returned to an initial state of
purity. For be it the Biblical "In the beginning" or Stevens' own "Begin,
ephebe," the beginning is always decreative, already "onomatoclas-
tic";[29] there always (already) were names for the sun, however far knowledge (or ignorance) delves into its past. It is only because "Notes"
implicitly argues that there never has been, never can be, a pure beginning, an originating act of baptism, that the ephebe can in fact begin.
"Notes" does evince an "appetite for newness." Far from being ideologically empty, however, it serves to expose our most canonical myth of
origin as itself the site of an effaced or forgotten ideological struggle. The
beginning was itself "invented," humanly constructed; it can be
changed; "It Must Change."[30]

If, however, beginnings are always decreative, they are not always
given to identical ideological ends, despite our various attempts—here
represented by Lentricchia—to return new beginnings to old ideologies:

The desire for original relation, face to face, unmediated by tradition—
my allusion is to the revolutionary desire for an American origin an-
nounced in the opening sentences of Emerson's "Nature" essay of 1836—
is the hope for rupture with Europe in the cultural as well as in the
political realm: revolutionary hope become a way of being in the world,

down to and maybe most essentially including that revolutionary freshness of perception enabled by what Emerson called "the transparent
eyeball." Freshness of perception is phenomenological rupture in the
wake of political rupture. . . . The transparent-eyeball passage in Emerson is father to the moment of vivid transparency in Stevens, but between
Emerson and Stevens falls not so much the struggle of fathers and sons—
this is not their chief difference—as a thorough commodification of everyday life. The appetite for American newness, in Emerson transcendental,
antihistorical, nature-oriented—become like the rose [sic] outside your
window, he urges, they are wholly themselves, they make no reference to
past or future roses. . . . [This] is thoroughly translated by later Stevens
into hope for the freshness of commodity consumption.[31]

Emerson's "appetite for newness" is not so much "anti-historical" as it is
blind to its own historicity: Lentricchia relates the phenomenological
break to the political rupture, but fails to note that rupture is itself a
governing trope of European history. The argument assumes, moreover,
that the political rupture is sufficient to transform an economic problem
into a perceptual one. (The difficulty is not becoming like the roses
outside your window, but possessing the economic resources to have a
window with roses outside it.) For Marx, nature becomes an object of
sensuous consciousness, or the senses "become directly theoreticians in
practice," only with the abolition of capitalist, property relations: "The
eye . . . become[s] a *human* eye when its *object* has become a *human*,
social object, created by man and destined for him."[32] "Revolutionary
freshness of perception" is not a "way of being in the world," of negotiat-
ing a compromise with things as they are, but the promise of transformation. "Marx has ruined Nature, / For the moment" (*CP*, 134) Stevens
complains in "Botanist on Alp (No. 1)," and he is right: Marx renders
nature historical. And while Stevens is not Marx, his own commitment to
a "revolutionary freshness of perception" also presupposes a "*human*,
social object," a "civil mundo." There can be no question, then, of
simply becoming "like the roses outside your window." On the contrary:
the ever-pre-givenness of flowers needs to be demystified.

Consider the "blue woman" of "It Must Give Pleasure," who has
apparently taken Emerson's injunction in earnest:

The blue woman, linked and lacquered, at her window
Did not desire that feathery argentines
Should be cold silver, neither that frothy clouds

Should foam, be foamy waves, should move like them,
Nor that the sexual blossoms should repose
Without their fierce addictions . . .

(CP, 399)

A blossom that is not a sexual adjunct is hardly a "veritable ding an sich": the restriction of metaphorical desire can only point to its restriction of desire metaphorically. And even in this "cold" and "clear" world the eye is never transparent:

The blue woman looked and from her window named

The corals of the dogwood, cold and clear,
Cold, coldly delineating, being real,
Clear and, except for the eye, without intrusion.

(CP, 399–400)

Emerson allegedly sees flowers wholly as themselves because he is of the party that has already made them wholly what they are: he is in the tradition of Adam, the subject who names. But the blue woman is of the party of Eve, the object that is named: to see the flowers wholly as themselves would be to forget that nature has already been produced for her, although not in her interests. Hence the necessity of the "exception": "except for the eye," except for the blue woman's own names. Nature is a commodity like anything else. Stevens' blue woman demystifies it. Emerson's "transparent eyeball" fetishizes it.

The "cold" and "clear" world of the opening movement of "Notes," however, would seem to be of the party of Emerson and transparence: "How clean the sun when seen in its idea, / Washed in the remotest cleanliness of a heaven / That has expelled us and our images . . ." (CP, 381). If the tercet is exclamatory, as it is conventionally assumed to be, the poem celebrates what "Credences of Summer" calls "the gold sun about the whitened sky," seen "Without evasion by a single meta-phor" (*CP*, 373). It is entirely possible, however, that the tercet is inter-rogative, a questioning of the very possibility of what "An Ordinary Evening in New Haven" calls "the poem of pure reality, untouched / By trope or deviation" (*CP*, 471). Certainly the blue woman of "It Must Give Pleasure" suggests that any search for a pure reality can only be a pure mystification, a conflation of the "ever-pre-givenness" of things with concrete objects. Her "cold" and "clear" world thus admits of an excep-tion, as does "the remotest cleanliness" of "It Must Be Abstract": "The sun / Must bear no name, gold flourisher, but be / In the difficulty of what it is to be" (*CP*, 381). The sun is cleansed of name "Phoebus" but only to be named "gold flourisher," which hardly suggests "the remotest clean-liness of a heaven / That has expelled us and our images" (*CP*, 381). This is not, then, simply a decreative Genesis, a reinscription of the sexual politics of the Adamic scene of nomination in photographic negative. For if the power to name is conventionally the Adamic prerogative, the power to unname, to undo the work of the first father, is conventionally the prerogative of his sons. The history of the "desire for original relation, unmediated by tradition" is part of the history of a sexual politics that genders imperfect states of mediation as feminine. The feminine is thus subject to denigration—illogically, but no less effectively—as both body and figure, matter and mediation.

Recall the Pythia's myth of origins in the *Oresteia*: Phoebe is to Phoe-bus not only as earth to sky, matter to spirit, but as reflection to source, image to substance. The play characterizes the goddess as chthonic, but she is also lunar, a secondary form of the presence or light that is Phoebus. Or, to substitute a Christian for a classical text, Phoebe is to Phoebus as Eve is to Adam, as Milton's redaction of Genesis suggests:

> What thou seest,
> What thou seest fair creature *is* thyself,
> With thee it came and goes: but follow me,
> And I will bring thee where no shadow stays
> Thy coming, and thy soft imbraces, hee
> Whose image thou art, him thou shalt enjoy
> Inseparably thine.[33]

If Eve is spared the fate of Narcissus only by turning to the one "Whose image" she is, Adam's fatal mistake will be to turn to the reflection of his own image in Eve and away from the God "Whose image" he is. The famous Miltonic hierarchy—"He for God only, shee for God in him"— posits Eve as a form of Ovidian *umbra* to Adam's *corpus*. Eve's dilated stay before her own image is thus the turning of *umbra* toward *umbra*, the meeting of shadow and shadow, which makes of Eve a figure for the dangers of figuration itself. Literary tradition has tended to follow 1 Corinthians 13 in identifying mirrors with imperfect states of mediation. And what is imperfect is gendered feminine.

But consider Stevens' redaction of Milton's redaction of Genesis:

> The first idea was not our own. Adam
> In Eden was the father of Descartes
> And Eve made air the mirror of herself,
>
> Of her sons and of her daughters. They found themselves
> In heaven as in a glass . . .
>
> (*CP*, 383)

In Milton's Eden, it is not until the fall, until point of view and perspective are introduced into Paradise, that subject and object break asunder. In Stevens' poem, however, Adam is already the father of Cartesian duality, and the poet who "cleans" the sun only to name it "gold flourisher" implicitly signs the sun as a son of Eve. For the downward gaze that reflects what is already *umbra* is not the symmetrical opposite of a sun seen in the remotest cleanliness of a heaven that has expelled us and our images: As the ephebe would well know, the sun cannot be clean when cleansed of the name "Phoebus," for the simple reason that *Phoibos*, the Greek form of the name "Phoebus," means, among other things, clean or pure. The *phoibos* of "Phoebus Apollo" is an epithet transformed into a proper name; the opening movement of "Notes" merely translates the proper name back into the epithet.[34] Plutarch assures us that Phoebus is indeed clean, that the proper name is in fact proper: "Phoebus, as is well known, is a name that men of old used to give everything pure and undefiled, even as the Thesselians, to this day

. . . when their priests, on prohibited days, are spending their time alone outside the temples, say the priests 'are keeping Phoebus' [*phebonomize*]."[35] The professorial voice that opens "It Must Be Abstract" assures the ephebe that Phoebus is not clean, and that to clean objects one must begin by eradicating tropes, names that are no longer or that never were proper. Yet to the ephebe, the appeal to the *phoibos* over and against *Phoibos* can only be yet another way of "keeping Phoebus," of extending the tradition in which fathers and sons do battle over the proper name Phoebus. It makes little difference if, like Milton, father and son share in the possession of the "divided god" or, like Wordsworth, the son rejects the name Phoebus, and hence the continuity between father and son. For as Lacan notes: "Aggression towards the father is at the principle of the Law." Stevens, however, refuses the conventional agon: "Between Emerson and Stevens falls not so much the struggle of fathers and sons" (Lentricchia is exactly if unwittingly right) but rather Stevens' refusal to conduct the struggle in patrilineal terms.

"It Must Be Abstract" attempts to negotiate the double and contradictory devaluation of women as flesh and figure, matter and mediation. The devaluation that "It Must Give Pleasure" rehabilitates in the figure of a new Eve is the "civil" or secular "mundo": the "Fat girl" is at once *corpus* ("fat") and *umbra* (the "more than natural figure"). Not that Stevens' "Fat girl" simply gains a self-presence or self-possession lacking in Milton: the purpose is not to posit an ontologically stable essence that can then be "named flatly" as what she is. The "Fat girl" is found "in difference"; she is not what Derrida calls the "eschatological meaning of being as presence, as parousia, as life without difference."[36] Nor is the poem in which she figures simply "notes toward" this (non)telos, what Derrida calls "arche-violence, loss of the proper, of absolute proximity, of self-presence." For if the poem refuses to acknowledge the incompatibility of flesh and figure—if it insists on the utopian possibility of sensuous consciousness—it also refuses the dichotomy between notes toward and telos, the very structure Romantic desire—that ambivalent pursuit of erotic relation or reciprocity—requires to sustain its own figurative life.

II   Accessible Bliss

In *The Sophist*, Plato defines the conditions under which we can properly speak of "the same" and "not the same": "Motion, then, is both the same and not the same. . . . We call it 'the same' on account of participation in the same with reference to itself but we call it 'not the same' because of its combination with difference, a combination that separates it off from the same and makes it not the same but different."[37] The "Fat girl" of "It Must Give Pleasure" is in motion; she is simultaneously "a change not quite completed" (*CP*, 406) and the citizen of a world in which "It Must Change," in which it cannot stop changing. But she is the same and not the same without the promise of a resolutive telos:

> They will get it straight one day at the Sorbonne.
> We shall return at twilight from the lecture
> Pleased that the irrational is rational,
>
> Until flicked by feeling, in a gildered street,
> I call you by name, my green, my fluent mundo.
> You will have stopped revolving except in crystal.
>
> (*CP*, 406–7)

This is at once the end of the poem proper (the last lines, excluding the epilogue); a beginning movement within the poem (a beginning leading toward the crystal, not an end in itself); a beginning that is an ending ("stopped" is the principal verb); and a beginning presented as already accomplished ("You will have stopped" is a future perfect, a grammatical presentation of a future action, or a future cessation of action, as already accomplished). "In difference" is here a retentional synthesis and a protentional opening, a movement toward an identity paradoxically accomplished in the movement toward, yet still contingent on a future presented as already accomplished. The famous passage from "The Noble Rider and the Sound of Words" ("There is, in fact, a world of poetry indistinguishable from the world in which we live, or I ought to say, no doubt, from the world in which we shall come to live" [*NA*, 31]) is frequently read as a reiteration of the temporal disjunction implicit in the title "Notes toward a Supreme Fiction." The concluding line of the poem, however, refuses the opposition between "notes toward" and telos, and implicitly argues the wisdom of "in difference" over and against "difference from" or disjunction.

This would seem a climactic revelation or moment toward which all progresses—an "end" as both termination of sequence and manifestation of purpose—yet it too is a fulfillment already accomplished in a beginning:

> And for what, except for you, do I feel love?
> Do I press the extremest book of the wisest man
> Close to me, hidden in me day and night?
> In the uncertain light of single, certain truth,
> Equal in living changingness to the light
> In which I meet you, in which we sit at rest,
> For a moment in the central of our being,
> The vivid transparence that you bring is peace.
>
> (*CP*, 380)

The "you" of the poem's prefatory stanza is without grammatical antecedent[38] but is itself both antecedent to and perhaps the antecedent of the poem "Notes toward a Supreme Fiction." Now a pronoun is a sign of grammatical substitution, the intelligibility of which depends on the stability of a fixed referent or antecedent. That the pronoun is antecedent to its referent or antecedent, or that the antecedent seems to be the poem "Notes toward a Supreme Fiction," a poem ostensibly in pursuit of its referent, is a paradox. But it is a paradox not unlike the future perfect of the concluding line of the poem, the grammatical presentation of a future action, or a future cessation of action, as already accomplished. "Notes" defines itself, by virtue of its title, as both spatially eccentric, as marginalia on some yet unwritten "extremest book," and as temporally prior or "toward." Yet if the "you" of the poem's opening and concluding cantos is at once latent and accomplished, if the poem pursues what is already and always is, then "Notes" dilates its own self-difference and does not move toward any destination. "Desire" is perhaps the most conventional term for narrative motivation, desire in the sense of the want of an elusive object or a deficiency in the desiring subject. Desire so conceived, however, is but a negative condition, and "Notes," despite the ironic "toward" of its title, is not a provisional structure, not the pursuit of something that is the transcendence of mere "notes."

Desire so conceived, moreover, is not complicit with the "hegemonic that capitalism attributes to the new qua new." For capitalism, at least in its late or consumer phase, is predicated on the operations of desire—or, better, on the systematic engendering of desire—that is either discontent with each and every fulfillment (the new is not the new once I possess it) or perpetually suspended on this side of fulfillment (the new is what I do not yet possess). But "Notes" is a poem of "accessible bliss," which is yet "hot" for another "accessible bliss" (*CP*, 395): It does not participate in the erotic pessimism that can conceive of satisfaction only as a consummation devoutly to be deferred. Certainly any simple notion of "toward," of "notes" as a provisional structure in relation to something that it is not, cannot survive the response to the question "What am I to believe?":

> If the angel in his cloud,
> Serenely gazing at the violent abyss,
> Plucks on his strings to pluck abysmal glory,
>
> Leaps downward through evening's revelations, and
> On his spredden wings, needs nothing but deep space,
> Forgets the gold centre, the golden destiny,
>
> Grows warm in the motionless motion of his flight,
> Am I that imagine this angel less satisfied?
>
> (*CP*, 404)

The directionality of "winged" that Stevens first introduces in "It Must Be Abstract"—the poem "sends us, winged by an unconscious will, / To an immaculate end" (*CP*, 382)—is here reiterated, but only to be forestalled in a suspension so fluid, a flight so protracted, that directionality is drained of all meaning. "Motionless motion" is the poem's paradoxical principle of (non)identity and is the poet's oxymoronic term for the trajectory—the angel who "forgets the gold centre" cannot be characterized as spatially eccentric; the angel who forgets the "golden destiny" cannot be temporally prior or toward. Self-unity and self-division, typographically dramatized in "I am and as I am, I am" (CP, 405), is Stevens' nonmonological response to Jehovah's radically monological *eyeh esher eyeh*, "I am that I am," Coleridge's idealization of the infinite "I AM" as the type of poetic identity, and the entire tradition of Cartesian metaphysics, the heritage of the *cogito* (in Stevens' poem, our Adamic bequest) that defines the self as the unproblematic possessor of the self. In a Cartesian metaphysic, the question "Is it he or is it I that experience this?" (CP, 404), the imagined angel or the imagining subject, can have no meaning, as the subject is itself posited as a stable locus prior to its imaginings. For Stevens, however, the answer to the question is but another question: "Is it I then that . . . am satisfied[?]," although it is a question sufficiently assertive to do without the question mark. The luminous melody of "proper sound" is ambiguously the property of both the imagined angel and the imagining subject, if indeed it is the property of either (proper derives from the Latin *proprius*, the peculiar, the distinct, that which belongs only to the self; hence, the self's private property). Were it not that Plato's characterization of motion posited a telos of noncontradiction, the transformation of "the same and not the same" into presence as the selfsame, it might properly be applied to the trajectory of Stevens' angel.

A self that is at once realized and yet to be produced is not a stable essence: "I am and as I am, I am" divides and defers identity even as it asserts it. It follows from this that the relation of self to self is not one of essence to essence:

Two things of opposite natures seem to depend
On one another, as a man depends
On a woman, day on night, the imagined

On the real.

(CP, 392)

The appositional structure of this rather wooden allegory posits a form of oppositional difference: man is related to woman not through any active process of differentiation and unification but as one stable entity to another. Stevens reverses the characteristic Miltonic formulation—the "imagined" is here the male, one of the things of "opposite nature" that is said to depend on the "real" or female—yet follows Milton in positing an opposition contingent on gender stratification. What is in Stevens first formulated as "difference from," however, is soon to become "in difference" or infolded: "And North and South are an intrinsic couple / And sun and rain a plural, like two lovers / That walk away as one in the greenest body" (*CP*, 392). And what is "in difference" in one "greenest body" is a radical revision of the Biblical "taken out of" or "differentiated from," perhaps our most canonical formulation of sexual difference: "And Adam said, 'This is now bone of my bones, and flesh of my flesh: she shall be called Woman, because she was taken out of [differentiated from] man'" (Gen. 2:23).[39]

To "differentiate from" is to posit both a standard of monological unity, a norm from which it is in fact possible to differ, and the ultimate goal of reassimilating the differentiated, of re-pairing the provisional or secondary with the norm. This is at once the relation of Milton's Eve to Adam, *imago* to *corpus*, and the relation of Milton's Adam to God, *imago* to transcendent *corpus:*

Man's nourishment, by gradual scale sublim'd
To vital spirits aspire, to animal,
To intellectual, give both life and sense,
Fancy and understanding, whence the Soul
Reason receives, and reason is her being,
Discursive, or Intuitive; discourse
Is oftest yours, the latter most is ours,
Differing but in degree, of kind the same.
Wonder not then, what God for you saw good
If I refuse not, but convert, as you,
To proper substance; time may come when men
With Angels may participate, and find
No inconvenient Diet, nor too light Fare.[40]

The time that will come is also the time that will overcome: men will then be converted not only to "proper substance," the transcendent *corpus* that is angelic existence, but will return to proper names. Miltonic temporality, in its broadest formulation, is the promise of repairing the damage attendant upon the Fall, of closing the gap between "meaning" and "Name" and realizing the eschatology of the proper. "Difference from" a transcendent or angelic standard of the proper is at the heart of Milton's poem, which in Stevens' sleight-of-hand revision of his precursor becomes precisely the mark of his difference from Milton: "Angel, / Be silent in your luminous cloud and hear / The luminous melody of proper sound" (*CP*, 404). Angelic existence is not the goal of temporal process but the silenced auditor of a melody; the proper is not a standard from which to measure deviance or difference but is itself the melodic product of differences: "Is it he or is it I that experience this?" The Miltonic relation of the imagined to the real or the metaphorical to the proper is at once the relation of woman to man, man to God, and Milton's own poem to a truth posited beyond its limited system of signs. Time will come when the first term in each opposition will be effaced before or repaired with the standard from which it is derived, and the prospective mode of the concluding book of *Paradise Lost* will give way to a final and definitive conversion. In book XIII of Augustine's *Confessions*, angels are said to enjoy access to the Word without the mediation of syllables, syntax, or difference: "They always behold your face, and, without any syllables of time, they read upon it what your eternal will decrees." In book VII of *Paradise Lost*, the Angel Gabriel explains that although the divine Word is "Immediate," it can be expressed to "human ears" only through the mediation of linguistic process: "Immediate are the Acts of God, more swift / Than time or motion, but to human ears / Cannot without process of speech be told." For the great theologian of the city of God and the great poet of heaven and hell, language is the diaspora, a region of "unlikeness" or difference, a sign of our distance from the proper, the divine, the One. For the great poet of earth, however, difference from an angelic or transcendent standard of the proper gives way to "in difference," difference within itself.

Stevens' revision of the Miltonic "proper substance" anticipates the concluding moments of "Notes," the celebration of "in difference" in the figure of a "Fat girl," but is itself anticipated by Wordsworth's revision of Milton, the concluding moments of *The Prelude:*

> The power, which all
> Acknowledge when thus moved, which Nature thus
> To bodily sense exhibits, is the express
> Resemblance of that glorious faculty
> That higher minds bear with them as their own.
> This is the very spirit in which they deal
> With the whole compass of the universe:
> They from their native selves can send abroad
> Kindred mutations; for themselves create
> A like existence; and, whene'er it dawns
> Created for them, catch it, or are caught
> By its inevitable mastery.
> Like angels stopped upon the wing by sound
> Of harmony from Heaven's remotest spheres.[41]

It is by a radical assertion of identity, not "gradual scale sublim'd," that the Wordsworthian "I" participates in the "proper substance" of angelic existence. The Miltonic "demarcations" between angelic and human existence are rendered "ghostlier" (*CP,* 130), and Wordsworth moves tentatively toward Stevens' unqualified "I can / Do all that angels can" (*CP,* 405). There is a sense, however, in which the Wordsworthian poetic does not evade hierarchical gradation but merely reverses the terms of Milton's "scale of Nature," "whereon / In contemplation of created things / By steps we may ascend to God."[42] The Wordsworthian reversal is not the descendental analogue of this *scala naturae,* the "lik'ning" of "spiritual to corporal forms" advanced by Raphael in book V of *Paradise Lost,* but a radical displacement of "created things," a celebration of consciousness or creative powers rather than divine creation. Wordsworth's reading of Milton is in this sense "Satanic"—the rejection of "scale" or hierarchy implicitly repeats the error of the Angel who thought "one step higher" would set him "highest"—but is in its gender determinants distinctly orthodox. For if the initial point of potential impasse in the Miltonic scale of contemplation is Eve, the woman whose dilated stay before her own image threatens to subvert the *scala naturae* or "conversion" to "higher presence," the final object of effacement in the Wordsworthian celebration of creative powers is an unnamed woman.

III   The Fat Girl

In the *Prelude* of 1799, the young Wordsworth happens upon a scene or "spot of time"

> where in former times
> A man, the murderer of his wife, was hung
> In irons. Mouldered was the gibbet-mast;
> The bones were gone, the iron and the wood;
> Only a long green ridge of turf remained
> Whose shape was like a grave.[43]

The "spot," as Cynthia Chase has argued, is the scene of a double effacement, the erosion of the remnants of an execution, which is itself the effacement of a murder.[44] In the text of 1799, nature registers the violence in "her" own terms, as a "ridge of turf . . . / Whose shape was like a grave." In the revised text of 1850, however, the violence assumes the explicitly textual form of "monumental letters," which is itself a form of violence directed against nature:

> on the turf
> Hard by, soon after that fell deed was wrought,
> Some unknown hand had carved the murderer's name.
> The monumental letters were inscribed
> In times long past; but still, from year to year,
> By superstition of the neighborhood,
> The grass is cleared away, and to that hour
> The characters were fresh and visible.[45]

Responsibility for the "monumental letters," which are first introduced
in the revisions and expansions of 1805, is clearly the poet's own. In the
revised poem, the inscribed name implies both the death of its bearer,
the absence to which it stands as testimony, and the "death" or effacement of the natural object on which it is inscribed, the "ridge of turf"
that is only tentatively "like a grave" in the poem of 1799, but which
becomes a kind of textual epitaph to its demise as the merely natural: the
"characters" are "fresh and visible" in the text of 1850 only because the
grass is "cleared away," because the natural object is effaced or super-
seded by "monumental letters." The effacement the 1850 *Prelude* identifies with textuality or inscribed names is, then, precisely the effacement
that the revisions of 1850 accomplish. The movement is not, as it is in
Milton, the movement of image toward substance or fuller presence, the
turning of the *imago* Eve toward the Adam whose image she is. Instead it
is the displacement of an object by the poet's own inscriptions or images.
And as the initial effacement in the Miltonic trajectory is directed
against Eve, the final victim in the Wordsworthian trajectory is an
unnamed woman: the 1850 *Prelude* not only "murders" a natural object by transforming it into a text, but literally expurgates or effaces the
original story of the murdered woman, the wife of the man whose inscribed name survives his death, but who is herself finally unmarked or
uninscribed.

The history of the text's revisions thus enacts the effacement the
Prelude itself advances as the condition or prerequisite of its own existence:

> For him, in one dear Presence, there exists
> A virtue which irradiates and exalts
> Objects through widest intercourse of sense.
> No outcast he, bewildered and depressed:
> Along his infant veins are interfused
> The gravitation and the filial bond
> Of nature that connect him with the world.[46]

The infant initially enjoys unmediated contact with a maternal "Presence," which is also irradiation by all that the mother sees and feels.

Through "intercourse of touch," "mute dialogues" conducted with the "Mother's heart," the child participates in a "filial bond" that extends to all of nature. But the intercourse is interrupted, interdicted; it is granted only to the infant who is literally *in-fans*, innocent of speech: "For now a trouble came into my mind / From unknown causes. I was left alone / Seeking the visible world, nor knowing why."[47] The "trouble" that leaves the poet an "outcast," "bewildered and depressed," is at once the death of his mother and the consequent movement from "mute dialogues" to articulate speech (consequent, of course, not in any literal sense, but in terms of the gender determinants of a poem that consistently identifies speech and textuality with the loss of the maternal). The "visible world," which was previously experienced in and through the mother, henceforth functions as a distanced or absent object of desire: In the gap that separates the desiring subject from the elusive object of his desires, a gap that involves both the loss of the maternal and the literal or natural with which she is identified, the child is born, or born again, into language. This second birth is thematized in terms of loss and pain, yet the formal prerequisite of the thematization, of expression itself, remains precisely the loss or effacement that is the source of the pain. As with the transformation of the "ridge of turf" into "monumental letters," of nature into writing, words can only be where the maternal is not.

This transposition of sexual difference unto language—the gendering of the tropological, the textual, as the loss of the feminine—finds perhaps its fullest theoretical articulation in the work of Jacques Lacan: "Freud reveals to us that it is thanks to the Name of the Father that man does not remain in the sexual service of the mother, that aggression towards the father is at the principal of the Law, and that the Law is at the service of desire, which it institutes through the prohibition of incest. It is, therefore, the assumption of castration which creates the lack through which desire is instituted. . . . Desire reproduces the subject's relation to the lost object."[48] The child remains what Wordsworth calls "mute" so long as "he" (the child is here constitutively male) remains in the "sexual service of the mother," in a dyadic and unmediated relationship with a maternal body. But "grâce au," both thanks to and due to the intervention of the father and the prohibition against incest (the *non* latent in the paternal *nom*), the dyadic relation is triangulated, and desire henceforth articulates itself in relation to a lost or absent object, the prohibited maternal body. The mere "assumption of castration," the prohibition against the incestuous use of the phallus, the extreme form of what Wordsworth calls the "intercourse of touch," creates both the lack through which desire is instituted and the conditions under which it is articulated. Desire, which dares not speak the name of its interdicted object, is thus condemned to metonyms or meta-names, language in a state of perpetual displacement. (I say "condemned," but only in the sense in which the poet of *The Prelude* says the death of his mother leaves him "bewildered and depressed"; again, what is born of loss or absence proves to be more than adequate compensation for the loss.) The appropriately named "nom du père," the realm of the figurative or symbolic, cannot, then, name or name properly its excluded Other, a point Lacan makes abundantly and crudely clear: "There is woman only as excluded by the nature of things which is the nature of words, and it has to be said that if there is one thing women themselves are now complaining about, it is well and truly that—only they don't know what they are saying, which is all the difference between them and me."[49] The appeal to the criterion of "nature" is little more than an alibi for an ideologically motivated exclusion, and the argument merely rehearses our most canonical formulation of sexual difference: "She shall be called Woman, because she has been differentiated from man." Lacan remains helpful, however, if only for the light he sheds on a question posed by Harold Bloom: Why is there no figure comparable to Milton's Eve in the poetry of the High Romantics?[50] For if Lacan is indeed an apologist for the gender determinants implicit in Wordsworth—if Lacan and Wordsworth are agreed that the exclusion of women from words can be explained simply by the nature of words—then Eve cannot be wherever words are.

Lacan and Wordworth are agreed, but Milton is not; the Wordsworthian myth of language, to risk a literally pre-posterous formulation, is present in Milton only as something Satanic, as figuration in its fallen state:

> O thou that with surpassing Glory crown'd,
> Look'st from thy sole Dominion like the God
> Of this new World; at whose sight all the Stars
> Hide their diminisht heads; to thee I call,
> But with no friendly voice, and add thy name
> O Sun, to tell thee how I hate thy beams
> That bring to my remembrance from what state
> I fell, how glorious once above thy Sphere.[51]

After the revolt in Heaven, Satan never utters the name of the Son, except in this single metonym, in which an innocent sun bears the burden of a projected hatred.[52] Here too there is "project for the sun," a pro-jection onto the sun of an animosity more properly (at least from the point of view of Satan) directed against the Son, the object or Other now lost to the fallen angel. Because Satanic metonymy exacerbates the distance between "meaning" and "Name," it would seem opposed to the Miltonic eschatology of the proper, the attempt to repair the linguistic damage attendant upon the Fall. But as if to point to his affinities with the fallen Angel, Milton himself never calls the Son, at least when the Son is outside the confines of heaven, by any name denoting "Sonship";[53] rather, he is simply "God," which in terms of Milton's own theology the Son clearly is not. Scripture ascribes to the Son "the name and attributes and works of God, as well as divine honours," but for Milton, or at least the Milton of *The Christian Doctrine*, these are "easily understood to be attributable in their original and proper sense to the Father alone."[54] For the Son to participate in or partake of the Name of the Father—for Milton to call the Son "God"—is thus the most radical of linguistic im-proprieties. Yet if misnaming unites poet and fallen angel, Milton is not necessarily of the devil's party.

In the invocation to book VII of *Paradise Lost*, for example, Milton entertains, but only to reject, the not quite proper name "Urania":

> Descend from Heav'n Urania, by that name
> If rightly thou art call'd, whose Voice divine
> Following, above th' Olympian Hill I soar,

Above the flight of Pegasean wing.
The meaning, not the Name I call. [55]

It is to the "meaning" and not the "Name" that the poet finally calls, which means that the name "Urania" is not quite proper, not "rightly . . . called." The literal influx of inspiration—and Milton insists that he is inspired, that the influx is literal—can only be adumbrated by a "nominal absence,"[56] the rejection of a name that in fallen discourse can only be "alien" or "alias." In *The Second Defense*, Milton praises Cromwell for virtues that "soar above the possibilities of titular commendation," for despising the name of king for a majesty far more "transcendent"[57]: a nominal absence again guarantees, or seeks to guarantee, a reality greater than the name. And while nominal absence cannot sustain narrative life—metonymic substitutes for the Word are no less characteristic of Milton than of Satan—a reality "greater than" fallen discourse remains the object of Milton's poetic. In Satan's address to the Son/sun, the greater reality, the Messiah, is elided: As if reverting to the "idolatrous" confusion of common noun and divine name that the creation narrative of Genesis is at pains to avoid, Satan sees the sun as "like the god / Of this new World," less as a name than as a god. In the invocation to book VII, however, the lesser reality, the not quite proper name Urania, is elided or cancelled: the literal or proper source of inspiration is not to be confused with the name that only imperfectly adumbrates it. Like Eve, Urania is tolerated within the Miltonic eschatology only to the extent that it works toward her effacement. "All Classical Literature," Foucault argues, "resides in the movement that proceeds from the figure of the name to the name itself, passing from the task of naming the same thing yet again by means of new figures . . . to that of finding words that will at last name accurately."[58] Had Milton found names that at last named accurately, the not quite proper name "Urania," the figure of the name rather than the name itself, would have been rendered superfluous.

Milton's Urania and Eve as but provisional figures in an eschatology of the proper; Wordsworth's unnamed woman as the absence that engenders figuration: it is in the context of this double and contradictory devaluation that I would like to place, by way of conclusion, an observation of Walter Benjamin's: "To be named—even if the name-giver is god-like and saintly—perhaps always carries with it a presentiment of mourning. But how much more so not to be named."[59] The Eve of Milton's punning "O Eve, in evil hour," the woman who is etymologized as "woe to man,"[60] would doubtless understand the "mourning" involved in the names given by even the "god-like and saintly." The expurgated wife of the 1850 *Prelude*, the woman whose original effacement or murder engenders the text in which she does not finally figure, would doubtless understand the "mourning" involved in not being named. There is a sense in which the Wordsworthian revision of Milton renders woman implicitly unnameable or innominate—she is now the presence that endangers figuration, not the danger that is figuration—but it is in the excluded middle between the two poetics that Stevens imagines his "fluent mundo." "I should name you flatly," but the "Fat girl" bears no proper name.

The Fat girl is not named because naming is apotropaic: it places at a distance; it defines the named as "different from." To name would be to divide "my green, my fluent mundo" and reinscribe sexual difference as male creator and female creation. The word "requires" governs both "I should name you flatly" and "Check your evasions, hold you to yourself" (*CP*, 406); to name would be to reduce the "Fat girl" to an atemporal and unitary entity. But she is found "in difference," not in unity; she is the citizen of a world in which "It Must Change," not progress toward the selfsame. Thus she bears no proper name. The Adam of Biblical and Miltonic fame is granted dominion over the objects he names. The poet of "It Must Give Pleasure," however, does not accept the sexual politics of the Adamic/Miltonic scene of nomination. "How is it I find you in difference?": you have been differentiated from your Miltonic counterpart.

But you are differentiated also from your Wordsworthian counterpart, or the counterpart you do not possess in Wordsworth: You are differentiated from the poetic in which the figurative or "fluent" is constructed on the ruins of a female "mundo." Here not to name would be the greater presentiment of mourning, and if the "Fat girl" does not bear a proper name, she is yet something other than an alien or alias figure for her own absence. Not to name or not to achieve a trope of contact with a substantial female body would be to affirm the loss of the feminine in and to an implicitly male structure of figuration; not to achieve contact would be to participate in that most familiar of romantic trajectories, the pursuit of a female presence distanced or displaced by the tropological nature of the pursuit itself. Romantic quests tend either to be interminable, perpetual "notes toward" or "preludes," or to end in some form of what Northrop Frye, following Blake, calls the "crystal cabinet," the radical closing up of the object that is perhaps the most frequent analogy for symbolic fixation.[61] Yet in Stevens' own "notes toward" (his romantic quest that is also a critique of romantic quests) it is only in crystal that the "Fat girl" will not stop revolving, and distance or difference from a female presence gives way to a woman who is herself found "in difference." The "excepted" or excluded in Wordsworth and Milton—the feminine as other than the materiality that endangers figuration, the feminine as other than the danger that is figuration—is in Stevens infolded. "Notes toward a Supreme Fiction" thus becomes the exception in the tradition of supreme fictions. "And for what, except for you, do I feel love?"

Part II

CONTEXTS

6

Wallace Stevens
The Concealed Self

C. Roland Wagner

What more is there to love than I have loved?
— Wallace Stevens, "Montrachet-le-Jardin"

Many have been fascinated by what Helen Vendler terms "Stevens' Secrecies."[1] Now that Stevens' secrets are emerging, also emerging are differences of opinion about what to do with them. Traditional literary critics try to keep their eyes averted from the merely "personal" elements in Stevens' poetry, or at least keep them from corrupting the pure act of literary understanding. Both Vendler and Milton J. Bates[2] take a position approximately midway between a psychoanalytic approach to Stevens' poetry and a purely literary one, curbing their fascination with Stevens' secrets by avoiding psychoanalytic interpretation (although Vendler has lately shown unusual responsiveness to the person as well as the poet). Nevertheless, their caution, admirable as it is in some respects, can interfere with adequate understanding of Stevens' life and work.[3] For example, an extraordinary instance of a secret that needs investigation is Stevens' supposed conversion to Roman Catholicism during the last months of his illness.[4] Bates, who believes it did occur (rendered "plausible" by the late poems), sees it as a mature act, an "adult accommodation with religion" that "affirmed his belief in the church as an institution, though probably not in his childhood God."[5] Vendler, who is severely skeptical of the conversion, argues that, even if it occurred, "the life work had been brought to a close before Stevens' last days . . . and any judgment on [his] work must find those irrelevant events occurring after it was complete."[6] But if the last poetry, and perhaps all the poetry, makes the conversion plausible, as I strongly believe it does, it is insufficient to explore the merely adult reasons for such a highly significant act. We need to uncover its infantile roots as well as the roots of Stevens' more complex acts of poetic creation. We need to understand better Stevens' susceptivity to the nurturing female others of his mind—his wife, his mother, his secret childhood divinities—a susceptivity which informs his poetry throughout and establishes a clear and fruitful link between Stevens' life and work. Stevens' mature poetic achievement need not be threatened by our knowledge of his immaturity but should rather be enhanced by it.

I

Stevens' religious beliefs were rooted in his ambivalence, an ambivalence that was fundamental to every aspect of his life. The possible conversion might be perceived as the last stage in a lifetime of ambivalence. Many critics of Stevens, myself among them, have in the past seen him as a strict naturalist, one who "surrendered all residual belief in religion."[7] But over the years there have been a variety of opinions on the subject of Stevens' beliefs, a spectrum extending from those who see him as a strict naturalist, through those who see him as a loose naturalist yet find radical inconsistency between his naturalism and his mysticism, to those who assert that he is a pantheist of sorts, to those, finally, who see him as a Christian. Harold Bloom alone seems to grasp some of the range of Stevens' emotional beliefs. He is willing, so to speak, to place this spectrum of criticism inside Stevens' mind. But he is not willing to include Christianity in the spectrum,[8] and Christianity is the key to the deepest layer of Stevens' mind, for it carried with it all the vital emotional ties of his childhood.[9]

There is a mixture of piety and skepticism in all his writings from 1898 to the year of his marriage in 1909 (and afterward). This was a period of shift from traditional religious beliefs to a less orthodox piety. Nature and St. Patrick's Cathedral, Emersonianism and Christianity confront one another: the house of God provided protection as Stevens discarded—but never completely—outworn beliefs. He both hates and loves his Bible as he throws away "the silly thing" (L, 102). The "church is a mother for them [others]—and for us [his fiancée and himself]" (L, 96), and yet nature is superior to the church. Although he denied the church's consolatory value after taking Communion in Reading, Pennsylvania, one Sunday during his youth—"Love is consolation, Nature is consolation," he defiantly asserted in his journal, not "Gloria in excelsis!" (L, 82)—Stevens found he was still susceptible to its magic when he attended Communion in 1913: "How thrilling it was to go to the old church last Sunday!" he wrote to his wife; "I had no idea I was so susceptible" (L, 181); and perhaps Stevens rediscovered consolation in the church if he in fact converted in 1955.

Even after his naturalism was intellectually established, his statements of naturalism often seemed defensive. For example, what can one do with Stevens' response to—as he puts it—the modernist "annihilation" of the "gods"? First he persuasively depicts the feeling of emptiness that followed their annihilation, the feeling "that in a measure, we, too, had been annihilated . . . dispossessed and alone . . . like children without parents." But then he goes on to make the astonishing claim that "no man ever muttered a petition in his heart for the restoration of those unreal shapes" (OP89, 260). It is precisely those "unreal shapes," even those that are out of date, that make the world go round, not least Stevens' world.

Those ghosts of the past continued to haunt Stevens even when he seemed to be saying that he was free of them. Nostalgia for his childhood beliefs is expressed in both open and hidden ways: his empathy for the exiled Jew in "Winter Bells," attracted by the glamour of a Catholic Mass, is clear (CP, 141).[10] More hidden is his persisting attachment to an "all-too-human" god in the Nietzschean "Less and Less Human, O Savage Spirit." On one level, he seems to be rejecting any kind of

anthropomorphic deity and, like the Snow Man, attaching himself to
nothingness:

> It is the human that is the alien,
> The human that has no cousin in the moon.
>
> It is the human that demands his speech
> From beasts or from the incommunicable mass.
>
> If there must be a god in the house, let him be one
> That will not hear us when we speak: a coolness,
>
> A vermilioned nothingness, any stick of the mass
> Of which we are too distantly a part.
>
> (*CP*, 328)

But what is this god? It can be the spirit of unimagined reality or,
possibly, the spirit of a reality transformed by the imagination, but
whether one or the other, it is a reality that is beyond us and our needs.
(Is there a hint, also, of a reality wholly beyond the imagination?) Yet
this forceful attack on traditional religious beliefs appears to contradict
itself and contains possibilities of connection with the divine object. The
connection is defined by the words "too" and "a part" in the last line.
The various meanings of "too" multiply the possibilities. Thus we are
also a part of that distant, divine reality; we are, *to an excessive extent*,
away from it; and we are, *more than we should be*, separated from it. And
the multiplications continue if we read "a part" as "apart."

If the god is simple, natural but irrational fact (the mass as disor-
derly), we are part of it but had best keep our distance from it. Or we are
part of it and cannot deny our connection with it. If, however, the god is
more than irrational fact (the mass as coherent), then our distance from it
is bad if we still demand salvation, but good if we assert our natural
separateness from it and stay within the limits of our humanity. Finally,
there is the distinct possibility that the "incommunicable mass" hints at
Holy Communion in the Catholic Mass, and bears all the weight and
complexity of the various meanings of distance and closeness already

noted.[11] But this would never have occurred to me—particularly the implied wish to participate in the Mass—if not for the claim that Stevens had converted. An appreciation of Stevens' ambivalence deepens our understanding of his empathy for the Jew in "Winter Bells" as it does our response to his lively interest in Pascal's deathbed communion, which he sees as contradicted by the philosopher's attack throughout his life on the "deceptions" of the imagination (NA, 133–36).

At the core of Stevens' ambivalent attachment to Christianity is a mystical yearning (also ambivalent) for union, a union only achievable in moments and always accompanied by a tragic sense of separation, "the dumbfoundering abyss between us and the object." Vendler argues that Stevens is a poet of hunger, desire, and passion, not the "cold and cerebral" poet that many find.[12] She argues that he seems inhuman to many readers because his poetry is mainly "second-order" rather than "first-order" poetry, that is, poetry that reflects on experience rather than responds directly and immediately to experience.[13] But why is Stevens so exclusively a second-order poet? I would suggest that his primal hunger is for union with the ideal regressive and forbidden object, and that this hunger for first-order experience, or, better, for the foundation of all first-order experience, is defensively transformed into a second-order experience of meditation and poetic dialectic. But Stevens' second-order poetry is not philosophical in the sense of a Lucretius or a Dante: it is a poetry of endless struggle with the naked wishes of the first level.

What alienates many readers is not the reflective poetry in itself but its restricted subject matter, its inbred focus, its Poe-like obsessive concern with primal experience. Stevens cannot allow himself to be interested in real people in his poetry because that would distract him from the central struggle with fantasies. (It might also, perhaps, tempt him toward the forbidden object). His difficult relations with other people, so well documented by himself and others, reflect this. As he wrote to his fiancée: "I do not get on well with my equals, not at all with my superiors. Ergo, I have no friends."[14] He also wrote to her that "most people are a great nuisance. . . . Perhaps that is why my own likes are often for things than for people: because of intolerance" (L, 107). Later on, after he was established, he got along rather well with his "inferiors," mostly male, where he was always in control, but he continued to have minor difficulties with superiors and equals. His greatest problem, of course, was with young, unmarried women. He was often hostile to them at work, especially during the difficult, middle period of his marriage. One of his favorite occupations was embarrassing new female employees at the office.[15] Considering his exquisitely civilized sensibility and his customary kindness and courtesy, his occasional boorishness is noteworthy and suggests a need to strike at what threatened him.

Stevens' separation from others pervaded all aspects of his life. Even his prose style and speech reflected a certain withdrawal from reality. There was a strong component of primary process thinking in his secondary process discourse, typical certainly of the mental life of the creative artist, but also perhaps symptomatic of neurosis or some developmental failure.[16] Elder Olson reports that "He didn't argue. He meditated. . . . He spoke in sentences, not in paragraphs. There was no such thing as a connected argument. What you had instead was a series of intuitive and highly perceptive remarks. . . . That was not a man who thought consecutively. . . . His real style was the 'Adagia,' and that was very much his conversational way."[17] And Harry Levin asserts that he didn't "take him very seriously as a philosopher. I think he was doing almost the converse in those critical essays, using prose discourse but making a kind of poetry out of that."[18]

The balance between satisfying wholly inward needs and satisfying needs that had to take account of both inward and outward reality often tilted toward inwardness at the cost of adequate communication. Stevens' meditations are in no sense developed arguments but repetitions—often glorious—on his central compulsive theme. His critical-rational faculties partly withdraw when this theme takes center stage. The complaint of those who find Stevens too cerebral should be rather that he is fixated on too narrow an aspect of experience. It is not so much that reason is getting in the way of immediate experience—although this does sometimes occur—but almost the reverse: that he lacks the mature, indeed, the *rational* capacity to respond in a unified way to a variety of experiences.

THE CONCEALED SELF / 123

The central relationship from which Stevens retreated was his relationship with his wife. Bates and Richardson have discussed the
complexities of that somewhat strange affair, and its details need not be
discussed here. The essence of it, as Bates writes, is that Stevens was
deeply uncomfortable with the Elsie of flesh and blood and so transformed her into an ideal fantasy, the inspiration of his early poetry and
his imaginative life.[19] As Stevens himself explained to Elsie well before
their marriage why they were "easier in [their] letters" than "when [they]
are together": "It must be because you are more perfectly yourself to me
when I am writing to you, and that makes me more perfectly myself to
you. You know that I do with you as I like in my thoughts. . . . You are
my Elsie there. —Yet it is the real Elsie, all the time" (L, 96). The "real"
Elsie is the interior Elsie: the idealized object of desire is already
beginning to separate from the Elsie of flesh and blood and to be prefer-
able to her. But not until the terrible clash between Stevens and his wife
after they began to live together did the split widen between the inner
and the outer Elsie. The center of gravity shifted from the wife in the
apartment to the illicit lover (the "interior paramour") in the mind.
Finding his subject and his voice as a poet meant for Stevens spiritually
separating from his wife. As Bates shrewdly observes, she felt that "she
had been supplanted" by her husband's poetry and perhaps poetry itself
might have qualified in her eyes as "metaphysical adultery."[20]

Bates goes on to argue, however, that the incompatibility between
Stevens and his wife was the result more of fate than of will. "He was
betrayed less by Elsie than by his own imagination; she was betrayed
more by insecurity than by her spouse."[21] With all due regard to whatever inadequacies Elsie herself brought to the marriage, Stevens' need to
idealize is not sufficient to explain his share in the failure. Of course,
Bates is aware of Stevens' "Doubts and Fears," his need for disguises and
his preference for fantasy over reality, which he discusses in great detail.
But curiously he never plainly asserts that Stevens was afraid of Elsie.
He perhaps prefers to have the reader come to this obvious conclusion
himself. But the indirect approach creates an atmosphere of thinness in
his interpretation of Stevens' motives. For example, Bates's explanation
of Stevens' encouragement of his wife's desire to escape from the city in

the early years of their marriage seems superficial. He attributes it to a husband's concern for his wife's welfare: his distaste for the crowded city and the lack of the family and social life she was accustomed to in Reading.[22] In his understated way, Bates remarks that Stevens "also appreciated the solitude—as opposed to the loneliness—of these summers," and even "suggested that Elsie prolong her vacation in the country." That he was "having an affair with her rival," the "interior paramour," is poetic and accurate but incomplete.[23] It says nothing about Stevens' terrible fear of intimacy. But his fear was not completely hidden. Stevens himself understood it to an extent. A more important motive, because more repressed and therefore more the critical cause of the failure of the marriage, was Stevens' unacknowledged anger.

Richardson's study is quite helpful in its understanding of the various shapes and forms of Stevens' anger—especially in the forms of irony and skepticism. She postulates a "deep pool of violence from which he drew his periodic indirect attacks on [Elsie]," and particularly his attacks on (her) orthodox religious beliefs.[24] Yet he had also praised the church as a "mother for them—and for us" (L, 96) and had "strongly urged" Elsie to "join a church," thus revealing his ambivalence toward both Christianity and his wife. Richardson intelligently guesses that Stevens might well have unconsciously seen his relationship with Elsie spelled out in James's *Washington Square*, in the sadistic, manipulating egotists and the vulnerable Catherine. He had hoped to send her the book "if it [was] any good," but found it disappointing because he could only allow himself to respond to its externals and avoided its deeper implications.[25] Richardson, however, misses or downplays Elsie's ability to recognize her husband's hostility. Certainly she sometimes realized that his irony—what she called the "mocking" and "affected" manner of his poetry[26]—was directed against her. Perhaps, among the sophisticated modernists in Walter Arensberg's apartment, she "could not see what others saw,"[27] but she could perhaps see what they could *not* see—that the need in her husband to tear down established structures of belief had a personal and prejudiced edge to it.

I wonder too if Richardson is correct when she asserts that Elsie did not appreciate that her husband's concern with food (at the time he was visiting his dying mother) was a sign of his deep wish for his own home and his wife's cooking? Even if it is true that Elsie "probably found this preoccupation annoying," because no direct expression of intimacy was joined to it, she knew how important food was to Stevens and would intuitively recognize it without needing to "remember what he had once written her about how[,] ever since he had left Reading for Harvard, thoughts of home were always associated with food."28

II

Ambivalent attachment to the nurturing, pre-Oedipal mother is central to our understanding of Stevens. It helps to explain his marriage, his religious beliefs and the roots—the strength and weaknesses—of his poetry. Let us begin with the image and the concept of the "face." In elucidating for a correspondent in 1943 a section of "Notes toward a Supreme Fiction" ("It Must Give Pleasure," III), Stevens interprets the face as the "elementary idea of God . . . We struggle with the face, see it everywhere & try to express the changes" (L, 438). The image is found in a number of places in the poetry and can be traced back to an earlier period in Stevens' life (1907), when he describes to his fiancée a Romantic face in nature that he saw during one of his walks in the woods in the rain:

> Once I stopped and smelled the earth and the rain and looked around me—and recognized it all, as if I had seen the face of my dearest friend. I said to myself, "It is like seeing the face of a friend" . . . the little wilderness all my own, shared with nobody, not even with you—it made me myself. It was friendly so much deeper than anything else could be.— You are different. I play a silver lute for you, when I am good, and Elsie is a soft name to sing, and you make a lover of me, so that I can be nothing else.—But to-day I escaped and enjoyed every breath of liberty. . . . To-day was so much of an Odyssey for me that you must forgive my truancy and, also, because I am penitent now. (L, 99)

Clearly Stevens here recognized the face as competing with his feeling for Elsie (although at this point she, not the face, is his poetic muse). He even implies that his feeling for the face is deeper than his feeling for

Elsie. Thus, well before the actual disappointments of the marriage, he was already anticipating trouble and even providing a path of retreat for himself. The "interior paramour," his "inamorata," was preparing him for "metaphysical adultery."

The romantic object was apparently recognized by Stevens later in life as stemming from attachment to the ideal mother, perhaps to his actual mother. Harold Bloom in fact argues that Stevens moved from an early indirect naming of "his own mother as the origin and purpose of his poetry" (as in "To the One of Fictive Music" [*CP*, 87–88]) to the "startling epiphany" of "The Auroras of Autumn" (section 3), where he "takes the Oedipal risk, as Keats and Whitman did, and invokes his muse as his actual mother and the other women of his family."[29] But although he must have linked the face of his mother with the divine face, it does not seem likely that Stevens saw her image as the source of his marital difficulties. If anything he saw its persistence as the consequence of those difficulties. The logic of equivalence between the ideal and the real mother was surely there but not all of its implications were conscious:

Farewell to an idea . . . The mother's face,
The purpose of the poem, fills the room.
They are together, here, and it is warm,

With none of the prescience of oncoming dreams,
It is evening. The house is evening, half-dissolved.
Only the half they can never possess remains,

Still-starred. It is the mother they possess,
Who gives transparence to their present peace.
She makes that gentler that can be gentle be.

And yet she too is dissolved, she is destroyed.
She gives transparence. But she has grown old.
The necklace is a carving not a kiss.

The soft hands are a motion not a touch.
The house will crumble and the books will burn.
They are at ease in a shelter of the mind . . .

(*CP*, 413)

The farewell is complex. it stands for many farewells, many "Forms of farewell" (*CP*, 482). In part it is seasonal and cyclical, in part related to old age, in part it continues Stevens' farewells to traditional religion, that "cemetery of forms" that no longer works for modernists. It expresses the perpetual and necessary movement from imagination to reality. Stevens is thus saying farewell to his own mother as a permanent nurturer and turning to adult satisfactions. He speaks for all of us as we move, or ought to move, from childhood to maturity. But he is also, narrowly, within the special limits of his own life, continuing to say farewell to a wife and a marriage and a home. He is saying farewell to normal love, a normal central relationship; he is attempting to adapt himself to what Bates calls a life of "emotional deprivation."[30] As he declares in the very late poem, "Local Objects":

> He knew that he was a spirit without a foyer
> And that, in his knowledge, local objects become
> More precious than the most precious objects of home:
>
> The local objects of a world without a foyer,
> Without a remembered past, a present past,
> Or a present future, hoped for in present hope . . .

> (*OP89*, 137)

Thus when Stevens endlessly writes of his loss of the comforts of the religious past, he is also alluding to his loss of a nurturing family past, his family of orientation, and alluding to his failed family of procreation, which surely provided some pleasures and compensations, but not the "absolute foyer beyond romance," the "mystic marriage" that would replace his own marriage—"love's characters come face to face" (*CP*, 401).[31]

In the above quoted section (3) from "Auroras" the verbal accent is on reconciliation, not on the unending quest. But does the tone of lonely sadness suggest the opposite, the pressure of the unreconciled wish? Certainly accepting mother as an old woman, as an inappropriate object of adult love, can be prime evidence that one has resolved Oedipal (and pre-Oedipal) conflict. Nevertheless, the question remains: How fully is that reality accepted? Before we turn to other late poems for evidence of unresolved yearnings, let us look again at this poem and consider whether Stevens' *wife* might be seen as the mother who "has grown old," whose "soft hands are a motion not a touch," "a carving not a kiss." These then would become images of despair rather than of disenthrallment, with Elsie standing in Stevens' mind for the *unavailable mother,* she who supplied him with the food of love, but not with love? This becomes more likely once we appreciate the fluidity of Stevens' conception of the mother figure. We are never entirely certain which he is speaking of: the mother inside himself—"a mother fierce / In his body" (*CP*, 321); the real mother that once lived and died and nourished him; or the mother that his wife represented to him.

Stevens' supreme self-consciousness, his apparent awareness of the extent and variousness and even some of the depth of his projections, can mislead us into assuming that he had an effective understanding of them. Self-consciousness is not the same as self-understanding or self-control. Because he asserts that the mother "has grown old," we may assume that he has stopped reaching for her as a young woman. Because he asserts that "the necklace is a carving not a kiss," we may assume that he accepts the limits that adult vision imposes on infantile longing. Because he asserts that "the soft hands are a motion not a touch," we may assume that he has reconciled himself to the tragic limitations that symbolic truth imposes. But adult recognition of symbolic truth does not cancel the persistent infantile need for literal truth. There is a dimension of literalness in Stevens, a yearning for romantic communion, finally expressed perhaps in his reputed conversion, that prevents us from taking his reference to the "touch" of the "inamorata," she that "Touches, as one hand touches another hand" (*CP*, 484), in only a vague symbolic sense. He means that touch to be literal, to be concrete. It is nevertheless the touch of a fantasy: in reality Stevens must settle for sight, for sound, for symbolic distance.[32] In his real world, "she that he loved turns cold at his light touch," in his bare world, the only object he can "touch, touch every way" is the snow (*OP89*, 117).

The two explicit references to his wife in the later poetry imply, through the fluidity of the imagery, that wife and mother were joined in

Stevens' unconscious and that the wife as bad mother was the reverse of the ideal, interior paramour—but she was still the mother, still deeply needed. "She that he loved," she who "turns cold at his light touch," of "World without Peculiarity" (*CP*, 453), is really similar to the responsive mother of "Auroras" (and of so many other poems) "who gives transparence to their present peace" (*CP*, 413). In the other positive poems the mother is somehow always unavailable (or available only for a moment), but the emphasis is not on harsh and cold rejection but on realistic limitation. In this poem the wife (the "hating woman") is the bad mother and represents the terrible negation, the incompleteness that spoils the perfection of the earth. But the actual mother and the father are also at odds with perfection, perhaps because of the wife. The father "lies now in the poverty of dirt," the dissatisfied mother "cries on his breast," and he, the alienated spirit, fails to find his center. But sometimes negativity is overcome ("difference disappears") and father, mother, and wife come together in harmony: "And the poverty of dirt, the thing upon his breast, / The hating woman, the meaningless place, / Become a single being, sure and true" (*CP*, 454). Although this Hegelian synthesis seems forced, it does reveal Stevens' urge to join the bad with the good mother as his ultimate object of love. He could only succeed in this when the figure of the bad mother was more hidden, more adequately defended against.

She is certainly not adequately defended against in "Madame La Fleurie," even with her strange disguise, for he insists on the difference between the good and bad mother and tries to keep them further apart than in "World without Peculiarity." Unlike most of Stevens' poems this one does not even aim at a synthesis. It sets the good "parent" of the "earth" side by side and at odds with the bad, the hating wife (the "bearded queen") at the other end of the house ("that distant chamber"), although the aspect of the good mother featured is the devouring figure of death. The poet's grief is not over the fact that mother death will devour him but that she will be sullied by ingesting the image of the evil wife that lies in his own heart together with the terrible truths of relationships "he had found in the handbook of heartbreak":

His grief is that his mother should feed on him, himself
  and what he saw,
In that distant chamber, a bearded queen, wicked in her dead
  light.

(CP, 507)

After a lifetime of being fed (nurtured) by both the good and bad mothers, the poet is disturbed by the thought that his body and mind, with all
they contain of the evil mother (and perhaps his own unacknowledged
hatred as well), will now nourish the good mother. Again the fluid images
may tell still more. Isn't the devouring aspect of the good mother in
keeping with the masculinity associated with the wicked queen? Isn't the
feeding mother also a bearded queen (a sort of witch, perhaps)? The poet
finds himself joining together what he wills to keep apart. The beard
suggests the pre-Oedipal, phallic (or hermaphroditic) mother, the woman
with a penis, whose masculinity is at once a threat to the male child
and a reassurance that protects it from the frightening thought that
creatures exist without penises.[33] Thus the "flowering" of the mother
("La Fleurie") may not only be associated with the good mother but with
the growing beard of the bad mother (the "wicked" queen).[34]

So let me repeat: the unavailable mother may become the wicked
mother. A universe described as indifferent to human concerns may not
be rigorously and objectively neutral, or even sublime, but may serve as
a spurning parental figure projected onto the universe in the guise of a
pure naturalism. When, "nothing himself," the poet as "listener" in the
snow "beholds / Nothing that is not there and the nothing that is"
(CP, 10), he may be thought of as responding stoically to a dehumanized
universe that refuses to love him. But like the ancient Stoics, he suppresses (and represses) his wishes, rather than clarifying his understanding. If Stevens had faced more of the truth of the interior sources of the
rejecting parent, the fluid images of the mother figure would have begun
to solidify and a real externality together with a more rigorous internality
would have emerged. By a rigorous internality I mean one in which
Oedipal and pre-Oedipal wishes are detected in ever-widening circles of
understanding. The external world could then have been more fully

distinguishable from internal needs and the internal needs could have been seen for what they really are. Most significantly, the intensity of the mystic quest, Freud's oceanic feeling, could have been reduced, and objects *of a different order* might have emerged.

Stevens' problems with his wife were not simply the reflection of a bad marriage. Rather, the bad marriage was a reflection of his underlying emotional inadequacy. Outside observers noticed two contradictory kinds of behavior in Stevens' treatment of his wife: Some saw contempt or at least arrogance and authoritarianism[35] (which probably contributed to Elsie's infantilization); others saw fearful submission to her wishes and jealous protectiveness.[36] Even when she became the "hating woman," he remained in awe of Elsie and overrated her, as he had before they were married, and yet, at the same time, he underrated her.

As negative feelings replaced positive ones, the angel became a sort of witch in his mind:

> If she is like the moon, she never clears
> But spreads an evil lustre whose increase
> Is evil, crisply bright, disclosing you
> Stooped in a night of vast inquietude.
> Observe her shining in the deadly trees.

(OP89, 66)

But now the real Elsie became more and more like the fantasized Elsie. "She insults everybody," Stevens complained, after an outburst of hers at Robert Frost.[37] He felt that he had to keep her hidden from view because of her dangerous impulses. Was she part of the "violence [from] without" that he had to protect himself from with "a violence from within" (*NA*, 36)? Stevens' view of his wife was now much like that of some children in their Hartford neighborhood, who would cry out at Elsie's strange appearance, "There's the witch!" She was "never nasty," but she was odd. "Don't come near me" was implied in her behavior.[38] Her transformation from the "most beautiful girl in Reading" into the witch of Hartford made it all the more difficult for Stevens to see and understand her as a real person. He could not recognize what she *was* before he married her, what she *became* because of him, and what she *would have become* with almost any other partner. Increasingly she became what he most dreaded, and society at large collaborated in maintaining his distortions, yet he continued to insist that she was a "damn good cook and a faithful wife."

That offhand remark brings to a focus the whole of Stevens' ambivalence toward his wife. It comes at the end of a conversation with his nephew John Sauer, who remembers that it took place in a "very fine little French restaurant" in New York. Stevens ordered for his nephew in French and they discussed "how fond he [Stevens] was of good music, . . . that he had quite a collection of records. I told him that I had some good records, too—the Philadelphia Orchestra and some light operatic music. 'Oh, good lord, John, I'm not speaking of that.' It was all this heavy stuff. He was very proud of his record collection; it must have been quite something. He said it thoroughly relaxed him. Elsie didn't appreciate the music. Elsie was a good cook. 'That's why I've got this obese look about me.' Very conscious of his big belly, very conscious. He said Elsie couldn't appreciate the things he does. 'She's a damn good cook and a faithful wife.'"[39] Superficially this is a compliment to Elsie, even with the complaint; less obviously, and semiconsciously, it suggests the edge of contempt for the domestic woman, unable to appreciate the finer things; most deeply, and unconsciously, it perhaps intimates something dimly remembered from an earlier life, Stevens' strong, latent attachment to the nurturing, yet dangerous mother—Was she poisoning him?—the bond stronger than steel preserved by a failed marriage.[40]

III

Stevens' poetry moves from the various disguises of *Harmonium*, through the more direct language of the 1930s and early 1940s, to the elastic, fluent and naked style of his old age. Did he resolve some of his conflicts? He had always believed in the necessity of "a kind of secrecy between the poet and his poem which, once violated, affects the integrity of the poet" (*L*, 361). The poem as defense stops functioning as defense if it is too clearly understood by others (and by the poet). In this sense the later poems are less secretive, less defensive, and hint at a major resolution of conflicts, at least regarding artistic creation. They even suggest some reduction in ambivalence in Stevens' marriage and in his religious beliefs, though here we must be cautious. Certainly the great late poems are less ironical, less "mocking." Bates calls them more "innocent,"[41] and this implies that the underlying anger has been reduced. In the early poems Stevens contained his anger with difficulty (see the rejected lines from "Le Monocle" [OP89, 39]) as he laboriously reconstructed the ideal object. The best of the late poems speak with increased maturity; the poorer ones the opposite. If we examine some of the former, with their characteristic boundaries, we may be able to appreciate how their sources both nourished and limited their greatness.

At his worst Stevens gets bogged down by tortuous symbolism and heavy diction that give delight only to selected graduate students (including myself years ago). I find some of this in all the long poems, even the greatest, as well as in too many of the shorter poems.[42] Let us bury the Canon Aspirin (despite Harold Bloom) together with the MacCullough and perhaps even Professor Eucalyptus. Let us turn away from the "mythology of modern death" in "The Owl in the Sarcophagus," although the symbolism may be helpful for understanding other, better poems by Stevens. I have already mentioned the failure of the intended synthesis in "World without Peculiarity" and the lack of clarity of the unresolved feelings toward mother and wife in "Madame La Fleurie." Other failures from the later poems are "Two Versions of the Same Poem" (especially section 1), "Someone Puts a Pineapple Together," "Of Ideal Time and Choice," and "The Ultimate Poem Is Abstract."

The "daily majesty of meditation" is at its height in a number of sections of each of the long poems, for example, the intensely moving section 9 and the fine sections 11 and 12 of "An Ordinary Evening in New Haven." The limpid perfection of "The House Was Quiet and the World Was Calm" and "The Course of a Particular" have been celebrated by many readers. The nobility and intensity of feeling of "Large Red Man Reading" and section 1 of "Two Letters" ("A Letter From") should be mentioned, as well as the unusual power and control of "Reality Is an

Activity of the Most August Imagination" and "Of Mere Being." Finally there is the exquisite plainness of "The World as Meditation" and the culminating glory of "To an Old Philosopher in Rome."

Of what are these successes composed? I should like to say a few words about the last two without pretending to completeness of understanding. The Santayana poem succeeds for some of the same reasons that the others do but goes beyond them in a direction that Stevens was normally not inclined to go. Its balance between thought and physical reality, its meditative music flowing from the accumulated wisdom of old age, is like the other successful poems, but even better. It is better, I think, because Stevens forgets himself in doing what he does nowhere else: he addresses and gives character to another real person. It is certainly true that Stevens identified with the old philosopher ready to die in the Convent of the Blue Nuns, that he is celebrating the best in himself in celebrating Santayana. But he does not seem to me to be consciously thinking of himself. This is a poem of love, the love of another human being, such as Stevens never wrote before. Although he had no present real relationship with the philosopher, the extra dimension of objectivity comes from the fact that Santayana was a real person whom he once knew (and exchanged poems with) and that subjectivity and objectivity here are in perfect balance. In contrast, for example, to the vague object of love in the dedicatory section of "Notes toward a Supreme Fiction"—"And for what, except for you, do I feel love?" (*CP*, 380)—that is often confused by new readers with Henry Church, there is a clearly defined object in "To an Old Philosopher in Rome," a poem of adult love of a real person living in a real time and place: "The bed, the books, the chair, the moving nuns, / The candle as it evades the sight, these are / The sources of happiness in the shape of Rome" (*CP*, 508). It is a celebration of Santayana's commitment, even in the face of death, to the naturalistic imagination. Stevens is honoring the life of a philosopher who he believed lived wholly within the imagination and wholly within the natural world: "With every visible thing enlarged and yet / No more than a bed, a chair and moving nuns" (*CP*, 510).

But did the picture of Santayana near death, surrounded by the blue nuns, arouse in Stevens some concern about his own end, about a death without viaticum? There is nothing in the poem that would make one think so. Its serenity is complete, its objectivity assured. Yet if we go outside the poem and consider the history of Stevens' involvement with Christianity and Catholicism up to the time of the poem (1952), we might indulge in a conjecture. Was there something about the scene, the Anglican convent surrounded by Catholic Rome, the ringing bells (cf. "Winter Bells" and "The Old Lutheran Bells of Home"), the nuns themselves, so like "the sisterhood of the living dead" and the "fragrant mothers" of "To the One of Fictive Music" (*CP*, 87), that stirred Stevens' latent ambivalence toward naturalistic purity, that touched his need to believe in more than the human imagination? Consciously the scene served to reaffirm his humanistic naturalism; unconsciously it may have helped him turn slowly from that naturalism. [43]

"The World as Meditation" is also clear and concrete and a love poem. But it is neither addressed to nor is it about a real person. It projects Stevens' ideas and feelings about love onto the tale of Ulysses and Penelope, who also represent (and are represented by) the reality of sun and earth. It transcends the soliloquizing of "The Sail of Ulysses" by dramatizing the poet's conception of imaginative love. It is a more successful embodiment of Stevens' dream of an alternative to his failed marriage because his primary identification is with Penelope rather than with Ulysses. His customary stance is taken from the male perspective, with the female as imagined object—the mind's eye and its "fluent mundo"—but in this poem Stevens makes delicate use of his own femininity, his passivity, in a way that achieves fuller actuality and a more convincing balance between lover and loved one. Instead of expressing the longing of the subject to reach an unattainable object, Penelope expresses "the longing of the object to be reached by the subject."[44] "She would talk a little to herself as she combed her hair, / Repeating his name with its patient syllables, / Never forgetting him that kept coming constantly so near" (*CP*, 521). Although Ulysses never arrives, the incompleteness is kept in tender yet firm control in this classic statement of romantic feeling.

But what kind of love is this? Is it like the adult love glimpsed in the Santayana poem? I don't think so. Lucy Beckett writes of love beyond the ordinary here.[45] But is it not less? Its serenity, as in almost every Stevens poem, is the serenity of a single mind in relation to itself, not of a mind in relation to another mind. It is the quiet acceptance of separation, of not having, of loneliness:

> But was it Ulysses? Or was it only the warmth of the sun
> On her pillow? The thought kept beating in her like her heart.
> The two kept beating together. It was only day.
>
> It was Ulysses and it was not.

(CP, 521)

The epigraph from Georges Enesco interprets Stevens' meaning in a more general way than the poem itself does.

> J'ai passé trop de temps à travailler mon violon, à
> voyager. Mais l'exercice essential du
> compositeur—la méditation—rien ne l'a jamais
> suspendu en moi . . . Je vis un rêve permanent, qui ne
> s'arrête ni nuit ni jour. (CP, 520)

When Stevens was asked why he never traveled outside the country, he usually replied that Mrs. Stevens was a poor traveler. In addition, for Stevens foreign lands were unspoiled places of the imagination ("Bergamo on a postcard"), parts of that perpetual "meditation" which sustained him in the face of an unsatisfying reality. But the epigraph may suggest another, opposite reason, not inconsistent with the first two. Foreign travel might have represented not only a fantasy to indulge in but a dangerous reality to avoid. Travel perhaps stood for an external danger situation symbolic of breaking from both the exterior wife-mother and the interior Mother.

Whether Stevens, then, identified with Ulysses, "the interminable adventurer" of the mind, as in "The Sail of Ulysses," or with Penelope, "Companion to his self for her," the outcome is the same: "His mind presents the world / And in his mind the world revolves" (OP89, 129). Penelope, as representative of the world—indeed, as the world itself—

is finally seen to be revolving inside the mind, if not inside the mind of Ulysses then inside the mind of Wallace Stevens. Stevens, however, could not be satisfied with such an image. He needed more. He wanted to break out of his permanent dream, out of the solitariness of his life and into a marriage and everything symbolized by marriage. That is part of what he meant, I think, by his repeated demand, in both his poetry and his prose, for normality and centrality in great poetry. He distinguished extreme and abnormal poetry—which he also equated with explorations into the mystical—from central poetry, a poetry that may begin with the mystical and the abnormal but whose "desire" and ambition is "to press away from mysticism toward that ultimate good sense which we term civilization" (NA, 115–16, 153–56).

Stevens seems to have recognized within himself an inherent solitariness, a detachment from other human beings, and longed to overcome this with a true marriage. Perhaps he realized that his mystical yearnings were too intense to be "normal," and poetry became a dialectical struggle to reattain centrality. But full centrality was beyond him, the idea of marriage was only a symbolic one, a marriage of self and the world, not a literal relationship with any human being. In "The World as Meditation," he attempts to leap over the gap between subject and object and achieve by *identification love* what he failed to achieve by *object love*. (In a sense his mysticism was too literal, his marriage, and his idea of marriage, too symbolic.) In the guise of Penelope he could wait indefinitely for a consummation devoutly to be avoided, resigning himself to incompleteness, and "Never forgetting him that kept coming constantly so near." Certainly there is a delicate sense of intimacy here but it is all inside the mind.

This is a poet *inherently* lonely, not lonely because of specific and later losses or rejections imposed by the "undulations" of time. ("Let the place of solitaires / Be a place of perpetual undulation" [CP, 60]). The loneliness is intrinsic to Stevens' identity, a sense of separateness that goes back to the roots of life, to the original separation from ("apart from"?) the maternal wellspring. Only one sort of marriage can correct, or seem to correct, that fundamental "solitude of the self" (CP, 494): the marriage of the self with the source of its being. And that is not really marriage at all but symbiosis, a blotting out of all distinct identity, a return to a time when "differences lost / Difference and were one . . . / A zone of time without the ticking of clocks" (*CP*, 494).

Paul Weiss's remarks on Stevens to Peter Brazeau bring out the problem simply and beautifully, with sympathetic clear-mindedness and without any depth psychology. He told Brazeau that Stevens' "ultimate passion was to try to get to the clean, clear ultimate reality, which required a thrust through everything that we are thinking, naming, using, saying. What I'm not clear about is what he saw when he got there."[46] Weiss, I think, is puzzled by the nature of the reality beyond the intimation of it in each individual poem. The reason for the uncertainty may be that, like the Romantic he still remained, Stevens' quest for the ultimate object is so powerful that it often refuses to remain in touch with the specific set of compromises that we term the poem. It often partly succeeds and always partly fails to reveal itself in the poem. Whatever may be the favorable balance of forces in each work, the totality of Stevens' output does not add up to the sought-for reality. It does not in fact add up to a real world. It is precisely *untrue* that Stevens' corpus, as Bates concludes, "explores all ramifications of the self, ranging freely between the sphere of the *paysan* and that of the visionary."[47] It is only the sphere of the visionary that Stevens explores. Contemplation is his subject and only those aspects of reality that feed a narrowly focused if tough-minded contemplation. Family, social (whether narrowly or widely conceived), and political realities are mainly excluded, and even when these are represented in the poetry, it need hardly be emphasized, they are generally denuded of their actuality and abundance.

Stevens' spirituality is not the byproduct of a rich and complex life, the crown of human existence, but rather its narrow, single purpose, to the exclusion of all else. His greatness lies in his ability to make us believe that he has encompassed everything that matters in the moment of vision, and that the moment of vision is the moment of truth. But the contradictory and obscure hints of the poetry and prose make it likely that we have been misled. We have been persuaded by the same fantasy, the same need for fusion with the ideal object, and by the poet's mastery of language.

His putative deathbed conversion, if it took place, was the remarkable conclusion to an ambiguous, contradictory, and secretive life. The fact that his own family knew nothing about it does not suggest to me the unlikelihood of the event but rather that it could so plausibly exemplify that ambiguity, that contradictoriness, and that secretiveness. At the same time the supposed conversion could also imply a strong need on Stevens' part to end the ambiguity, to eliminate the frustration of doubt, and to repossess in fantasy the childhood "mother . . . for us" all. It suggests indeed an abandonment of the conditions of modern reality. Although the poetry, to the last, appears to accept those conditions and remains dialectical and modern, the acceptance is far from wholehearted; the late poems are often betrayed by a painful accommodation, a secret dissatisfaction, a residual yearning for the unattainable. There remains a tantalizing obscurity even in Stevens' best poems, a sense that all that wisdom, that joyous celebration joined with hard acceptance, "the grandeur . . . / In so much misery . . . / the afflatus of ruin" (*CP,* 509), is not enough.

Still, the disciplined force of some of his greatest poems masters us so effectively that we only discover the incompleteness—"the fragments found in the grass" (*CP,* 515)—afterward, when we are no longer under its sway. "We reason of these things with later reason" (*CP,* 401). We learn that the creator of the poems was more complex than the most complex of his poems.

7

Getting Wisdom
The "Rabbi's" Devotion to *Weisheit* and its Implications for Feminists

Rosamond Rosenmeier

The house is empty. But here is where she sat
To comb her dewy hair
     —Wallace Stevens, "The Beginning"

I

The 1930s were a personally turbulent decade for Wallace Stevens.[1] The worldwide economic depression coincided with a personal depression of the kind Stevens seems to have suffered periodically.[2] "The Sun This March" (1930), appearing after a six-year silence, suggests "how dark" the poet "ha[d] become." Relief for this condition comes as light—from the sun's "exceeding brightness." Stevens locates this brightness in the past; it used to be "a part / Of a turning spirit in an earlier self" (*CP*, 134). It does not simply illuminate things now; its "re-illumines things that used to turn" (*CP*, 133).

Similarly in "Owl's Clover" (1936), an unwieldy poem played on the scale of cosmic history, something "within us" as a "second self" returns out of the past to restore momentum to history and language to the poem. In "The Sun This March" "voices" come down, and in "Owl's Clover" parents who "have never died" bear the poet's "self"; their "lives return, simply, upon our lips, / Their words and ours" (*CP*, 67). The word "parents" in this passage, Stevens later explained, refers to "all generations of ancestors" (*L*, 374). "Needs" that are at once psychological, cultural, and poetic have led the poet into an exercise in retrieval.

In both of these poems, Stevens specifically personifies this ancestral source as "rabbi"; he summons the rabbi to preside over the present period. In "The Sun This March" the rabbi is to be the "true savant" of the poet's "dark nature" and in "Owl's Clover" he is to be a similar, but quasi-political alter ego, a "Metropolitan Rabbi," as he explained to Ronald Latimer (*L*, 292–93). The rabbi is to bring about change and to "fend" the poet's "soul" as change occurs.

With the ever-elaborating consistency that is his hallmark, Stevens continued to invoke and assume the persona of rabbi. In "Things of August" Stevens puts on that persona when he declares, "We'll give the week-end to wisdom, to Weisheit" (*CP*, 492). Stevens suggests that weekends spent with *Weisheit*/poetry transform the rabbi/poet into light and joy; the rabbi/poet becomes the "lucidity of his city," and the "joy of his nation" (or in effect, again, "metropolitan"). The staginess of the theosophical references in "Things of August" should not distract us from noting the basic strategy here: the poet is being likened to the alchemist/ sorcerer of Pennsylvania German culture.[3] The devotional study of Wisdom was the occupation of those pietistic German groups in Pennsylvania that Stevens considered to be, particularly, his mother's forbears.[4] In "Things of August" the poet is clothed in the insignia of the deuterocanonical Dame Wisdom: in diamonds, red garments to the floor, and a ring that guides him. Ecclesiasticus predicts that the son will "wear [Wisdom] like a gorgeous robe / and put her on like a crown of gladness" (Ecclus. 6:31). The poet/rabbi of "Things of August" does just that.

Stevens, in 1952, explains to Bernard Heringman that he has "never referred to rabbis as religious figures but always as scholars." He also says, "In view of Mr. [C. Roland] Wagner's very philosophical papers on my things, I am beginning to feel like a rabbi myself." Here Stevens stresses not only the identification he feels with rabbis, but the fact that his childhood upbringing provided his education on this subject: "When

I was a boy I was brought up to think that rabbis were men who spent their time getting wisdom" (L, 751). In Stevens' mind, then, these rabbis, these ancestral scholars, are larger than life, and in comparison, the modern poet gives voice to a lesser Wisdom ditty, a "Lebensweisheitspielerei" played by those who are "left," since the "proud and the strong / Have departed" (CP, 504).

Portrayals of the poet in the likeness of rabbis occur throughout the Collected Poems, but with renewed vigor and emphasis after the 1940s. Despite its having "almost the color of comedy," this analogy has a "strength at the centre" that is "serious" (CP, 477), as Stevens writes in "An Ordinary Evening in New Haven." Wisdom as mirror, clothed in several of her chief attributes (gold, gems, belts) and projected as "blessed beams from out a blessed bush" is the predicate of the implicit "wasted figurations" that are "saved and beholden" by the poet, "in a robe of rays." He warns us that poetry as "the serious reflection" is "composed / Neither of comic nor tragic but of commonplace" (CP, 477–78). Elsewhere he said that the purpose of the poet's role is "to help people to live their lives" (NA, 29). Stevens' sense of the rabbi prototype was not simply that the modern poet was a "new scholar replacing an older one" (CP, 519), but that he was a commonplace, familiar figure whose purpose was to make life more livable. One aspect of proverbial wisdom is, of course, practical advice for day-to-day living. Stevens wrote to Renato Poggioli that "the figure of the rabbi has always been an exceedingly attractive one to me because it is the figure of a man devoted in the extreme to scholarship and at the same time to making some use of it for human purposes" (L, 786).

The rabbi savant who had emerged out of an earlier self to "fend" the poet's soul is only one of many such "custodians of the glory of the scene" (CP, 469). In Harmonium Stevens had suggested that there are different colors for rabbis. In "Le Monocle de Mon Oncle" the poet who began as a "dark rabbi" grew to become a "rose" one. In "An Ordinary Evening in New Haven" the poet is both "infant A" and "hierophant Omega"; he stands in the shoes of both of these opposite "interpreters of life," who together ensure an ongoing interpretation of the scene by assuring the circularity of the dialogue. Stevens' verbs frequently indicate that the poet is doing what rabbis do: he looks, beholds, expects, sees (often for just an instant). He studies, broods, and remembers a beloved object. And although the object of his pursuit is feminine, she nevertheless has the power to become one with the scholar and to play a role in his androgynous creativity.[5] When Stevens declared in "Le Monocle de Mon Oncle" that "I behold, in love, / An ancient aspect touching a new mind" (CP, 16), he was describing the characteristic action of rabbis who study texts lovingly for the affecting wisdom hidden there. For Stevens it was not so much that Wisdom hides herself, but that she has been part of all that has been forgotten. Stevens explained the phrase "disregarded plate" (from "Sunday Morning") to Harriet Monroe as a reference "to the disuse into which things fall that have been possessed for a long time" and that "the young inherit and make use of." By "plate," he said he meant "family plate" (L, 183). In the later poetry, particularly, the adjectives "used-to," "waste," and "disused" describe parts of a world that had been all but lost from Stevens' memory. However "eccentric" or out of the way parts of that regional world seemed, these provided a center for the later work.

II

It is the purpose of this essay not only to reassert the finding others have made that Stevens turned particularly to the family past in his search for a "gorging good" (CP, 440), but also to delineate the feminine identity of that "good." The retrieval of precious materials for poetry meant the rediscovery and the readaptation of the role of scholar/rabbi as well as a return to the multiple appearances of the female figure, Wisdom—the wisdom that the rabbi "gets." For feminists, the importance of this return lies in the fact that the Palatinate German refugees to Pennsylvania with whom Stevens identified were infused with the biblical and Apocryphal Wisdom tradition.[6] The Hermits of the Wissahickon Brotherhood, the Ephratans, and the Philadelphia Society—led by the seventeenth-century apocalyptic, Jane Leade—were all in addition followers of the "countertraditional"[7] works of the 17th-century shoemaker mystic, Jacob Boehme, whose florid reconstruction of the cosmos centered on the dialectical and sexual relationship between God and the Sophia, *die Jungfrau der Weisheit*.

Compounding the influence of the divine female on Stevens' family past is the fact that "returning" is used as a metaphor for his increasing identification with his mother and with what he called "her people." Stevens was certain that Margaretha Catherine Zeller's predecessors came to Pennsylvania in the early eighteenth century. The critic's task is complicated by the fact that when Stevens refers, for example, to "Bald heads with their mother's voice still in their ears" (*OP*, 82), or to "the goodness of lying in a maternal sound" (*CP*, 482), or to "the origin of a mother tongue / With which to speak to her" (*CP*, 470–71), the referents cannot easily be fully "disentangled" (*CP*, 322).

I do not recommend that we attempt to disentangle one "mother" from another; I approach this complication, particularly in the poetry after *Harmonium*, with the assumption that Stevens is layering his central figures for poetry, and that the first, the original, the "mother" layer has some of the essential characteristics of the Behmenist's Sophia and is marked as well by the quality of feeling that Stevens had for his own real mother.[8] "A pleasure, an indulgence, an infatuation" (*CP*, 158) were the words he used to express what he "found" in the nostalgic poem, "Like Decorations in a Nigger Cemetery." By "return" Stevens did not mean a trip to a literal place. (His actual visits to Reading in these years proved disappointing.) His voyage back rather resembled H.D.'s, and one is tempted to suggest that Stevens' female figures for poetry are composed, like H.D.'s, as a "palimpsest." But in Stevens' use of the wisdom paradigm, it is Wisdom as an ongoing androgynous process that is emphasized more than her realizable presence as a "solid" figure.[9] Yet both poets chose as central, an ever-changing goddess-mother whom they seek and expect to find again. In H.D.'s work Athene is a Wisdom figure.

It is important to focus briefly on the usefulness of the Wisdom tradition as a counter for the expression of feelings that Stevens would not express about real life occasions. He denigrated autobiographical writing as "laborious reportage" (*L*, 624). Yet as Stevens proceeded to "make" something of the study of family history (*L*, 457), he also developed and enlarged his sense of the suggestive power of the paradigms for poetry that were latent in that history. As both mothers and brides, Stevens' female figures frequently promise or suggest renewal or reconciliation. But images of fulfillment are as frequently wiped away or erased by his use of verbs in the subjunctive, by his use of sentences that do not finish or that finish contrary to fact. [10] In this most characteristic Stevens gesture (the soldier knocks the table and the bouquet falls on the floor), Stevens is faithful to a principal feature of Wisdom tradition. Not only is the certainty of loss suggested in Ecclesiastes' "a season to every thing and every purpose," but (particularly in Gnosticism and Behmenism) Wisdom herself regularly dies, disappears, or changes. Wisdom thus provides a model for a female figure who is both the soul-destroying mother, "Madame La Fleurie," as well as the Christ-like Eulalia who speaks the mystery of the incarnation to the "dark-syllabled" rabbi/poet Semiramide (*CP*, 287). This embodiment of contrariety in Wisdom requires more discussion than is covered here. But it follows the Wisdom tradition for Stevens to say with resignation, as he said to Delmore Schwartz, that "the Drang nach den Gut is really not much different from the Drang nach den opposite" (*L*, 693). The coupling of longing and loss, the repeated assurances that nothing is sure, are central to this heritage. Wisdom provides a peculiarly deconstructive undercurrent to the Torah and the Gospel by uttering the male testament writers' feelings that the certainty of *ultimate* blessings may elude us, but meanwhile we can "learn to hold fast" (*L*, 558) and work to "restore the status quo ante" (*L*, 615). Stevens' comments about the hopelessness of restoring "savor to life when life has lost it" echo the tradition. He wrote, as a true devotee of Wisdom, to Barbara Church that "these moments of despair can best be controlled by the regimen of life: exercise, sleep and a will not to see the spots in one's eyes" (a reference to his eye disease) (*L*, 615).

These states of feeling, so vividly present (if we read through the dark glass of his persistent self-irony), are the *noeud vital* of the poetry: the crying out of needs, and then the questioning whether "Seelensfriede [is] something that [can] be pursued and caught up with" (*L*, 615). Such statements dimly embody, but must not be understood only as references to, life's real disappointments.[11] They must be understood as the expressions of a layered discourse to which the poet felt native, and which he adopted and adapted because it so eloquently portrayed states of life and mind that were powerfully in him from his earliest days. "One writes about [life]," Stevens wrote to Rodriguez Feo, "when it is one's own life provided one is a good barbarian, a true Cuban, or a true Pennsylvania Dutchman, in the linguistics of that soul" (*L*, 624–25). The amalgam of this "linguistics" had been forged early and deep. In the example of John Crowe Ransom, Stevens found a poet similarly true to the region of his birth. Stevens insists that "A Tennessean has no choice." He then adds a cry like that of the exiled Psalmist, a cry that betrays Stevens' feelings at a very deep level: "O Jerusalem. O Appalachia." Stevens says that Ransom cannot help but pursue the "legend" of his region. "This is what happens," Stevens reflects, "to things we love" (*OP*, 261).

One implication of these findings is the recognition that Stevens' poetry was indeed grounded in *paideuma*, exactly in the way Hugh Kenner, borrowing from Leo Frobenius, used that term to distinguish Pound's work. Stevens turned to his people's "whole congeries of patterned energies, from their 'ideas' to the things they know in their bones," precisely in the sense Frobenius intended.[12] When Stevens made reference to the Pennsylvania pietists, he did not focus on theology. He made analogies; he drew often facetious parallels between his situation and the situation of the ancestor: between, say, "waiting in New York" and "wait[ing] in Jerusalem the Golden" (*L*, 511). He found Sachse's two-volume study of the German sectarians and pietists in Pennsylvania "precious." But that finding did not send him into theological speculation, it sent him back into his personal past for sounds and sights to which he could feel connected. "When I was a boy," he wrote to Henry Church, "I met one of these sisters in Ephrata. She was then 90 and her father could very well have gone back to the time when the vital characters were still alive" (*L*, 511). He wanted to find his way back, to feel attached. Of the "Low-German" girls of his childhood acquaintance, he wrote to Elsie Moll (apparently his wife-to-be was not among this group), "I love them, my dear. You must not think that I do nothing but poke fun at them . . . I feel my kinship, my race. To study them, is to realize one's own identity. It is subtly fascinating" (*L*, 127). This is the self-described "common yellow dog" who found more in "our Pennsylvania Anjou" than in the "'fronts audacieux' of New York," but who "never intended to admit" that he was a "common yellow dog" (*L*, 181). Later he did say that "there may be something to [the] idea that my colors are the colors of my origin" (*L*, 753). There he did not mean the color yellow. He meant to indicate that he knew things about his Pennsylvania past "in his bones" but, like a good Pennsylvania pietist, intended to keep these "hidden before the world."

The fact is that this *paideuma* has been neglected by historians in general. And, further, that "poking fun" at Pennsylvania Germans seems to have been the tradition among the educated English of that region—a practice that Stevens shared. A more significant factor leading to neglect may be the central role given to the Divine Female by various of the leading religious sects of the Pennsylvania Germans. In this unusual emphasis the sectarians were distinguished from the mainstream Protestant Reformed churches. To Stevens' great delight these German and Dutch denominations made determined efforts to correct the sectarian heresies, but to little avail. [13] The parallel Stevens was fond of speculating about—between the "fictive abstract . . . as immanent in the mind of the poet, as the idea of God is immanent in the mind of the theologian" (*L*, 434)—has not yet been interpreted as suggesting two female figures, one on each side of that analogy. The statement that Stevens found poetry a "substitute for religion," as he wrote to Hi Simons (*L*, 348), has prompted much theological and epistemological interpretation. But the evidence that by religion Stevens did not mean Protestant orthodoxy but something else, something closer, perhaps, to "the sisterhood of the living dead" (*CP*, 87) has not been fully explored. It is true that Stevens' early training in Lutheranism was a significant episode in his life. And it is true too that, as he said, "the First Presbyterian church [in Reading] was very important [to him in childhood]," but, as he also pointed out, "a [bike] ride to Ephrata was like an excursion into an unmapped country" (*L*, 125). We should take Stevens seriously, I think, when he reports to Bernard Heringman that he is a "dried-up Presbyterian" (*L*, 792) and when he declares in "The Blue Buildings in the Summer Air" that

"Cotton Mather died when I was a boy" (*CP*, 216). There is abundant evidence that ultimately, these "dead" structures did not provide the fruitful analogues for poetry that the rabbi sought.

Stevens gives us every indication of where to travel to find what he meant by the "gods" for which his poetry was intended as a substitute. When he disavows orthodoxy, he nevertheless adopts scriptural analogy to construe what he calls "a sustenance itself enough" (*CP*, 316). In "Esthétique du Mal," the poet's stanzas are "firm," and they "hang like hives" (*CP*, 315). Where they hang has changed, however, since "both heaven and hell / Are one, and here, O terra infidel" (*CP*, 315). There is, nevertheless, a "health" in the presumably unbelieving "world," of which the "golden combs" of the poet's hive *seem as if* "part." The biblical figure of honey and honeycombs to express the writer's "pleasant words" is a deliberate echo here, and Stevens' claim for poetry recalls the Solomonic claim that words can be "sweet to the soul and health to the bones" (Pr. 16:24; also Ps. 19:10, and Cant. 5:1). In Luke 24:42, Christ likens honeycomb to his promises of fulfillment. In Ecclus. 24, Wisdom asserts that "remembrance of me is sweeter than honey, and my inheritance sweeter than the honeycomb."

The use of honey and honeycomb as figures for poetry is central to "The Blue Buildings in the Summer Air" and helps clarify the role of a disavowed Protestant orthodoxy in a poetry that depends nevertheless on scriptural references in the "activity of resemblance." Stevens increasingly defined this poetry as a "satisfying of the desire for resemblance" (*NA*, 77). In "Blue Buildings," Stevens draws a comparison between two seekers, the mouse in the wall, who is a wisdom or honey-seeking pietist and Cotton Mather, who is a doubt-driven representative of "wooden Boston" Protestantism. Mather preaches louder and louder in order to silence the sound of the mouse: his nibbling, described in the God-like phrase "eminent thunder." The two figures are on a parallel quest, but Mather's reading "all day, all night and all the nights, / Had got him nowhere." In contrast, the mouse is exhorted in the last lines of the poem also to search all day, all night, but for the honeycomb. Mather had gotten nowhere, that is, only to a realm described as "the blank" where he continues to insist that heaven must be where he thought it was. The differences between the two seekers lie in how and what they seek and where they seek it. The mouse seeks a nourishing substance; Mather, a bodiless abstraction.

Poetry, that nourishing substance, belongs to "the seeing man" and here the exemplar of that man is not Mather but Lenin whom the mouse is instructed to "go nibble at." Elsewhere Stevens has said that "with the collapse of other beliefs, this grubby faith [communism] promises a practicable earthly paradise" (NA, 143). Similarly Mather is instructed to look on earth for his heaven, which is often just glimpsed, or encountered by chance. It is the "brilliance through the lattices," as Wisdom was glimpsed in Proverbs 7:6. It is also where Jacob Boehme found it to be: "in an apple on a plate." It is found on earth and yet expressed in a line that perfectly resembles scripture: "It is the leaf [like the olive twig] the bird [like the dove] brings back to the boat [like Noah's ark]" (CP, 217).

In "The Blue Buildings in the Summer Air," however, Stevens goes a step further than simply identifying earth as his "fluent mundo," the place of true wisdom/poetry (CP, 406–7). He makes clear the peculiar avenue of religious tradition that he would have us explore. He understands Cotton Mather's longing for something to "quiet that mouse in the wall"; he even offers comfort to Cotton Mather or to those he represents; the comfort is named in stanza 2: "Over wooden Boston" rises the "sparkling Byzantine." In the context of the numerous Wisdom references, the great monument to the Sancta Sophia in Constantinople is evoked to assure the likes of Cotton Mather that, although the mouse decreates his churches, the overarching presence of Wisdom's/poetry's spirit still precludes or still includes everything Mather is and represents. In Proverbs 8, Wisdom gives rulers the "authority and ability to rule." And there, too, she lays claim to being "the first of God's creatures." When Stevens tapped into the Wisdom traditions of his pietistic forbears he met (probably again) the idea developed by Boehme that the "female ground of being is prior to and then coexistent with the creating, masculine deity."[14] He met a divine figure found in earth, not simply in heaven. For Behmenists she was indelibly imprinted in nature as "the signature in all things" and was specifically called mother or matrix.[15]

III

There are direct and indirect indications of the nature of the maternal voice that Stevens called "the mother's voice" still in the ears of "children and old men" (*OP*, 82). In "Esthétique du Mal" Stevens tells us that "He had studied the nostalgias," and "In these / He sought the most grossly maternal . . . / Who most fecundly assuaged him" (*CP*, 321). While researching his family's genealogy in the 1940s, Stevens read a number of histories and biographies of early settlers to Pennsylvania. It is clear that this reading served to refresh the sound of the German his mother spoke (*L*, 417, 521). The representative texts of the pietists and sectarians were laced with the discourse of Wisdom scriptures.[16] The Wissahickon Brotherhood gave particular significance to Revelation 12, which describes the "woman in the wilderness"—the woman "clothed with sun" who brought forth a man child and then fled into the wilderness where she is said to be nourished and protected until the time of Christ's Second Coming. Millennial expectations throughout mark the writing of the pietists, so much so that the Wissahickon hermits were known as "The Society of the Woman in the Wilderness." Wisdom is both a heavenly figure (associated with clouds and sun and moon) and an earthly one (with equally strong associations with dew and mists, with water, fire, and with flowers). The rabbi's task was to protect and study the scriptural promises of Her Coming, and through alchemy and astronomy, try to detect the natural evidences of her "dawning redness" in the wilderness of this world. "She," like Stevens' figures for the supreme fiction, is a now-you-see-her, now-you-don't figure.

Stevens' citations of biblical language tend to center on Wisdom texts. In addition, Stevens' poetic and prose discourse is marked by the language habits and the literary forms common to Pennsylvania German culture. The proverb is considered "the very bone and sinew of [Pennsylvania German] dialect," and is said to "play a prominent role in the speech of Pennsylvania Germans."[17] Stevens' "Adagia" thus can be said to be one expression of the "mother tongue." The emergence of the epigrammatic phrasing in "Like Decorations in a Nigger Cemetery" is a clear reenforcement, in terms of style, of the remembrances of the child-

hood *"pays"* that the poem evokes. "Owl's Clover" was to have been
called "Aphorisms On Society," again suggesting the rediscovery of the
family voices celebrated in that poem. The change to "Owl's Clover" tells
us that Stevens preferred the more expressive bird of wisdom in his title.
These interrelations are again suggested in the late poem "Adult Epigram," a title that might be transcribed as "the poem in final or complete
form." The "epigram" tells us that poetry is Wisdom's analogue: "the
ever-never-changing same, / An appearance of Again, the diva-dame"
(*CP*, 353).

One aspect of the parallel Stevens drew to the German pietists served
to describe the quality of the poet's devotion over time. In a review titled
"Rubbings of Reality," Stevens focuses his comments, ostensibly about
William Carlos Williams' *Collected Poems*, on the man who "writes a
little every day." This man writes, Stevens says, because (again) "he
needs to." And, Stevens explains, "what he really does is to bring, or try
to bring, his subject into that degree of focus at which he sees it, for a
moment, as it is and at which he is able to represent it in exact definition." Writing like a true pietist astronomer watching from his watch-
tower, Stevens describes writing as "the grinding of a glass, the polishing
of a lens by means of which he hopes to be able to see clearly." Stevens'
modern example of such an artist is Picasso, but then he asserts, "the
world of the past was equally the result of such activity." He then cites
the Wissahickon hermits as his example of artists out of the past: "Thus
the German pietists of the early 1700's who came to Pennsylvania to live
in the caves of the Wissahickon and to dwell in solitude and meditation
were proceeding, in their way, from the chromatic to the clear." Stevens
then asks, "Is not Williams in a sense a literary pietist, chastening
himself, incessantly, along the Passaic?" (*OP*, 257–59). To this rhetorical
question, the answer is surely only a qualified "yes." The truer literary
pietist is Stevens himself.

Stevens here falls into a discourse that bears the mark of the "linguistics of the soul" of the true Pennsylvania German. The phrase "who came
to dwell in solitude and meditation" and the description of the poet's
"chastening himself, incessantly" bear that stamp. Similarly, the prose
and poetry of this period are dotted with the words "piety" and "good-

ness," and these are often given the ancestral tincture. "I write poetry," Stevens said, "because it is part of my piety: because, for me, it is the good of life" (*L*, 473). When Stevens, in 1948, angered by a publisher's loss of some poems, expressed his outrage to Thomas McGreavy, he lapsed into the ancestral vernacular: "One should constantly confront the machinations of the devil and the contumely of his courts. These confrontations make one shrink back into one's own virtue. The poet must always desire the pure good of poetry just as the sinner desires only the pure good of the blood of the lamb. Without thee, O Sophia, what value has anything? The poet lives only in and for the world of poetry. Nicht wahr?" (*L*, 625).

Stevens in effect seems, in the *Collected Poems*, to proceed "from the chromatic to the clear" in his handling of the figure of the Sophia as the "pure good of poetry" that the poet "must desire." His first representations of her in *Harmonium* were ones he later rejected in "The Sail of Ulysses" as not the (presumably true or real) "shape of the sibyl." This later reference to the "englistered woman, seated / In colorings harmonious, dewed and dashed" (*OP*, 104) points back to the earlier more "chromatic" renderings of Her in "To the One of Fictive Music" and "Le Monocle de Mon Oncle." Although Wisdom's likeness continues to inform Stevens' queens, women, brides, spouses, nuns, and dames, she is gradually "disembodied" (*CP*, 445). In fact, each of the major volumes extends the likeness between Sophia and poetry beyond previous likenesses. "She" is a harmony, an idea of order, a world, a summer, an aurora, and a rock. Finally, she is, fittingly, embodied as the "sibyl of the self." She began as someone external to the poet; she ends as an internal presence. She ends as a self in need. The tone of the poet's disappointment deepens, but the discourse, and the legends imbedded in that discourse, continue "to bear" (*CP*, 393). From the early "voice cr[ying] in the Wilderness," the letterhead of a letter to Elsie in 1909 (*L*, 115), to the last "critic of God, the world / And human nature, pensively seated / On the waste throne of his own wilderness" (*OP*, 115), the same "intimations . . . derived from analogies" (*L*, 494) served him. The legendary materials of Wisdom enabled Stevens to continue to perfect a voice "To

speak humanly from the height or from the depth / Of human things"
(*CP*, 300).

In so few pages I have been able barely to touch on the Wisdom
parallel and its implications for Stevens' criticism in general, and for
Stevens' feminist critics in particular. I hope that these pages will serve
as an invitation to feminists to look to the female presence in the Palatinate Christian groups in Pennsylvania—a presence that differed significantly from the Christ of the dominant groups in New England during the
same period.[18] One last point should be made about Stevens' uses of
female tradition. Stevens was not, in many of the ways we mean the term,
a feminist. When the budding poet wished (to himself in his journal) for a
wife, he confessed his feeling on the subject but obliterated the person
from the portrait: "The proverbial apron-strings have a devil of a firm
hold on me + as a result I am unhappy at such a distance from the
apron." He said he wished "a thousand times a day" that he had a wife,
explaining that he begins "to feel the vacuum that wives fill." By "wife"
he says he means "a delightful companion who would make a fuss over
me" (*L*, 43). Such a wife is without self; she is an extension of the poet's
self, and a response, particularly, to the need to be fussed over. Stevens'
undifferentiated "most beautiful maid / And mother" (*CP*, 461) follows
the outline of Wisdom as bride / mother. But Stevens' uses of the paradigm seem to weigh heavily on her maternal, not her bridal, likeness.
Stevens remains "a child that sings itself to sleep" at the end of his life
(*CP*, 436).

And for that very reason, the first letter in the *Letters* is a fitting
document with which to launch that volume. He writes to his mother
from Ephrata, where he was vacationing, that he is "in depressed spirits"
and wants to come home. He says he "hate[s] <u>ladies</u>? (such as are here)"
(*L*, 5), and then he proceeds to recount what he has eaten and express
how impatient he is to have her response to his letter. He later puts the
intimacy with his mother as a matter of identity: "I am more like my
mother than my father," Stevens writes Elsie in 1919 (*L*, 213–14). The
solace of a maternal presence, his shared identity with her, and even his
need to denigrate women, all persist as characterizations of the female

presence who is nameless, or "So-and-so," or simply "the desired one" (*CP*, 505). But in the magnificent life-review that is part of "The Auroras of Autumn" it is the mother who "invites humanity to her house / And table" (*CP*, 415). She, not the father, is the God-like presence. Her portrayal echoes Wisdom's inviting the elect to her "house" (she has spiced her wine, and she has spread her table in Proverbs 9:2). The father, in "The Auroras of Autumn," is by contrast a poet of sorts. He fetches the "tellers of tales" who give forth a "clawing . . . sing-song." They are, like many of the ancestral singers in *Parts of a World*, a "loud, disordered mooch." The portrayal suggests Stevens' father's poeticizing with his cronies who loved to mimic Pennsylvania song and poetry. Here Stevens enlarges the portrait of the mother and writes about her with an unmixed quality of reverence and affection. "The mother's face" has become "the purpose of the poem." He writes with none of the sexual unease he has fallen into in his earlier imaginings of the fulfillment of his wishes: They are, simply, "together, here, and it is warm" (*CP*, 413). Stevens had called his own mother's house, "a huge volume full of the story of her thirty-five years or more within it" (*L*, 173). The biblical echoes, the indirect references to literal parents, the enlargement of the domain of the mother and her presence as the poem's "purpose," all tellingly illustrate what the "pastoral nun" meant when she said that "poetry and apotheosis are one" (*CP*, 378). In his understanding of "apotheosis" Stevens did not follow the orthodox elders who "Pulse[d] pizzicati of Hosanna." Instead, he felt "Susanna's music," especially "now," when "in its immortality, it plays / On the clear viol of her memory" (*OP*, 92). And therein lies a tale for the annals of feminism.

8

Aesthetics and Politics
Marianne Moore's Reading of Stevens

Celeste Goodridge

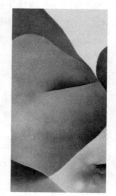

Several years ago I wrote about Marianne Moore and Wallace Stevens in a book concerning Moore's role as a poet-critic in the high modernist community.[1] I argued that Moore's reviews of Stevens' poetry, beginning with her 1924 assessment of *Harmonium* and ending with her 1964 retrospective musing for the *New York Review of Books*, were a tribute to and a defense of Stevens' aesthetic preference for the hint, the disguise, and the mask. When she felt uneasy about some aspect of Stevens' enterprise, Moore tended, particularly after her review of *Harmonium*, to mute or mask her discomfort. Moore's reading of Stevens, I suggested, made visible the link between her own poetic project and his. Given her own desire for detachment, reserve, and the public performance of alternating between controlled disclosure and concealment, Moore supported Stevens' distance from his readers, championing his "achieved remoteness"[2] in her own, at times, impenetrable style of approaching his work. Moore's benign acceptance and gentle indulgence of Stevens' tendencies to be obscure, aloof, and evasive, I contended, emerged in her imitative appreciation. (Her criticism of the High Modernist poets she admired most, often took the form of imitating in her own prose style some stylistic quality or temperamental affinity of the writer under consideration.)

The problem with a reading designed primarily to highlight the consanguinity between Moore's and Stevens' projects is that it could not fully bring to the foreground Moore's reservations. I will argue now that the things Moore objected to in Stevens' early poetry from *Harmonium*—his representations of both the torments and delights of desire, his voyeurism or watching of the other from a distance, his tendency to overindulge his imagination, and his turning inward toward a romantic core of self under the guise of self-mockery—led to his endorsement of a politics in the thirties that made him turn toward the world, only to turn away from its "cry for help." This posture enabled Stevens to advocate in "A Fading of the Sun" that individuals in the face of fascism and oppression turn inward and look "within themselves / And cry and cry for help" (*CP*, 139).

A private exchange that Moore had with T. C. Wilson in 1935 after *Ideas of Order* was published by the Alcestis Press will show that she approved of Stevens' recommendation in "A Fading of the Sun," and in doing so supported what Wilson and others viewed as Stevens' elitist ivory-tower disregard for those not graced with his or other artists' resources. Even though Moore defended Stevens she did not assume that he was indifferent to the events of the time or those who cried for help; but, unlike Wilson, she did not believe that Stevens or other poets had a social and moral obligation to use their art to affect political action, to alleviate suffering, to feed those who were hungry. In short, Moore echoed Stevens' statements in the thirties concerning poetry's function. On the jacket of *The Man with the Blue Guitar and Other Poems* (1937), for example, Stevens wrote: "While the poems [in *Owl's Clover*] reflect what was then going on in the world, that reflection is merely for the purpose of seizing and stating what makes life intelligible and desirable in the midst of great change and great confusion. The effect of *Owl's Clover* is to emphasize the opposition between things as they are and things imagined; in short, to isolate poetry" (*OP*89, 233).[3]

I am interested in mapping the relationship between Stevens' aesthetic in *Harmonium*, one that Moore at times found repugnant, and Stevens' politics as expressed in his poems from the thirties, particularly those in *Ideas of Order*, which she almost wholly supported. I will focus on the continuity between Stevens' economies of desire in *Harmonium* and his representations of the artist in his poetry during the thirties. In her 1924 review of *Harmonium*, for example, Moore referred to Stevens' poetry as "aristocratic cipher."[4] Still later, in 1935, when she wrote to Stevens thanking him for sending her *Owl's Clover*, she made a similar comment when she equated his success with both his disguises—a hallmark of his poetic in *Harmonium*—and his implicit allegiance with "still persisting members of an aristocracy." Moore playfully identified herself and by extension Stevens' other readers with "the tenantry." "The world probably is not owl enough to thank you for troubling about it," Moore wrote, "but an unkilled and tough-lived fortitude is a great help to us, conveyed as it is by your disguises, and may I say as the tenantry say to still persisting members of an aristocracy, 'long life to it,' to this hero which you exemplify."[5]

Although Moore did not make the connection, we can see that this hierarchical division between the poet as aristocrat and the reader as tenant was in keeping with Stevens' sinister and often sexist attitudes toward his poetic subjects in *Harmonium*. Flirting with his muse from afar, he portrays her as simultaneously tempting and threatening, seductive and dangerous, enticing and tormenting. Thus he entreats "Florida," when she is most tempting, to be "a scholar of darkness, / Sequestered over the sea" (*CP*, 48); or he commands the muse to "speak, even, as if I did not hear you speaking, / But spoke for you perfectly in my thoughts" (*CP*, 86). In poems like "O Florida, Venereal Soil," "Two Figures in Dense Violet Night," "The Apostrophe to Vincentine," "Another Weeping Woman," and "Floral Decorations For Bananas," Stevens positions himself in relation to his subjects so that he can objectify them from a safe distance. From this vantage, he frequently watches, stills, silences, dehumanizes, and transforms his objects of desire. Desire is fueled by an avoidance of contact. Finally, Stevens' inner torment—colored by both his fears and haughtiness—may have prompted him to advance toward his subjects only to retreat.

Moore could not tolerate this construction of desire when it was used in certain poems from *Harmonium* like "The Apostrophe to Vincentine" or "Last Looks at the Lilacs." Nevertheless, when Stevens vacillated between an engagement with the world and a retreat from it as an endorsement of a particular politics in *Ideas of Order*, she defended his right to do so. While I make no claim that Moore would have said "the personal is political" or that she saw the unsettling link between Stevens' disturbed, often divided habit of mind in *Harmonium* and his prescriptions for surviving and being an artist in the thirties, her readings enable us to see the connection. Most important, Moore's readings give us additional insights into the relationship between Stevens' poetics and politics, allowing us to see that Stevens' politics were implicit in his early aesthetic.

Before establishing this linkage the record of their friendship and interaction over the years must be considered. Although Moore and Stevens did not meet until 1943 when they attended the Entretien de Pontigny at Mount Holyoke—Stevens as a speaker and Moore as a member of the audience—they were aware of each other's poetry from the start. When *Poems* was published by the Egoist Press in London in 1921 Moore wrote to James Sibley Watson at the *Dial,* suggesting Stevens as a reviewer of her first book of verse. Nothing came of this suggestion because at this time Stevens did not think highly of Moore's poetic efforts. In 1922 we find him confiding to Alice Corbin Henderson, an assistant editor of *Poetry* between 1912 and 1916 and a poet and reviewer, that he thought Moore was too concerned with "form" and with disavowing that concern.[6] Thirteen years later, however, Stevens did in fact write about Moore, reviewing her *Selected Poems* in 1935 for *Life and Letters Today.* When he called Moore a "romantic" in this review, Stevens implicitly examined her need to create "a world elsewhere"—a need he shared. He also wrote about Moore for the 1948 Marianne Moore issue of the *Quarterly Review of Literature,* this time citing her desire to find "an individual reality" in her surroundings. Finally, as late as 1953 Stevens suggested to Herbert Weinstock, his editor at Knopf, that Moore choose the poems for the proposed Faber and Faber edition of his *Selected Poems.*[7]

Moore followed Stevens' poetry with care and interest over many decades. As early as 1916 she wrote to H.D., then assistant editor of the *Egoist,* expressing an interest in writing about Stevens.[8] In 1924 she reviewed *Harmonium* for the *Dial;* this was followed by reviews of *Ideas of Order* (1936), *Ideas of Order* and *Owl's Clover* (1937), *Parts of a World* and *Notes toward a Supreme Fiction* (1943), and *The Auroras of Autumn* (1951).

While Moore clearly admired Stevens' work beginning with *Harmonium*, she also had reservations. These have been consistently overlooked by critics who seem to believe that perceptive, illuminating reviews—particularly those reviews that attend to formalist issues as Moore's review of *Harmonium* did—are necessarily favorable and supportive of the project at hand. Most readers, therefore, have missed or ignored Moore's criticism of Stevens, choosing instead to focus on her praise of his craft. When Moore's objections to Stevens are highlighted in her first review and in her manuscript notes, we can begin to recover the nagging dissonance in Stevens' poetic sensibility between his masks and disclosures, his expressions of pleasure and of pain, his advance toward his subjects and his retreat; we can also begin to see that these tensions in *Harmonium* anticipate some of those found in *Ideas of Order*—most notably, Stevens' hunger for engagement with the world and his need for withdrawal.

Moore's first review both constructs and makes visible the emotional underpinnings of Stevens' "mythology of self / Blotched out beyond unblotching" (*CP*, 28). In doing so she anticipates James Merrill's perceptive contention that Stevens "had a private life, despite—or thanks to—all the bizarreness of his vocabulary and idiom."[9] In addition, she allows us to see that the central oppositions governing Stevens' temperament and aesthetic in *Harmonium* led to his politics in the thirties.

In her 1924 review of Stevens' *Harmonium*, "Well Moused, Lion," Moore praises his craftsmanship, yet at every turn she points to the private torments and divisions that underlie his art. Moore begins by focusing on Stevens' repeated attempts to use his imagination to escape from the real world: "In his book, he calls imagination 'the will of things,' 'the magnificent cause of being,' and demonstrates how imagination may evade 'the world without imagination'; effecting an escape which, in certain manifestations of *bravura*, is uneasy rather than bold."[10] The references to Stevens' poetry here serve to illuminate Moore's awareness of his disturbing inner landscape. "The magnificent cause of being" sends us to "Another Weeping Woman"—a poem that suggests that the pain and grief experienced by the weeping woman will not be alleviated by "the imagination, the one reality / In this imagined world" because she is left "with him for whom no phantasy moves, / And [thus is] pierced by a death" (*CP*, 25). The man's deprivation, or lack of phantasy, eclipses the restorative power of the weeping woman's imagination. Their non-meeting becomes an emblem of the pervasive disjunction between reality and the world of the imagination. (We are reminded of Stevens' plea at the end of "To the One of Fictive Music": "Unreal, give back to us what once you gave: / The imagination that we spurned and crave" [*CP*, 88].) The phrase "[the] imagination 'the will of things'" (*CP*, 84) refers us to "Colloquy with a Polish Aunt." In this poem a dialogue takes place between a "She" and a "He" in which *she* asserts that *he* uses his imagination to "dream of women, swathed in indigo, / Holding their books toward the nearer stars, / To read, in secret, burning secrecies . . ." (*CP*, 84). *He* becomes something of a voyeur as he watches these women "read, in secret"—as he observes them turn toward a world apart from this one.

Moore was the first reader to imply that Stevens' extravagant devices for escaping from "the world without imagination" (*CP*, 27) grew out of an emotional discomfort with the world he inhabited. Unlike Stevens' early readers who saw him as a self-assured aesthete, Moore recognized that Stevens' poetic depended upon the gap, or friction between the imagination and reality, and that Stevens' negotiations were fraught with difficulty.[11] Stevens, Moore implied, masked his uneasiness with bold displays of bravura, but he did not always achieve a balance in "his voyaging" (*CP*, 35). His crossings were not an easy "fluctuating between sun and moon, / A sally into gold and crimson forms" (*CP*, 35).

Moore highlights this in her assessment of "'Sunday Morning," which, she maintains, appears to be governed by a well-orchestrated equilibrium, but in fact exhibits a tension between this world and the intangible. Moore's verbs, "disturbed" and "oppressed," point to Stevens' inability to move comfortably between these realms. "'Sunday Morning' on the other hand—a poem so suggestive of a masterly equipoise—gives ultimately the effect of the mind disturbed by the intangible; of a mind oppressed by the properties of the world which it is expert in manipulating."[12]

While Moore recognized that Stevens worked hard and with some success at creating "an achieved remoteness"[13] akin to Crispin's desired "flourishing tropic" (*CP*, 35)—a refuge in his art from the pain of his thwarted desires in the ordinary world—she did not condone the excessive flights: "The riot of gorgeousness in which Mr. Stevens' imagination takes refuge, recalls Balzac's reputed attitude to money, to which he was indifferent unless he could have it 'in heaps or by the ton.'"[14] Balzac, who was obsessed with earning money and spending it, was frequently on the verge of bankruptcy, often spending in excess of what he actually possessed. Moore implies in her analogy that Stevens' indulgence of his imagination led him to overspend and overindulge his appetites.

In *A Future For Astyanax* Leo Bersani points out that "the psychology of desire in [Balzac's] work faithfully reflects his reckless financial gamblings. . . . Desire in the society of *La Comedie humaine* swings crazily back and forth between catastrophic explosion and a panicky retentiveness. . . . The most successful profiteer—both psychologically and economically—is the hoarder. . . . To spend and to desire are to be exploited and finally devoured."[15] Moore's identification of Stevens with Balzac complements Bersani's analysis as she invites us to see Stevens as someone who accumulates debts that he refuses to be accountable for—whose psychology of desire in his poems forced him to vacillate between reckless spending and fastidious hoarding. Like his "manifestations of *bravura*,"[16] Stevens' constructions of desire, his advancing toward and retreating from his subjects, served to mask his unhappiness with his circumstances.

When Moore describes Stevens' appetite for "a flourishing tropic," (*CP*, 35) as exemplified in Crispin's journey in "The Comedian as the Letter C," she gives us some concrete examples of Stevens' potentially excessive, and perhaps disruptive imaginative flights to "exotic" climes:

One is excited by the sense of proximity to Java peacocks, golden pheasants, South American macaw feather capes, Chilcat blankets, hair seal needlework, Singalese masks, and Rousseau's paintings of banana leaves and alligators. . . .

. . . moonlight on the thick, cadaverous bloom
That yuccas breed . . .

. . . with serpent-kin encoiled
Among the purple tufts, the scarlet crowns.[17]

Moore's examples from the poem suggest that this landscape, like Rousseau's paintings, contains threatening and dissonant energies: moonlight is inseparable from the diseased, if not deathly "thick, cadaverous bloom / That yuccas breed and of the panther's tread" (CP, 31); and serpent-kin are lurking ominously "among the purple tufts" of the jungle (CP, 32). These images come from section 2 of the poem "Concerning the Thunderstorms of Yucatan" where we are told Crispin's "violence was for aggrandizement"—a noticeable increase in power, position and riches—and that he desired "an aesthetic tough, diverse, untamed, / Incredible to prudes" (CP, 31). Such an aesthetic would lead to "elemental potencies and pangs / And beautiful barenesses as yet unseen" (CP, 31).

Moore's reservations concerning Crispin's (or Stevens') "simple jaunt" (CP, 29) in the Yucatan and his movement toward an "aesthetic . . . incredible to prudes" (CP, 31) can be seen in a comment she made in her manuscript notes for her review. Beside the phrase "an aesthetic incredible to prudes" she has written "an objectionable bearishness surliness."[18]

Just what Moore was after privately can be seen in her public assessment of some of Stevens' poems in Harmonium: "One resents the temper of certain of these poems. Mr. Stevens is never inadvertently crude; one is conscious, however, of a deliberate bearishness—a shadow of acrimonious, unprovoked contumely. Despite the sweet—Clementine will—you—be—mine nonchalance of the 'Apostrophe to Vincentine,' one feels oneself to be in danger of unearthing the ogre and in 'Last Looks at the Lilacs,' a pride in unserviceableness is suggested which makes it a microcosm of cannibalism."[19] In poems like "The Apostrophe to Vincentine" and "Last Looks at the Lilacs" Moore suggests that Stevens' posture is reprehensible, inexcusable, gratuitously cruel, and deeply disturbing. When reading "The Apostrophe to Vincentine," Moore asserts that we may be lulled by the seemingly benign distance that Stevens' speaker creates between himself and his subject, the heavenly Vincentine who is both animal and human. Stevens' speaker initially presents Vincentine as "nude," "small," "lean," and "nameless"; she does not compete with "monotonous earth and dark blue sky" (*CP*, 52). In the next three sections he invites us to see her as human: "as warm as flesh" (*CP*, 52), as a brunette, "as clean" (*CP*, 52), and as dressed in green. In part 3 she is seen "walking / In a group" and can be heard (*CP*, 53). It is only by part 4 of the poem, however, that we realize that Stevens' first configuration of Vincentine in part 1 was that of an unnamed "white animal, so lean" (*CP*, 53). This turn in the final section of the poem may be where Moore feels we are "in danger of unearthing the ogre." The withholding of this information until the end makes his gradual transformation of Vincentine appear to be innocent when in fact it conceals a dissonance between what Vendler calls "the animal and the heavenly."[20] As Vendler points out:

> Brutality and apotheosis end in a stalemate. We remember Vincentine at least as powerfully in her repellent incarnation as a white animal so lean as in her named and transfigured state, brunette, dressed, walking, talking, and feeling. The poem shows us a mind willing and welcoming the decor of thought and fancy, while unable to rid itself of primal reductiveness and visual disgust. The reductive diction, telling us in itself that poetry and apotheosis are *not* one, but remain in a problematic relation, marks the speaker as a man caught between the nameless lean, on the one hand, and illimitable spheres of the beloved, on the other.[21]

Moore did not find an aesthetic justification for Stevens' disturbing objectification of Vincentine—one that safely consigned him to the periphery as still voyeur, watching but not participating. For Moore, the human beloved—the muse herself—is eclipsed by Stevens' insistence on the animal nature of the object of desire. She could not tolerate the dual nature of Stevens' muse, the commingling of the heavenly with the "white animal, so lean" (*CP*, 53).

Moore's description of "Last Looks at the Lilacs" as "a pride in unserviceableness . . . which makes it a microcosm of cannibalism" is probably connected to both the speaker's indulgent attitude toward the subject as well as the behavior of the subject: the "well-booted, rugged, arrogantly male, / Patron and imager of the gold Don John, / Who will embrace her before summer comes" (*CP*, 49). Stevens' Don John may be

Mozart's Don Giovanni, whose arrogant "pride in unserviceableness" acts as a foil to Donna Elvira's willingness to serve and oblige as she tries, with no success, to persuade him to reform his ways.[22]

Moore's manuscript notes also illustrate just how disturbing and repellent she found Stevens' unwillingness to attend to anyone but himself; she did not find his self-involvement synonymous with self-reliance. Stevens' vacillation between being "the fairy" and "the brute" allowed him to repress or dismiss basic emotions that others might well confront.

> W. Stevens—a pride in unserviceableness
> that is not synon. with the beauty of
> aloofness selfsufficiency
> the fairy & the brute
> a bg ogre stalking toward one w a knobbed
> club . . .

Stevens recoils from admitting the force of the basic emotions.[23]

When Moore compares Stevens to a snake in her review of *Harmonium* she also forces us to confront Stevens' tendency to move in contradictory and unsettling directions in his poems; nevertheless, she implies that his imagination demanded this sort of opposition: "Imagination implies energy and imagination of the finest type involves an energy which results in order 'as the motion of a snake's body goes through all parts at once, and its volition acts at the same instant in coils that go contrary ways.'"[24] Moore's conceit captures the divisive energy of Stevens' poetic. The snake also conjures up images of deception, betrayal, rebellion, danger, sexual temptation, seduction, and phallic potency. We think of a poem like "O Florida, Venereal Soil" where Stevens' muse is lascivious, tempting, tormenting, and insatiable—on the side of excessive spending— only to be reimagined and stilled as "a scholar of darkness / Sequestered over the sea": "Sparkling, solitary, still, / In the high sea-shadow" (*CP*, 48).

Moore's second reference to a snake in her review underlines the extent to which she associated that image with danger, unpredictability, and the uncontainable. Comparing Stevens' "poised uninterrupted harmony" to the studied harmony of figure skating, tight-rope dancing, and certain undefined medieval dances, Moore shifts from these images of learned harmony to the natural harmony of a snake's motion and the sea's movement after a storm: "It recalls the snake in *Far Away and Long Ago*, 'moving like quicksilver in a rope-like stream' or the conflict at sea when after a storm, the wind shifts and waves are formed counter to those still running."[25] Moore's source, W. H. Hudson's "A Serpent Mystery" in *Far Away and Long Ago*, is worth examining; "I stood thrilled with terror, not daring to make the slightest movement, gazing down upon it. Although so long it was not a thick snake, and as it moved on over the white ground it had the appearance of a coal-black current flowing past me—a current not of water or other liquid but of some such element as quicksilver moving on in a rope-like stream. At last it vanished, and turning I fled from the ground, thinking that never again would I venture into or near that frightfully dangerous spot in spite of its fascination."[26] Hudson's serpent cannot be predicted: "dangerous on occasion as when attacked or insulted, and able in some cases to inflict death with a sudden blow, but harmless and even friendly or beneficent towards those who regarded it with kindly and reverent feelings in place of hatred."[27] We may infer from Moore's analogy that she believed Stevens' postures in some of his poems led him to be both dangerous and harmless, defensive and unguarded, elusive and accessible.

When Moore reviewed *Ideas of Order* in 1936 for Eliot's *Criterion*, she departed from her assessments of *Harmonium*, and defended Stevens' internal divisions and conflicts as integral to his poetic project; for Moore, Stevens' poetic project had changed as he began to respond with feeling to the events around him and to withdraw from them.

> They [the poems in *Ideas of Order*] are a series of guarded definitions but also the unembarrassing souvenirs of a man and
>
> . . . the time when he stood alone,
> When to be and delight to be seemed to be one.[28]

Unlike many of the poems in *Harmonium* in which the poet was engaged in some fashion with his relation to others, Stevens was often alone in these poems, offering prescriptions for "How to Live. What to Do" or confronting how "dark [he had] become" (*CP*, 133). Some of Moore's private exchanges indicate that she applauded Stevens for turning his attention to the artist's role in the world at large, even while retreating from attempting to assuage the pain he undoubtedly confronted. She was not troubled by his increasing desire to look within and be a "true savant of this dark nature" (*CP*, 134). Nor was she troubled by his imagining in poems like "Waving Adieu, Adieu, Adieu" what it would be like "just to stand still without moving a hand" (*CP*, 127). Moore's manuscript notes reveal that she admired Stevens' "great depth of emotion" in "Waving Adieu, Adieu, Adieu."[29]

Shortly after *Ideas of Order* was published by Alcestis Press in 1935, Moore corresponded with T. C. Wilson, then associate editor of the *Westminster Magazine,* concerning some of these issues raised by Stevens' new poems. Two of their exchanges are particularly noteworthy. On June 26, 1935, Wilson wrote to Moore about Stevens' "precision as regards imagery and rhythm." He noted the "beauty, elegance, and lyrical ardor" of Stevens' new poems. Then he went on to express some serious reservations about Stevens' current enterprise:

> Perhaps it is captious to say so, especially when the poems have given me so much pleasure, but I find Stevens' direction, as expressed in these poems and other recent poems, somewhat disturbing. I mean, these poems are evening songs, spoken with a "dying fall," very beautiful and even perfect of their kind, but pervaded by a willingness to accept defeat or the next best thing to it. All of them seem to me the words of a man who is "bidding farewell, bidding farewell," in lovely cadences, yet nevertheless "saying farewell" and "meaning farewell"—"farewell in the eyes and farewell at the center." My objection, I suppose, is not so much an aesthetic as a moral one—yet so fine a poet as Stevens must submit to moral judgment, I think. . . . When he says:
>
> What is there here but weather, what spirit
> Have I except it comes from the sun?
>
> the attitude is one which is distasteful to me, which is, in my opinion, basically anti-intellectual, amounting to a denial of the poet's real and

greatest function—and when a poet of Wallace Stevens' calibre is led to deny the intellectual aspects of his subject matter and to affirm or attend only to those of the senses, one can understand how he can say:

But I am, in any case,
A most inappropriate man
In a most unpropitious place.

The irony implicit in these lines (in their context) may make my objection less valid, but I do not think that it invalidates it very seriously.[30]

Wilson felt that in poems like "Waving Adieu, Adieu, Adieu" Stevens had turned away from the world and its troubles under the guise of rehearsing a farewell. He found this posture self-serving, immoral, distasteful, and anti-intellectual. To turn inward as Stevens had done was unacceptable to Wilson; it was in short "a denial of the poet's real and greatest function," the implication being that the poet had a moral obligation to respond to the physical and economical impoverishment of others. How, Wilson might have said, could Stevens—or indeed any artist at this time—afford to write poems about a search for an "American Sublime": "What is there here but weather, what spirit / Have I except it comes from the sun?" (CP, 128). For Wilson, "the ever-jubilant weather" did not deserve Stevens' attention at this time.

Moore held other opinions. She wrote back to Wilson on July 5, 1935:

His great accuracy and refracted images and averted manner indicate to me a certain interior reconcentration of being. One who has borne heat and burden as well as he has, and as long as he has, is very deeplaid [sic]. I feel sure that the support he needs would not come from general society but from men—men whom he likes, who are aware of his mental strife and are not on the surface with regard to his interior debts and insufficiencies. A man like Bernard Shaw does not consider dying by inches permissible. Men of compulsions and poetic respects, like Donne and Gerard Hopkins, or Dante, would undoubtedly have been swine if they had not been able to assert that life that amounts to anything is a matter of being colossally inconvenienced.[31]

Moore finds Stevens' "averted manner," his need to turn away, acceptable and of a piece with his struggle to make sense of his life; for her, it is an emblem of his great strength, "his interior reconcentration of being." Stevens is not on the side of defeat; he is not evading or ignoring his duty as a poet. His poetry she reminds us grows out of his "mental strife . . . the opposition between things as they are and things imagined" (*OP89*, 233)—and a sense of his distance from "general society." For Moore, it was not Stevens' or any artist's responsibility to take care of those who were suffering. That Stevens was willing to take stock of his own place in the world was enough. Rescuing Stevens from Wilson's charge that Stevens abdicated his responsibility as an artist, Moore places Stevens in the august company of Donne, Hopkins, and Dante. By allying Stevens' with these poets who attended to their own inner spiritual development and sustenance, who did not seek, as Shaw did and Wilson might, to feed the body before the soul, Moore justified Stevens' "compulsions"— his need to look inward, to attend to his own needs before those of others.

Later that fall Wilson and Moore again exchanged letters concerning Stevens' poetry; he may have known Moore was writing a review of *Ideas of Order* for the *Criterion*, and he may have believed, despite her earlier response, that she would finally come around to his position. In his letter of October 27, 1935, Wilson made it clear that the implicit relationship between Stevens' poetic and his politics in "A Fading of the Sun" caused him some concern.

The book [*Ideas of Order*] has been a great thing to me; Wallace Stevens' humility is surely not the least of his qualities, and his composure, which must have been obtained not without struggle, shows itself in his ability to look a thing full in the face, no matter how disrupting it may be, and have his own spirit strengthened thereby rather than, as happens in so many cases, be overcome by what he has seen. A poem like "A Fading of the Sun" indicates that Wallace Stevens is alert to what I cannot but think it must give him pain to look upon. I myself, should I come to write on the subject of this poem, should not be capable of the reserve and certitude which Mr. Stevens displays. What he says here is truer than what I should be forced to say—that is, it is *ultimately* true to say that "If they will look

/ Within themselves" ". . . they will not die." Yet I think that it is first necessary to make it possible for those people to look within themselves, and I at any rate could not in looking upon their misery and incomprehension speak as Wallace Stevens does. Such misery is not [to] be borne, and will not be much longer, and those who have made thousands of souls crippled in spirit, body, and vision will have to answer for it.[32]

For Wilson, Stevens' reserve and certitude allowed him to advocate that those who were oppressed and suffering might turn inward as a means of removing themselves from this degradation. Stevens' "search for a tranquil belief" (CP, 151) in the face of what he witnessed constituted for Wilson an acceptance of the misery, not a call for active change. Acceptance made one complicitous with those who actively caused the suffering, with those who "will have to answer for it." Wilson recognized and implicitly lamented the gulf that stood between these people and Stevens, finding it hard to imagine how they could follow Stevens' suggestion. Moore, on the other hand, saw nothing incongruous in Stevens' recommendation; in fact, her manuscript notes indicate that she read the poem as exemplifying Stevens' fortitude in the face of the pain and misery surrounding him. "Where W. Stevens has got his fortitude," Moore wrote, "one does not know but he has it."[33]

In her letter to Wilson on November 29, 1935 she avoided discussing his response to Stevens' poem; instead she focused on his more general assessment of the collection: "Purblindness regarding Wallace Stevens ought not to be one of our current misfortunes in letters and I wish I had succeeded in saying in my notice of Ideas of Order what you say clearly and so impressively in your letter—about looking things in the face and about Wallace Stevens' composure as the result of struggle. I hope you will be presenting these thoughts yourself."[34]

It was of course Stevens' composure in "A Fading of the Sun," and his distance from those he addressed, that had disturbed Wilson. Knowing what he did, Stevens failed for Wilson, as he would have for Shaw, because he did not call for political action in the face of the misery he confronted. For Moore, it was Stevens' equilibrium, his "certain interior reconcentration of being," and his reluctance to politicize the role of the poet and the social function of poetry that allowed her to celebrate these poems from *Ideas of Order* and later those from *Owl's Clover*. As she maintained in "Unanimity and Fortitude," her 1937 review of *Ideas of Order* and *Owl's Clover*: "Despite this awareness of the world of sense—which at some points, to a prudish aestheticism, approximates wicked-ness—one notices the frequent recurrence of the word *heaven*. In each clime which the author visits and under each disguise, it is the dilemma of tested hope which confronts him. In *Owl's Clover* 'the search for a tranquil belief,' and the protest against the actualities of experience, become a protest against the death of world hope; against the unorder and chaos of this 'age of concentric mobs.'"[35]

For Moore, the self-serving habit of mind that had fueled the poems of *Harmonium* had been replaced by a new engagement with the world—with "a protest against the death of world hope" and a renewed "search for a tranquil belief." She was not troubled by the fact that Stevens' "protest against the actualities of experience" led him to turn inward in the face of what he observed. Nor did she see a connection between his aesthetic in *Harmonium*—one that frequently necessitated a withdrawal from the world and a use of disguises—and his position in the thirties. Moore maintained at the end of her 1937 review of *Owl's Clover* and *Ideas of Order*: "As R. P. Blackmur has said, 'the poems rise in the mind like a tide.' They embody hope, which in being frustrated becomes fortitude; and they prove to us that the testament to emotion is not volubility. It is remarkable that a refusal to speak should result in such eloquence and that an implied heaven could be made so definite."[36]

It is significant that Moore ends her review with an unequivocal en-dorsement of Stevens' politics that might also describe his aesthetic; this makes sense inasmuch as both Stevens' aesthetic and his politics, as Moore read them, grew out of a sustained "achieved remoteness" from this "age of concentric mobs." Yet Moore was critical of this posture when it governed Stevens' aesthetic in *Harmonium*, when it had sexist implications, when a particular economy of desire was made visible. In his later poetry, however, she accepted Stevens' distance, disguises, and escapes as his much needed defense against "general society," the "sudden mobs of men" (*CP*, 122).

9

Views of the Political in the Poetics of Wallace Stevens and H.D.

Melita Schaum

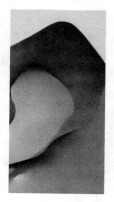

> A generation ago we should have said that the imagination is an aspect of the conflict between man and nature. Today we are more likely to say that it is an aspect of the conflict between man and organized society.
> —Wallace Stevens, "Imagination as Value"

One of the offshoots of the "new pluralism" in contemporary literary criticism is the tendency to locate texts in new, involved, even reciprocal relationships to a sociopolitical world. While the change suggests a welcome complexity in literary analysis, actual practice seems at times to devolve into reductive readings of literature or an equivocal understanding of political response. The impulse to place literature within the world of "real" events is capable of yielding strikingly contradictory products, leading us to reflect again on the complex links among aesthetics, history, and politics.

Two examinations of significant poems written during World War II illustrate the difficulties of such study: Marjorie Perloff's "Revolving in Crystal: The Supreme Fiction and the Impasse of Modernist Lyric" in *Wallace Stevens: The Poetics of Modernism* (1985) and Alicia Ostriker's "No Rule of Procedure: The Open Poetics of H.D.," delivered at the

June 1986 H.D. Centennial Conference in Orono, Maine. Both Wallace Stevens' "Notes toward a Supreme Fiction" and H.D.'s "The War Trilogy" are long poems composed around 1942, a time of accelerating wartime involvement and thus hypothetically a time fruitful for analyzing the interrelations between history and art. Yet both poems are examples, seemingly incongruous during this time of international upheaval, of lyric preoccupation, balanced form, artistic perfection, and the meditative personal voice. As such, they constitute almost a sub-genre of the contemplative, lyrical neo-epic in a time of war. But what is more striking than their structural similarity or their apparent historical incongruity is the discrepancy of responses given to these texts today—a difference that on the surface suggests a latent double standard in critical reception but more fundamentally questions the equivocal definition of "politics" in literary study.

Marjorie Perloff's analysis of Wallace Stevens' "Notes toward a Supreme Fiction" seeks to relocate the modernist lyric within its particular sociopolitical context, and in so doing relegate Stevens' poetics to a safe margin. Using a combination of correspondence, biography, publishing history, and an outline of wartime events occurring during the months of Stevens' composition of "Notes," Perloff indicts Stevens for his retreat from the monumental political events of his day. She calls this major poem "a kind of antimeditation, fearful and evasive, whose elaborate and daunting rhetoric is designed to convince both poet and reader that, despite the daily headlines and radio bulletins, the real action takes place in the country of metaphor."[1] By contrasting "the dark summer of 1942, when the Germans were pressing against the eastern front and the fighting in the Pacific was heavy," with Stevens' finicky design of the "perfect geometric whole" of "Notes," Perloff implies Stevens' removal from "the pressure of reality" in favor of the rhetorical "purity" of poetry—a dilemma she broadens to represent the general "impasse of Modernist lyric."[2]

Perloff invokes Mikhail Bakhtin's theory of the dialogic imagination to discriminate between the closed, "monologic," lyric authority attributed to Stevens and other High Modernist "aesthetes," versus the "rupture in the lyric paradigm" demonstrated by such collage-like poetry as Ezra

Pound's *Cantos*. In "Discourse in the Novel," Bakhtin had employed his concept of literature's inner drama of dialogue to distinguish between the style of the novel and the lyric—more specifically, to quote Bakhtin, between "artistic prose" and those genres that are "poetic in a narrow sense."[3] The former, in Bakhtin's paradigm, is identified by writing that puts to use the "sense of the boundedness, the historicity, the social determination and specificity" of language through an interaction with "alien discourse," allowing the entry and play of multiple "languages" within the work. Such a narrative's effect of equalizing discourse sets it against more narrowly "poetic" writing, which presumes the direct, unmediated power of the artist's language to assign meaning. The traditionally unified, "monologic" voice elevates poetic language as authoritative, "a pure and direct expression of [the author's] own intention."[4]

Despite Bakhtin's discrimination among genres, Perloff asserts that "today we can apply this distinction to poetry itself" and appropriates Bakhtin's complex terms "monologic" and "heteroglossic" to segregate what she terms the single-voiced "straight lyric" of such poets as Stevens from the multi-vocal "collage poetry of the Pound tradition." Pound and company, by inviting the entry of other "impure" discourses into poetry, undermine the polarity between art and life to move their work beyond the stylistic impasse and closed, monologic autotelism of Stevens' lyric voice. In the end, the concept of the Supreme Fiction—and Stevens' poem itself—is subject to severe political censure as a vehicle, however unsuccessful, by which to evade history.

The contemporary fascination with the poet's involvement—or lack of involvement—with the world touches a poet like H.D. as well. Like Perloff, Alicia Ostriker also attempts to define the connection between prosody and politics, but with remarkably different results. In her analysis of H.D's "breakthrough" epic, "The War Trilogy," Ostriker draws on Pound, Whitman, and Olson to establish a "politics" of open, improvisational poetics in which the lyric "I" is not erased but asserts itself in stylistic opposition to cultural expectations. Literary structure and its deviations here function as the artist's resistance to the social, psychic, and institutional restraints imposed by a dominant culture.

Ironically, in Ostriker's investigation the very elements that Perloff indicts in Stevens become commendations to the woman poet's craft and strength in a dissolute time. Treating "Trilogy" as a modern long poem by definition "philosophical, discursive, narrative, ultimately visionary," Ostriker points to its strategic difference from the works of other (male) artists. Unlike the "disorder" of *The Waste Land*, the *Cantos*, or *Paterson*, "Trilogy" reflects an older tradition with its fixed form, and its aim toward closure and coherence announces a "confidence in the poetic process" in antithesis to prevailing modes. The geometric verse-patterns of the poem represent, for Ostriker, beauty and coherence, yet constant variation tempers the whole: devices such as cadence, enjambment, and off-rhyme achieve the elusive effect of the poem's being "neither fixed nor free."

H.D.'s tone is described, along the same lines, as being light and intimate, not "authoritative" like that of her male contemporaries in the long poem genre. The momentum of her verse is one of "lightness and hesitation"; her form is dubbed a "slender-lined epic" both in an echo of the dictum to "write the body" and to show H.D.'s resistance to the long poem's tradition as public, doctrinally authoritative poetry. Even H.D.'s imagery bespeaks a feminine "poetics and politics of openness," consisting of repeated visions of womb-like enclosures opening from their apparent limits to a sense of the infinite. Ostriker points above all to the more "intimate" relationship of H.D. to her audience through the lyric voice: The sense of inclusion in the repeated use of "we" is balanced by the poem's general drive to be "exemplary, but not determinate," and the lyric "I" evades the strictures of authority and objectivity, as it "invites us to trust our own vision, ourselves. . . ." In the end, H.D.'s technique of patterned repetition leading to intense universal insight parallels the move from personal rumination to independent vision that manifests the woman poet's political utterance against the stress of cultural oppression and the chaos of war.[5]

To what can we attribute this virtual point-for-point discrepancy in analysis between the wartime lyric long poems of these two writers? Is there a qualitative difference between the "geometric precision" of a male poet which renders his endeavor a finicky escape from politics and the "impure" real world, while a similar formal patterning of a woman's verse becomes an assertion of coherence, insight, and expression? Can the meditative lyric intimacy of the former be indicted as monologic authoritarianism, while the very same quality in the latter is read as an outcry *against* the authoritative and a remedial intrusion of the personal and relative? Moreover, the implicit suggestion that a woman poet's personal vision *may* be an adequate response in a time of political upheaval, while a male poet's equally contemplative poetry is judged to be irresponsibly escapist throws us back into the stereotypic dualism of male activity versus female passivity, implying that women need have no "legitimate" political vision at all. But perhaps this apparent rupture is not merely a question of misdirected critical favoritism or double standards; rather, it forces the acknowledgment that poetics and politics involve each other in ways not yet fully examined.

One problem may lie with the term "politics" itself, often facilely taken to be synonymous with events in the "real" world. Perloff lists the battles of Midway, Bataan, and the Coral Sea to provide the historical context for the composition of "Notes," and offers such vaguely condemnatory juxtapositions as "On June 5, *the day after the Battle of Midway*, Stevens [writing to his publisher] adds, 'I shall be greatly pleased to have the unbound copy . . . done on hand-made paper if you have it.'"[6] Her emphasis on the neglected urgency of radio bulletins and headlines in Stevens' poetry and correspondence seems to propose that an artist's explicit recognition of specific current events is a necessary factor for his work to be political.

Here Perloff's analysis of "Notes" is consistent with a larger agenda, made evident in her collection *The Dance of the Intellect*. This work champions the prescient postmodernism of Poundian collage-poetry in contrast to the aesthetic isolation of the High Modernist lyric and the subsequent "extinction" of that neo-Romantic "species." For Perloff, postmodernism's salvation lies in its accommodation of the materials of the "real" world, in "the urge to return the material so rigidly excluded—political, ethical, historical, philosophical—to the domain of poetry. . . ."[7] In contrast to "straight" lyric poetry's presumed removal from actual history, the Pound tradition "wants to open the field so as to make contact with the *world* as well as the *word*."⁸ Two premises clearly underlie Perloff's position: (1) the concept of politics as *material* for poetic inclusion, and (2) the possibility of separating *word* and *world*.

Strictly speaking, however, one finds that politics covers a much broader, ultimately more abstract field than the inclusion of topical subjects or the reportage of international affairs. Events may be political in nature—symptoms of ideology, results of the momentum of international relationships—yet events do not in themselves constitute politics. War itself is not politics but the outcome of politics—or, as Wallace Stevens wrote, "war is the periodical failure of politics" (*OP,* 164), and further, war "is only part of a war-like whole" (*NA,* 21).

Here too the interrelationship of word and world elaborated by New Historicism bears reiteration. Such theories as Dominick LaCapra's unity of event and discourse, Hayden White's view that history is only a text, or Fredric Jameson's perspective that history is a limit "available only in textual form" contribute to a view of history that emphasizes its discursive, interpretive nature. If ideology is rhetoric (and history, in the Burkean paradigm, "a kind of conversation"), then the focus of our examination must involve the complex relationships between word and world, language and power. To become truly politicized, the critic and writer must recognize the field of political action as most fundamentally a "rhetorical war."

Subsequently, the metaphors that underlie our culture help constitute our politics—the ideological "texture of consensus" in society—and to these images and the concept itself of social consensus we must respond when we engage in political response deeper than a mere commiseration over headlines or a general keeping up with the news. Ideology at its root is language, is rhetoric—from the casual euphemism of the speech-maker, to the semiotics of propaganda, to the sinister dualism of "Us" and "Them" that makes up the figural backbone of military politics. The "poetic acts" of media and government create the fictions without which war could not exist: the images of heroism and service, the "good death," the hypostatization of countries, the bird's-eye view from the boardroom of international victory or defeat, war itself becoming truly "an abstraction blooded." Contrary to Perloff's antithesis of the "real" war versus

Stevens' "country of metaphor," the two are intimately involved: Politics is a cultural image-making which directs, interprets, rationalizes and abstracts the events of (in this case) military action. In its most basic sense, the theatre of war has always been a "Theatre of Trope."

In terms of the relationship between politics and art, a clearer denominator emerges between the forces of cultural troping and the resistance or compliance of individual trope—a battle fought on the field of the image. This understanding of the intersection of language and politics has strengthened and refined, for example, the best of feminist writing, in which political response frequently consists of unveiling and examining social metaphors themselves and the motives implicit behind cultural image-making. For feminist writers and critics, aware of the particular historical situation of women within a hegemonic discursive network, the very act of writing is a political act, a riot of the individual against a dominant discourse that silences. Art is a type of resistance that at its most powerful employs subtle textual strategies to "steal the language," undermine monolithic conceptions of form and expression, exercise the "politics of style." Literature seen on this level becomes a scrutiny of ideology through a subversion of its medium, a rupture of consensus, a sabotage of the patriarchal "universal" that questions the strictures of doctrine and subverts the notion of authority. Most important, an address to specific events or the inclusion of narrowly identified political material becomes secondary: a novel by Virginia Woolf about a woman organizing a party can be as integrally political as a critical study by Kate Millet or a tract on comparable worth.

The revisionist challenge issued by feminism, which goes beyond literary style to address the definition of politics itself, has shaped and influenced in a prototypical way the critical reception of H.D. Like Stevens, H.D. is a High Modernist poet difficult at first to assimilate into traditional views of the political, but her changing fortunes might afford a new perspective through which to view other modernist poets, including Stevens. H.D.'s cryptic lyrics, her aversion to mass movements, and her avowed distrust of public politics during two world wars made it initially easy for critics to dismiss her as "not of this world" (Hughes), a "poet of escape" (Bush) who either "avoided politics of any kind" (Guest)

or practiced a type of political "indifferentism" (Watts). Remarks like
C. H. Sisson's of 1975 were common: "In her essence H.D. is a slight,
extremely feminine figure, whose battles are all inward, and who
scarcely thought to link her thought with the public preoccupations of
the age. She lived obscurely with the illusion . . . that if the artist gets
on with his art all will be well."[9] No major overview was needed to
motivate Susan Stanford Friedman's sardonic summary a decade later, of
H.D. perceived by the literary establishment as an "escapist dryad too
fragile for the modern world." Those critics of the 1980s who wished to
reexamine H.D.'s unique orientation to the turmoil of her day found they
needed to dismantle the narrow definition of the political as a touchstone
for literary study. As Friedman and others clearly saw, the reevalua-
tion of H.D. demonstrated that "the concept of politics itself needs revision."[10]

That revision took a number of directions in H.D. scholarship, but all
were grounded on the inseparability of word and world (the power of
discourse) and on the subsequent political motivation behind the individual's relationship to language (the power of the contextualized "I" to
redirect rhetoric). For Friedman, the traditional concept of politics as
public activism directed toward international issues and conforming to
mass movements perpetuated the trivialization of women and other marginal members of society by failing to recognize the more intrinsic politics of gender and culture. As an alternative to the narrow view of
political involvement, Friedman saw a "larger gender-based pattern"
demonstrated by certain modernist women writers in which they "expressed a progressive politics originating in an exploration of the power
structures underlying the personal. The private domain of the individual
self in relationship to others . . . served as the point of political origins.
How far each woman took her political analysis as expressed in her life
and work—particularly how much she made connections between gender and issues of race, class, religion, sexual preference, and state
power—is a matter of individual variation."[11] In the case of H.D. in
particular, the structure and themes of her work represented a critique of
oppressive sociopolitical structures on a worldwide level and a challenge
to the "madness of the mainstream." By realigning the power of the word

with worldly action, "H.D.'s writing itself constituted her action against the dominant culture."[12]

Rachel Blau du Plessis further elaborated ways in which the political struggle takes place in a rhetorical arena for H.D. and other women writers, a drama of verbal power and revolution which Friedman elsewhere called "textual entrapment and liberation."[13] Du Plessis saw H.D.'s escape from rhetorical "thralldom" as representative of the larger struggle involving human identity and resistance. To survive in the face of a culture that negates her (both as woman and as poet), H.D. must gain "cultural control of her own story," must "struggle with . . . the voices of culture to retain control," must resist being reduced, defined, and thereby "colonized" by a patriarchy "which would appropriate her."[14] And H.D. must address this challenge to selfhood on its most basic textual level: "She must de-story the old story, lift the weight of the accustomed tale so she can tell her own. Destroy."

> This is the central struggle of the woman writer. For
> every word, each cadence, each posture, the tone, the
> range of voices, the nature of plot, the rhythm of
> structures, the things that happen, events excluded, the
> reasons for writing, the ways she's impeded, the noises
> around her, vocabularies of feeling, scripts of behavior,
> choices of wisdom, voices inside her, body divided,
> image of wonder
>
> all must be re-made.[15]

This revisionist use of story and myth, moreover, moves beyond personal actualization to the arena of cultural change—from literary structure to social structure. Alicia Ostriker studies ways in which H.D. and other women poets pursue a feminist antiauthoritarianism expressed through aesthetic technique and aimed at subverting oppressive cultural and political structures. For Ostriker, H.D.'s long poems dismantle and invert the myths of heroism and patriarchy, and attempt to reclaim the power of history and story for the "altered ends" of "cultural change." H.D.'s long poem *Helen in Egypt*, for instance, both in theme and in structure "assails fascism and hero-worship" and gives form to an "uncompromising inwardness, [a] rejection of all authority."[16] On the one hand the poet's creative gesture stands as a "response to the chaos of history"[17]—a shaping, a healing of the "spiritual diaspora" endemic to a time of war. But in addition, and constituting perhaps its most political move, it insists upon breaking down imposed structures of thought, language, and social attitude by centralizing the marginal; displacing hierarchies of race, religion, and gender; effecting a return to the hetero-doxy of reality and truth.

Focusing on politics as the remedial intrusion of personal reality onto cultural abstraction and as the recapture of the vocabulary of that reality sets the lyric voice centrally in the sphere of political relevance. More-over, the "struggle not to be reduced" or negated by a dominant culture not only is a concern of women, but comprises perhaps the central concern underlying all individual political action and resistance. The feminist move from object to subject—escaping the dehumanization of being the passive object of language by reclaiming the active and "forbidden female identity as speaking subject"[18]—can be extended to the situation of human beings in general silenced and depersonalized by sociopolitical abstraction. The assertion of individual reality and the imposition of standards of accountability and humaneness on the collec-tive abstract may well constitute political engagement at its most intrin-sic level. Against the false determinism of war, inwardness becomes not escape but resistance; subject-ivity is revealed to be not solipsism but rebellion, the remedial intervention of human agency.

This concept surfaces in Robert Duncan's *H.D. Book,* itself a work in contention with the doctrinaire critical establishment and one that repre-sents the affective search for relevance by a poet and activist in the politically taut 1960s. Reading Duncan, we can begin to merge the female struggle against the oppressive "voices of culture" with the indi-vidual political struggle to retain independence of thought, to resist being "colonized" by "official culture." For Duncan, personal politics is the central—perhaps the only—politics to be feasibly enacted; it repre-sents, in brief, "the consensus of authority vs. the heresy of individual experience."[19] Analyzing H.D.'s sense of military and cultural evil in

"The War Trilogy," Duncan defines the agonistic equation: "Where we cannot identify with the will of powerful groups in the society we live in, we feel their power over us as an evil. The word *evil*, the O.E.D. suggests: 'usually referred to the root of *up, over*,' may then be whatever power [is] over us of outer or inner compulsion. As the power and presumption of authority by the State has increased in every nation, we are ill with it, for it surrounds us and, where it does not openly conscript, seeks by advertising, by education, by dogma or by terror, to seduce, enthrall, mould, command or coerce our inner will or conscience or inspiration to its own uses."[20] Such power on a rhetorical level—the seductive conscription by means of advertising, education, dogma— takes on sinister but admittedly familiar contours in a time of war: "'Rails gone (for guns),' the poem [*The Walls Do Not Fall*] begins, with the officers of the State, in the name of the War Effort, taking over all the conditions of personal reality into their own use. . . . With the declaration of war in the modern state, which claims to represent the authority of the people, the means and ends of the war become the ultimate reality."[21]

At issue for H.D. in the face of her detractors (both the fictive adversaries in the poem and the real-life critics of her poetic "escapism") are the survival of self and the centrality of language in shaping our realities. In a time of war, survival of the self is of immediate concern—not only physical survival but spiritual and intellectual endurance against the narcotic of group opinion and the national appropriation of personal realities and lives. As a woman in a patriarchial culture, a poet in a literal, utilitarian age, and an introspective individual in a time of mass ideology, H.D. faces negation through charges of irrelevance levelled at her from many directions by a powerful "official" culture: "'So what good are your scribblings?' the partisans of the Sword demand in *The Walls Do Not Fall*. The immediate contention means 'of what good for the War Effort?' but the accusation gives rise to answers in the poem that it is her very way of life, her ultimate individuality that is under question."[22] To her adversaries' contention that the Sword "fights for life," H.D. responds "that Writing too is part of the fight for life."[23]

The first phase in H.D.'s offensive is to reveal not only the relationship between particular uses of language and a culture that valorizes military action, but the primacy of discourse over event, its ability to create a self-fulfilling reality. Duncan sees it as the interaction of wish and world—fiction and actuality—in the creation of our distinctively human lives, which are contoured around such abstractions as history, identity, society, ideology, war. He recognizes that "all of human history appears to H.D. as if it were a Creation or fiction of reality, involving wish as well as world in its works—and here, the war as much as the writing is wish. . . ."[24] Moreover, "H.D.'s sense [was] that ultimately the War was to be subject to Writing itself as a higher prime of reality."[25]

> . . . remember, O Sword,
> you are the younger brother, the latter-born,
>
> your Triumph, however exultant,
> must one day be over,
>
> *in the beginning*
> *was the Word.*
>
> . . . . .
>
> Without thought, invention,
> you would not have been, O Sword,
>
> without idea and the Word's mediation,
> you would have remained
>
> unmanifest in the dim dimension
> where thought dwells . . .[26]

Acknowledging rhetoric's power to manipulate or to unveil the illusions that guide our actions divests political "reality" of its seamless, unimpeachable potency. At the same time, it warns of the danger of unexamined language, a danger which the poet, in her drive to challenge official discourse, can reveal and alleviate:

> . . . if you do not even understand what words say,
>
> how can you expect to pass judgement
> on what words conceal?
>
> . . . .

. . . for gods have been smashed before

and idols and their secret is stored
in man's very speech . . .[27]

The project of the poet, representative of the individual disen-
franchised by the dominant culture, is to recapture the integrity of self
by continually recapturing the discourse of personal reality. As Duncan
summarizes, "The problem throughout is one of translation between the
individual experience which is repressed in the official culture or ban-
ished to the realm of madness and the body of what is taken as authoritative."[28] This paradigm of resistance defines the politics of gender
and culture expressed in the writings of women. Yet the insight that
politics can and often must be addressed at the level of discourse, by the
individual voice in rebuttal to cultural consensus, seems not to have
extended to the consideration of general poets' response to international
politics and the workings of official culture in a time of war.

Here some statements of Wallace Stevens might be allowed to demonstrate how his own distrust of mass movements and avoidance of public
politics point to a more sophisticated concept of autonomy as political
gesture, and how his scrutiny of language reveals an awareness of the
complex ways in which discursive and sociohistorical events interact.
Critics have long seen in Wallace Stevens the epitome of the modernist
poet's removal from the sphere of political engagement. What is assumed
in much literary analysis is that the high modernist preoccupation with
lyric interiority always signifies an escape from history and the world: a
type of navel-gazing solipsism at odds with an era of world-changing
events. But what has been overlooked in Stevens' preoccupation with
poetry and the poetic is that far from illustrating a "guilty aestheticism"
removed from history, it provides startling insights into the fictions of
history, the rhetorical illusions by which we as social beings live and act.

In an address delivered at Bard College in 1948 titled "Poetic Acts,"
Stevens examined a fundamental communal phenomenon: the engagement with the "unreal," which makes up a central part of all social,
economic, religious, and political thinking. Much like H.D.'s conflation

of wish and world, this "projection of poetry into reality," the creation of fictions or generalizations that dominate our opinions and actions, is revealed to be both a fundamental drive of communal man and a simplification that must be repeatedly unmasked. Stevens explains the pervasiveness of imaginative projection in everyday life:

> When we go to the corner to catch a bus or walk down the block to post a letter, our acts in doing these things are direct. But when we gather together and become engaged with something unreal our act is not so much the act of gathering together as it is the act of becoming engaged with something unreal. We do this sort of thing on a large scale when we go to church on Sunday, when we celebrate days like Christmas or the much more impressive days of the end of Lent. . . . we [also] find the poetic act in lesser and everyday things, as for example, in the mere act of looking at a photograph of someone who is absent or in writing a letter to a person at a distance, or even in thinking of a remote figure. . . . Just as in space the air envelops objects far away with an ever-deepening blue, so in the dimension of the poetic act the unreal increasingly subtilizes experience and varies appearance. The real is constantly being engulfed in the unreal. But I want to be quite sure that you recognize that I am talking about something existing, not about something purely poetic. (*OP*, 236–37)

Stevens goes on to provide examples from social interpretation, our fictive projection into the nature of class that often determines social action: "The act of thinking of the life of the rich is a poetic act and this seems to be true whether one thinks of it with liking or with dislike. The same thing may be said of the act of thinking of the life of the poor. Most of us do not share the life of either the one or the other and for that reason both are unreal" (*OP*, 237). These lives—imagined but not directly known—become the foundation from which our opinions evolve and our prejudices often emerge. As Stevens says elsewhere, "If one collected instances of imaginative life as social form over a period of time, one might amass a prodigious number. . . . social attitudes, social distinctions and the insignia of social distinctions are instances. . . . people turn to the imagination without knowing it in life" (*NA*, 145, 147).

Other abstract areas of life can also be seen as poetic projections, perhaps necessary fictions for social existence, but nonetheless subject to the same dangers of reductiveness and unreality. Duncan has pointed out that "money and war are also fictional entities, for men believe in them, as they believe in elves and gods, to make real their lives."[29] Stevens, too, has called money "a kind of poetry" (*OP*, 165), and in "Poetic Acts" he goes so far as to label modern national economy a "poetico-economy"—a term we can undoubtedly appreciate today. Elsewhere, Stevens identifies the irrational nature of the electoral process (*OP*, 225) and culminates his examples with the ultimate "poem" of military action: "Surely for millions of men and women the act of joining the armed forces is measurably a poetic act, since for all of them it is a deviation from the normal, impelled by senses and necessities inoperative on the ordinary level of life" (*OP*, 237). And finally: "One wants to consider the imagination on its most momentous scale. Today this scale is not the scale of poetry, nor of any form of literature of art. *It is the scale of international politics . . .* we live today in a time dominated by great masses of men and while the reason of a few men may underlie what they do, they act as their imaginations impel them to act" (*NA*, 124, emphases added).

In the midst of this constant engagement with unreality, the poet paradoxically best embodies the individual's duty to return to reality, as the man of imagination who nonetheless "commits himself to reality, which then becomes his inescapable and ever-present difficulty and inamorata" (*OP*, 238). The poet, for Stevens as for H.D., here becomes the individual who through scrutiny has cultivated an "immunity to eloquence," who "has strengthened himself to resist the bogus" (*OP*, 238).

Stevens' concept of resistance—personal, poetic, and political—finds further analogies to the politics of recapturing personal reality. In his essay "The Irrational Element in Poetry," Stevens deals directly with the responsibility of the writer, clarifying the antithesis between poetic engagement and escape: "The pressure of the contemporaneous from the time of the beginning of the World War to the present time has been constant and extreme. No one can have lived apart in happy oblivion. . . . We are preoccupied with events, even when we do not observe them closely. We have a sense of upheaval. We feel threatened. We look from an uncertain present toward a more uncertain future. One feels the desire to collect oneself against all this in poetry as well as in politics. If politics is nearer to each of us because of the pressure of the contemporaneous, poetry, in its way, is no less so and for the same reason" (*OP,* 224). Reiterating the connection between the irrational impulse in social and political action as well as in poetry, Stevens points to this time of upheaval, when "the greater the pressure of the contemporaneous, the greater the resistance." But rather than an evasion of the real, for the man of responsible imagination, "*Resistance is the opposite of escape.* . . . Resistance to the pressure of ominous and destructive circumstance consists of its conversion, so far as possible, into a different, an explicable, an amenable circumstance" (*OP,* 225, emphases added).

While superficially the conversion of circumstance can be misread as precisely that poetic escape that Perloff and other critics indict—the falsifying of reality toward a more favorable vision—instead, the move toward engagement and accountability here must be appreciated. With characteristic lexical precision, Stevens chooses the word "amenable" as the goal of human conversion of circumstance, as that word denotes making circumstance answerable, responsible, accountable, able to be tested, responsive to examination. Elsewhere, Stevens makes scrupulously clear his definition of the "pressure of reality" as the force of contemporary events which overwhelm and evade us, which seek to conscript: "By the pressure of reality, I mean the pressure of an external event or events on the consciousness *to the exclusion of any power of contemplation.* The definition ought to be exact and, as it is, may be merely pretentious. But when one is trying to think of a whole generation and of a world at war . . . the plainest statement of what is happening can easily appear to be an affectation" (*NA,* 20). It is the difficult *contemplation* of events—converting or translating political irrationality and cultural abstraction back into a morally answerable set of concrete actions, assumptions, motives—which constitutes resistance at its most fundamental level. Again, the recapture of the integrity of self in the face of outer compulsion is at issue. In antithesis to the fictive soldier's "final aphorism" in Stevens' early "Lettres d'un Soldat"—"No introspective

chaos . . . I accept / War, too, although I do not understand" (*OP,* 11)—
Stevens pits the "great modern faith . . . faith in the truth and particularly in the idea that the truth is attainable" (*OP,* 235).

On a broad level, it can be argued that the examination of such "truth"
preoccupied Stevens' entire poetic career, with the understanding that it
is in the interplay between imagination and reality that truth perhaps
abides. On the one hand, Stevens recognized the empty yet powerful
inventions pervading history, severed from the real and the particular,
yet breeding through repetition their own actuality

> The civil fiction, the calico idea
> The Johnsonian composition, abstract man,
> All are evasions like a repeated phrase,
> Which, by its repetition, comes to bear
> A meaning without a meaning.
>
> (*OP,* 65)

These are the "descriptions without place," "the invention of a nation in
a phrase," Stevens' "seemings" of history. At the same time, although
the tendency toward invention of this nature continually evokes the
poet's near-obsessive scrutiny and suspicion, and often calls forth his
despair, his "truth-seeking" attitude must allow for the "beneficient
illusions" necessary to man's being in the world, resulting in a carefully
complex relationship to the powers of inventive abstraction. Abstraction
is a tendency to which we capitulate because we must, but which we
must also recognize for what it is and for the power it has in our lives. As
Stevens ominously declared for his time: "The world is at the mercy of
the strongest mind in it whether that strength is the strength of sanity or
insanity, cunning or good-will" (*OP,* 174). Yet equally, "If the mind is the
most terrible force in the world, it is also the only force that defends us
against terror. . . . it is the only force that can defend us against itself"
(*OP,* 173–74).

Given the intimate connections between politics and language, such
literature that studies the workings of language, human desire, and the
imagination in a time of war becomes centrally political, becomes a force

(as it were) defending us against itself. Within this context Stevens rightly saw, "it is the theory of description that matters most. / It is the theory of the word for those / From whom the word is the making of the world . . ." (*CP*, 345). The lyric itself—indicative of subjectivity, perspective, and the singular voice—takes on new relevance, denoting the resistance of the individual sensibility against an age which acts as "a barricade against the singular man / By the incalculably plural" (*CP*, 340). The lyric voice assumes a determined autonomy, not of the elitist artwork, but of the self in a time when the pressure of contemporary ideology and mass action is at its most extreme.

In a reply to *Yale Literary Magazine*'s query concerning the greatest problem facing the young writer in America in the 1940s, Stevens most clearly articulated this necessary battle fought by the individual against the pressures of political conformity:

> The role of the poet may be fixed by contrasting it to that of the politician. The poet absorbs the general life; the public life. The politician is absorbed by it. The poet is individual. The politician is general. It is the personal in the poet that is the origin of his poetry. . . . This does not mean that he is a private figure. On the other hand, it does mean that he must not allow himself to be absorbed as the politician is absorbed. He must remain individual. As individual he must remain free. The politician expects everyone to be absorbed as he himself is absorbed. This expectation is part of the sabotage of the individual. . . . the poet's problem, then, is to maintain his freedom. (*L*, 526)

In a paradigm of politics which not only includes but mandates the individual's recapture of the integrity of self through affirmation of the discourse of personal reality, the lyric voice becomes a central and relevant artistic vehicle of the modern age. Postmodernism's advocates, frequently self-congratulatory in their avoidance of the lyric "I's" authority and autonomy, may themselves be masking a nostalgia for a pure, unmediated presentation of the discourses of the "actual" world, an implosion of the mediating self into an innocence which is simply unavailable. Such poets as H.D. and Wallace Stevens, with their more difficult focus on the complexity and power of the lyric, on the rhetoric of history and politics, and on the directed language of resistance, present the lyric "I" in a subtler and ultimately more political light— as "the irrepressible revolutionist . . . the intelligence that endures" (*NA*, 152, 52).

10

The Houses of Fathers
Stevens and Emerson

Lisa M. Steinman

Critics have discussed Emerson's influence on Wallace Stevens, and more recently there have been a number of historically oriented studies of both poets, neither of whose writings seems on the surface to have been deeply influenced by contemporary historical events—other than Emersons' reactions to the slave question in the fifties.[1] My purpose here is to juxtapose some of the insights of the latter studies, to suggest how comparisons of these two American poets might involve discussing not only literary history but also history more literally conceived, including the historical place of poets in our culture. In particular, I will consider the situation of the male poet in America, not simply because of the special focus of this collection, but because questions of gender impinge on both Emerson's and Stevens' consideration of the poet's social role.

In "Spiritual Laws," Emerson wrote that we "call the poet inactive, because he is not a president, a merchant, or a porter. . . . real action is in silent moments. The epochs of our life are not in the visible facts of our choice of a calling, our marriage, our acquisition of an office, and the like."[2] Emerson then argues that to "think is to act," and concludes that poetic power is not simply comparable to but above "all that is reckoned solid and precious in the world,—palaces, gardens, money, navies, kingdoms."[3]

Yet while challenging the values of his culture, Emerson also reveals the need to defend poets against the charges that they are idle and deal with the insubstantial. Throughout essays such as "Spiritual Laws," Emerson addresses those who believe that lack of success in the political and economic world marks writing as an idle pastime. The argument is pointed, because Emerson himself never forgets that poetry does not yield economic power: "There are not in the world at any one time more than a dozen persons who read and understand Plato:—never enough to pay for an edition of his works."[4] Further, in 1853, Emerson wrote that his "quarrel with poets is that they do not believe in their own poetry," a recognition of the ways in which poets internalized cultural values.[5]

In 1836, in "Spirit," Emerson notes that even the "poet finds something ridiculous in his delight, until he is out of the sight of *men*" (emphasis added).[6] While Emerson's point is to resist the self-mistrust that is socially bred, his language suggests how poetic delight was viewed as part of the private domain—traditionally, a woman's sphere—in contrast to the apparently more valuable and solid world of public action (where a man might comfortably identify himself as "a president, a merchant, or a porter," but not as a poet). The penultimate paragraph of "Spiritual Laws" implicitly reaffirms Emerson's task as rescuing what is culturally defined as passive, unimportant, and feminine. He moves from a defense of writing, and specifically of poets, to the following: "Let the great soul incarnated in some woman's form, poor and sad and single, in some Dolly or Joan, go out to service, and sweep chambers and scour floors, and its effulgent daybeams cannot be muffled or hid, but to sweep and scour will instantly appear supreme and beautiful *actions*" (emphasis added).[7] Here, Emerson's awareness of the value American culture places on action in the material world, and of the concomitant depreciation of poetry, is explicitly framed in terms of gender as well as in terms of class. The passage above equates attempts to reclaim the importance of poetry with attempts to reclaim the importance of what is culturally defined as women's work. At the same time, however, it is only by redefining such work as active and powerful, that is, as important in the vocabulary of his culture, that Emerson can defend it.

Most often, Emerson suppresses or glosses over any mention of women's work. For example, again stressing the importance of "Self-Reliance," arguing against the pressure to conform, Emerson proposes as an ideal the "nonchalance of boys who are sure of a dinner, and would disdain as much as a lord to do or say aught to conciliate one. . . . [whereas] the man is, as it were, clapped into jail by his consciousness."[8] In his article on "The Politics of Emerson's Man-Making Words," David Leverenz argues that Emerson's point tacitly rests on the assurance that those who make dinner "sure"—always women—will not adopt a similar nonchalance about conforming to social expectations. In fact, in American culture, being certain of a meal most often rests on the assurance that there is *both* a cook and a breadwinner in the family, which is to say that the passage could be read as a willful (or perhaps wistful) suppression of social realities for men and women. Nonetheless, Leverenz finally seems right, given Emerson's biography (his mother played both roles); certainly Leverenz is right to make us pay attention to the importance of gender roles in the passage. Moreover, he is equally illuminating when he discusses Emerson's reconception of thinking as power. Pointing out the changes in social conditions in America between 1825 and 1850, Leverenz concludes that while Emerson's poetics are attractive, his language "resonates with the unresolved tensions of his life and time," in general by omitting women and their world in his attempt to reclaim a manly power for his own enterprise.[9]

Others, Quentin Anderson for example, have also noted that Emerson's vision of social reality is not his strong suit, often adding that Emerson's actual relationships with others—especially with his wife, Lidian, and with Margaret Fuller—were characterized by a related disregard for our collective social life. Anderson describes "the split American," whose practical and visionary sides have trouble with each other, noting that Emerson's internal divisions as well as his idealism devalue personal relations and sexual roles, both being seen as part of the practical world.[10] There are also other ways in which culturally defined gender roles are involved in the conflict Anderson identifies. For the male poet, this includes the internalization of what counts as a manly occupation and of the importance of being a material provider, which in turn entails seeing poetry as unmanly. To defend the visionary and the poetic thus often requires either repudiating the qualities culturally defined as feminine or appropriating such qualities by redefining them as masculine.

I have argued above that Emerson not only tried to resist the devaluation of poetry and the necessity of yielding to cultural expectations, but he tacitly acknowledged the connection between these two forms of resistance. Yet if Emerson's resistance and redefinitions allow him to celebrate the private sphere, he also slights the actual inhabitants of that sphere, or translates them into visionary terms, in order to proclaim the importance of his own activity. In other words, Emerson's defense of poetry involves establishing a distance between the private but valorized world of the poet, who withdraws from the public world, and the private life of the man, when he is at home. This is related to the healthy and unhealthy ways of distancing oneself from the world that Emerson explicitly discusses when he identifies a distancing he defines as a fact of spiritual existence, a distancing he advocates between the social and the spiritual worlds, and a "safe distance" from experience he deplores.

In "The Poet," for example, Emerson writes that "even the poets are contented with a civil and conformed manner of living, and to write poems from the fancy, at a safe distance from their own experience."[11] For Emerson, to be at a safe distance from real experience is to dwell in the illusory social world. But to explore experience is not to do away with all distance between the poet and the objects of the poet's attention: his description of higher minds as those who "never ceased to explore" suggests Emerson's celebration of exploration over discovery.[12] "Experience"—an essay that follows "The Poet" in Emerson's second series of essays—spells out the belief that "souls never touch their objects."[13] Specifically speaking of other people, in an argument for living in present experience, Emerson proposes that we should treat "men and women well: treat them as if they were real: perhaps they are."[14] He also notes that—like eating dinner (which boys take for granted in "Self-Reliance")—discussing "the household with our wives" is trivial compared with "the solitude to which every man is always returning."[15]

Two aspects of Emerson's difficulty with the practical world become apparent here. Not only are men and women necessarily distanced from even worthy objects of their attention, but the images used to describe unworthy objects of attention recall the lines from "Spiritual Laws" where Emerson writes that like worldly professions or politics, marriage is not truly important. So, Emerson argues not only for distance as an idealist condition of life, but also for another kind of distance, distance from the trivial. Defining the trivial, Emerson sees domestic life as the mirror image of public life; it is not the realm from which he will draw his vocabulary of approval (using terms like "action" or "power"), but it is part of that from which he requires a willed (rather than a necessary) distance. Thus, despite his celebration of the private, Emerson doubly distances himself from "mere" domesticity.

Given the ideal nature of the private realm Emerson defends, women are not banned from themselves seeking the solitude to which, Emerson says, "every man is always returning." Yet, such images assume that someone (presumably "our wives") will make dinner and run the household while men return to their solitude.[16] Moreover, the metaphors in which Emerson describes a more visionary reality reemphasize his unsettling reinforcement of gender stereotypes in his attempt to empower his own activity. In the 1844 "Nature," for instance, he writes: "It is the same among the men and women, as among the silent trees; always a referred existence, an absence, never a presence and satisfaction. Is it, that beauty can never be grasped? in persons and in landscape is equally inaccessible? The accepted and betrothed lover has lost the wildest charm of his maiden in her acceptance of him. She was heaven whilst he pursued her as a star: she cannot be heaven, if she stoops to such a one as he. . . . To the intelligent, nature converts itself into a vast promise, and will not be rashly explained. Her secret is untold. Many and many an Oedipus arrives."[17]

Once again, although Emerson's anatomy of desire is attractive, and although his other writings often imply he would protest any suggestion that his choice of metaphors was meant to exclude actual women, it is tempting to set against Emerson's myth, Muriel Rukeyser's recasting of the exchange between Oedipus and the Sphinx. In her poem, "Myth," Rukeyser's Oedipus says to the Sphinx, challenging her explanation that he has come to a tragic end because he answered her riddle incorrectly, "'When you say Man . . . you include women / too. Everyone knows that.' She said, 'That's what / you think.'"[18]

There *is* a difference in Emerson's thinking between the emblematic, astral maiden in the beginning of the passage from "Nature" quoted above and—for example—Lidian. Nonetheless, the passage suggests both that Emerson's idealism had repercussions in the social world he wanted to ignore (perhaps just because he ignored it) and that his attempt not to identify himself with the domestic informs even his most idealistic passages. After all, the maiden described in the passage from "Nature" begins as a figure, like the figures of the silent trees or the star. Emerson's larger argument is that the soul never gains its object. Trees and stars always do maintain their distance and their silence. Metaphorical maidens, though, must more willfully be kept at a distance from those who might want to discuss household affairs. And, on the other side of the coin, wives must be kept at a safe distance, in order that the poet's activity—which American culture allied with the private and the impractical—not be identified with (on interfered with by) actual domesticity.

The questions raised by this consideration of Emerson are relevant to Stevens, who unwittingly echoes Emerson's claim that poets find their own delight "ridiculous" until they are outside of the sight of other men. In 1913, Stevens wrote telling his wife Elsie to keep his attempt to put together a collection of poetry "a great secret"; the letter continues: "There is something absurd about all this writing of verses; but the truth is, it elates and satisfies me to do it. . . . So that, you see, my habits are positively lady-like" (*L*, 180).

It may be unfair to use the letter of a sixteen-year-old boy, written to his mother, to gloss the letter of a thirty-four-year-old man, written to his wife of less than four years. Still, one of Stevens' earliest preserved letters does seem a comment on his self-description of 1913. As a boy, Stevens wrote home from a summer resort: "I hate <u>ladies</u>? (such as are here)[.] [They] are all agreeable enough but familiarity breeds contempt—poor deluded females—they are contemptible without familiarity" (*L*, 5). Although there is absolutely no question of literary influence, Stevens' letter begins almost like Emerson's passage from "Nature," disclaiming "ladies" as a social category, and staving off any charges of "familiarity." But the young Stevens ends his letter with contempt even for ladies kept at a distance (which must have been a way of both reassuring and disconcerting the distant lady to whom he was writing, namely his mother). Again in 1913, Stevens describes being "lady-like" as absurd, if not contemptible. Once more, he seems at the same time to have felt his writing was protected from ridicule when he was writing to his wife or in his home; perhaps just because writing poetry seemed "lady-like," it could be shared, but could at first only be shared, within the family circle.[19] An early letter from Stevens' father makes clear that Stevens previously had the same habit of sharing not only letters but poetry with his mother. Garrett Stevens wrote to his son when Stevens was at Harvard: "I am convinced from the Poetry (?) you write your Mother that the afflatus is not serious—and does not interfere with some real hard work" (*L*, 23).

Stevens' internalization of and resistance to the idea that poetry and real work were at odds is clear in his journals, which wrestle with the categories his father provided. Three months after the letter cited above was sent, Stevens wrote to himself: "Those who say poetry is now the peculiar province of women say so because ideas about poetry are effeminate. . . . Poetry itself is unchanged" (*L*, 26).[20] The journal entry is labeled "Poetry and Manhood," and explicitly rejects as "effeminate" the poetry of "silly men" (*L*, 26). That is, in casting about for a definition of manly poetry, Stevens rejects not women who wrote, but the genteel poets whose work could be labeled effeminate.[21] At the same time, it seems clear that Stevens was also trying to protest his father's suggestion—a suggestion Stevens at first took to heart—the the effeminacy of poetry was connected with poetry being the kind of thing one sent to one's mother, and therefore "not serious." The implication is that serious poetry is not genteel poetry, and neither is it read primarily by women.

In his obituary for Stevens—"Comment: Wallace Stevens," published in *Poetry* in January 1956—William Carlos Williams compares his fellow writer not to Emerson, but to Emily Dickinson, "imprisoned by her conscience in her father's house for a lifetime."[22] The idea that Stevens and Dickinson were equally affected by internalizing the assumptions of patriarchal culture is illuminating. As Frank Lentricchia insists: "Male is not equivalent to patriarchy."[23] Yet Williams' comparison brings home the separate difficulties faced by male and female poets in American culture, even as it implies that these difficulties are related. Williams suggests that for Dickinson to have removed herself from marriage was for her to have been trapped in her father's house; for Stevens to have been trapped in his father's house was for him to have assumed the roles his father prescribed for him: as breadwinner, as professional, and as one whose "afflatus" did not interfere with "real work." Stevens could write in "The Plot against the Giant," in a way that would not have occurred to Dickinson, of "a curious puffing" that "will undo" (which is to say unman) his giant "yokel" (*CP*, 6–7).

Although the situations of Emerson, Dickinson, and Stevens are historically different, for all three socially prescribed gender roles affected their ability to declare themselves as poets in America. Emerson, of course, faced the assumptions of his culture from an unusual vantage point, biographically, having been raised and supported by women, from his mother to his first wife, Ellen Tucker, whose legacy after her death supported the poet. In the case of both Dickinson and Stevens, the problem of being trapped was more literally the problem of becoming or being supported by a father. Still, in trying to resist being trapped in the roles culturally prescribed for him, Emerson leaves women to carry on the household affairs and feels he must distance himself from domesticity. Despite Williams' perceptive comment, Emerson and Stevens, as male poets, have more in common with each other in their responses to cultural pressures than either has with Dickinson.

To quote from Marianne Moore's poem "Marriage": "She says, 'Men are monopolists,'" while "He says, . . . 'a wife is a coffin.'"[24] Moore's strategy is characteristic: her voices quote from others, indicative of the social nature of the different pressures brought to bear on men and women. Moreover, her quotations on both sides of the question carry weight, in part because they are drawn from others whom Moore admired, namely M. Carey Thomas, president of Mount Holyoke, and Ezra Pound. The portion of Thomas's 1921 address from which Moore quotes says men are monopolists because they "practically reserve for themselves" all affairs of state and of pomp—"membership in academies, medals, titles . . . and other shining baubles, so valueless in themselves." Thomas was aware not only that "men" did not mean "women," but that the baubles she dismissed on such an Emersonian note were nonetheless "infinitely desirable because . . . [they are] symbols of [public] recognition."[25] Pound, on the other hand, when he said that a wife was a coffin, might almost have been thinking of Stevens, who virtually gave up poetry in the period (1924–1933) during which he consolidated his position at work and had a child. Stevens gained some of that recognition Thomas said was denied women, but he also identified himself as a breadwinner, who gained recognition in the world of business, not of poetry. As Pound reported to Williams: Stevens "says he isn't writing any more. He has a daughter!"[26] I began with the suggestion that Stevens resembles Emerson in part because he faced similar cultural pressures. But more self-consciously than Emerson, Stevens was torn between his internalization of cultural commonplaces and his attempts to redefine or resist those commonplaces. Finally, as with Emerson, Stevens' very resistance exacted hidden costs from those closest to him.

The idea that artistic culture generally was the province of women, while men, to be successful, should be associated with business, was widely commented upon by the time of Moore, Pound, Williams, and Stevens. Thus, for example, even Edmund Clarence Stedman's influential and genteel collection of American poetry, *An American Anthology, 1787–1900,* published at the turn of the century, noted that in America economics was "a more fascinating study than letters." Stedman also mentions living "in a time half seriously styled 'the woman's age,'" a reference not only to the literary achievements of women, but also to what Ann Douglas has called the feminization of American culture.[27] In 1909, the year in which he published his first book, Williams wrote to his brother, defensively, that a "good many people think to like poetry is to be a molly coddle."[28] And Van Wyck Brooks, discussing "The Literary Life," in Harold Stearns's collection of critical essays on *Civilization in the United States,* suggests the culturally accepted belief that a man's place was in the public sphere of business and commerce explains "why our novelists take such pains to be mistaken for business men."[29]

Stevens obviously internalized such commonplaces; unlike Emerson, he deliberately took up residence in his father's house (metaphorically speaking), and with some self-awareness, seeing both the losses and the

THE HOUSES OF FATHERS / 199

gains therein. He wrote to Ronald Lane Latimer in 1937: "A good many years ago, when I really was a poet in the sense that I was all imagination, and so on, I deliberately gave up writing poetry because, much as I loved it, there were too many other things I wanted not to make an effort to have them. . . . I didn't like the idea of being bedeviled all the time about money and I didn't for a moment like the idea of poverty, so I went to work like anybody else and kept at it for a good many years" (L, 320). This is Stevens' acknowledgment of himself as a conformist ("like anybody else"), but also as a man, who by his own choice made himself conform. (He *deliberately* gave up writing.) If there is some wistfulness or self-justification in the passage, there is no sense (such as one finds from time to time in Williams' late interviews) that he would do anything differently.[30]

At the same time, Stevens' proposal in "Adagia" that "money is a kind of poetry" (OP, 165) might be seen as a late variation on Emerson's strategy of redefinition, although a peculiar one because although Stevens' statement subversively implies that poetry is that by which money might be measured, he could not have said the coinage of poetry granted him the power he sought, a power he was not willing to relinquish.[31] Moreover, in his letters, Stevens, unlike Emerson, rarely equates the need to work like anybody else (and to achieve a certain material comfort) with the demands of his domestic life, although he did apparently tell Pound that such demands kept him from writing. Still, as mentioned, early in his life, the domestic sphere served as a preserve for Stevens, a place where he could retreat from the pressures of reality (pressures he claimed later he deliberately accepted) and be himself, as poet.[32]

However, for Stevens to be a poet only at home was in some sense to yield to his father's definition of poetry as "not serious." And, whatever else he says, Stevens' early letters about wanting a family, or about wanting, once married, to observe the social conventions, suggest that his marriage became part of the reality that put pressure on him, not the escape his early letters sometimes envision.[33] Lastly, if Stevens increasingly internalized the feminine, as Joan Richardson proposes, it was not so much, as Frank Lentricchia suggests, because Elsie felt betrayed and turned away from him once he began publishing the poems he first identified as a private offering to her, but because in his quest to internalize the feminine, Stevens ultimately, like Emerson, distanced poetry from both the world of commerce and the actual domestic world.[34] As he came to claim he was a worldly success as a lawyer by choice—a self-made man—so too his appropriation of the "feminine" world of poetry was on his own terms, and to some degree at the expense of those who might claim to be exterior paramours. The ways in which Stevens insisted on composing Elsie before their marriage (telling her what to wear) and the ways in which he arranged to keep her, physically, at a distance after their marriage, suggest again that his desire to appropriate the feminine was evident well before the failures of his marriage, and, indeed, may have played some part in those failures.[35]

This is not to deny Frank Lentricchia's suggestion that we might read Wallace Stevens as a figure of patriarchy against itself, but it is to question the repercussions of Stevens' position. For example, Lentricchia denies that Elsie Stevens' appearance on the Liberty-head dime and the walking-Liberty half-dollar has relevance in considering Stevens' relationship to the feminine.[36] Certainly, that Stevens' wife sat for the sculptor Adolph Alexander Weinman is only an accidental emblem of Stevens' relationship to his economic responsibilities as husband and father. That is, he did not force his wife to pose. But the emblem thus formed seems quite relevant to Stevens' situation. Weinman, at the time, was also the Stevenses' landlord, for one. Also, in the same period, Stevens was paying very careful attention to finances (not least, as Joan Richardson notes, in trying to furnish and improve the apartment where the couple lived).[37] Economic "Liberty," the coin, then, was graphically bound up with marriage, and with landlords. It is difficult not to believe that Stevens noticed such an emblem, albeit an ambiguous one.[38] Is the coin a sign of how artistic freedom was, for the male poet, at odds with economic liberty: Stevens might have a wife and money, but only by deliberately choosing to give up writing poetry? Or is the coin a sign of how money is a kind of poetry? Weinman himself was a sculptor who made money as a landlord. Perhaps more to the point, Elsie is transfigured into a double-sided symbol—at times a sign of the pressure and need to conform, to be a breadwinner; at other times the sign of another kind of liberty, poetic freedom, as Stevens came to embody his interior muse in the figure of a woman for whom first his mother, then Elsie, modeled. In neither case, it should be pointed out, could Elsie figure as herself, or as a flesh-and-blood paramour.

There is evidence that Stevens thought about what it meant to have his wife's image thus within and without. In 1934, Stevens was just emerging from the period of relative silence as a poet, having foregone literary efforts (and for the time, literary recognition) while he struggled with career, family, and health. Indeed, Stevens' high blood pressure diagnosed in the late twenties meant he could not buy life insurance; his health problems may have been important as much because they made him work and save to provide for his family's long-term financial security as because of his actual effects of ill health—though these were real enough—on his time and energy.[39] It is in such a setting, then, that Stevens wrote "Lions in Sweden," proclaiming he

> was once
> A hunter of those sovereigns of the soul
> And savings banks, Fides, the sculptor's prize,
> All eyes and size, and galled Justitia,
> Trained to poise the tables of the law,
> Patentia, forever soothing wounds,
> And mighty Fortitudo, frantic bass."

(CP, 124)

This may be Stevens' comment on literary lions, as well as on the quest for those "medals" and "shining baubles" that Thomas characterizes as symbols of recognition. The poem also comments on the "manly" virtues Stevens had just spent roughly a decade trying to embody (fidelity, justice—as in practicing law—patience, and fortitude). Such virtues are turned into relics, decorations found on public institutions, suggesting that Stevens' commitment to the social roles he had been playing may have been "galled."

Significantly, in light of this reading, liberty is not mentioned. And yet Stevens' image of the "sovereigns of the soul / *And* savings banks . . . the sculptor's prize" (emphasis added) recalls Elsie's profile, both within

Stevens' life and on United States coins. "Sovereigns," in the poem, rule both the soul and the banks, as coinage, as ideals, and as images of personal identity; traditional sovereigns are also, by the end of the poem, rejected for more indigenous sovereign images, as if the poem were the prelude to a personal declaration of independence. As such, the poem is one of renewal, an attractive Stevensian gesture of self-fashioning. Nonetheless, it is significant that to make such a gesture, Stevens must proclaim that if "the fault is with the soul, the sovereigns / Of the soul must likewise be at fault, and first" (*CP*, 124). This may be, as with Emerson, a rejection of (among other things) patriarchy. But it also sounds a warning to those who unwittingly serve as the models for sovereigns of the soul, especially the "poor deluded females."

Notes

1. "Sister of the Minotaur": Sexism and Stevens

1. See Randall Jarrell, "The Collected Poems of Wallace Stevens," *The Third Book of Criticism* (New York: Farrar, Straus & Giroux, 1969), 55–73; first published in the *Yale Review* 44 (March 1955): 340–53. There he says of Stevens that "there is about him, under the translucent glazes, a Dutch solidity and weight; he sits surrounded by all the good things of this earth, with rosy cheeks and fresh clear blue eyes, eyes not going out at you but shining in their place, like fixed stars" (p. 67). A similar sense of Stevens' magnanimity is found in Marianne Moore's review of *Harmonium*, "Well Moused, Lion," *Dial* 76 (January 1924): 84–91; and Harriet Monroe's review of the same volume, "A Cavalier of Beauty," *Poetry* 23, no. 6 (March 1924): 322–27.

2. See Peter Brazeau, *Parts of a World: Wallace Stevens Remembered, an Oral Biography* (New York: Random House, 1983), in which Naaman Corn says not only that "Mr. Stevens was very dominating" and that "no one dictated anything else but Mr. Stevens," but that he also caused his wife to "quit talking" by "snapping" at her whenever she spoke (p. 248). With regard to Stevens' "scripting" of Elsie, see Joan Richardson, *Wallace Stevens: The Early Years, 1879–1923* (New York: William Morrow, 1986), especially chapter 5.

3. Mark Halliday, "Stevens and Heterosexual Love," *Essays in Literature* 13 (Spring 1986): 135–55.

204 / NOTES TO PAGES 4–9

4. Milton J. Bates has handled these, and other facts about Stevens' relationship with his wife, with great tact in *Wallace Stevens: A Mythology of Self* (Berkeley: University of California Press, 1985); and "Stevens in Love: The Woman Won, the Woman Lost," *Essays in Literature* 48 (Spring 1981): 231–55.

5. This phrase is taken from Sandra M. Gilbert and Susan Gubar, *Madwoman in the Attic: The Woman Writer and the Nineteenth-Century Imagination* (New Haven: Yale University Press, 1979). See all of chapter 2, "Infection in the Sentence," for a lengthy discussion of the "ill" consequences of our largely phallocentric language (pp. 45–92).

6. With regard to Stevens' attitude toward the "High-Toned Old Christian Woman," see George Lensing's remark that "she is never permitted to present her side in the poem, though the speaker ironically pretends her to represent that side for her" ("'A High-Toned Old Christian Woman': Wallace Stevens' Parable of the Supreme Fiction," *Notre Dame English Journal* 8 [Fall 1972]: 46).

7. Edna Kenton, "German Women and Feminism," *Trend* 7, no. 2 (May 1914): 147–52. See also "War and the French Working Woman," *New Republic*, June 1, 1918, 145–47; or "War and the Woman's College," *New Republic*, July 6, 1918, 285–87.

8. Louis Sherwin, "The Land of the Hen-Pecked," *Trend* 7, no. 4 (July 1914): 437–41; Cato Major, "Rule the Women or They'll Rule You," *Trend* 1, no. 2 (May 1911): 233–34.

9. Joan Kelly, *Women, History & Theory* (Chicago: University of Chicago Press, 1984), xix; and Sandra Gilbert, "Soldier's Heart: Literary Men, Literary Women, and the Great War," *Signs* 8 (1983): 422–50.

10. The first of these by H.D. is an especially antierotic poem; the second seems essentially a poem about rape; both are printed in *Glebe* 1, no. 5 (1914); Groff's poem appears in *Others* 2, no. 1 (1916): 121–22; Pound's are in *Others* 1, no. 5 (1915): 84–85; in Cannell's "Ikons," *Others* 2, no. 2 (1916): 149, woman's sexuality essentially equals man's *value* and *violence*; finally Burke's poem, addressed to a "Virgin," essentially enacts a verbal rape, *Others* 2, no. 3 (1916): 174.

11. Helen Hoyt, *Others* 1, no. 5 (191?): 79.

12. Titled the "Woman's Number," *Others* 3, no. 3 (1916).

13. An interesting point of comparison here is William Carlos Williams' essay, "For a New Magazine," in which he says that new literature should be "the machine of women and men" (thereby not only mentioning women as authors, but putting them first). Nevertheless, he goes on to say, much like Stevens, that "poetry is thus everything that a man of the greatest power could

wish to encompass" (*Blues* 1, no. 2 [March 1929]: 30–32). Similarly, George Oppen asserts that Ezra Pound was, at least in the early years, "caught in the idea of being 'macho' though the word didn't exist at that time. He was going to be the pounding poet, the masculine poet" (Burton Hatlen and Tom Mandel, "Poetry and Politics: A Conversation with George and Mary Oppen," in *George Oppen: Man and Poet*, ed. Burton Hatlen [Orono: University of Maine, 1981], 27).

14. In this regard, see Edward Kessler, *Images of Wallace Stevens* (New York: Gordian Press, 1983), who finds that Crispin of "The Comedian as the Letter C" accepts his "masculine and feminine natures" late in the poem (p. 66), and who also argues that the androgynous nature of the "creative imagination" also informs the invocation of "Le Monocle de Mon Oncle" (p. 238 n. 15). In contrast, Frank Lentricchia interprets the possibly androgynous nature of the speaker in "Final Soliloquy of the Interior Paramour" as something much more suspect—"a self-sustaining bisexual unit" that is specifically *not* an "enhanced" individuation (*Ariel and the Police: Michel Foucault, William James, Wallace Stevens* [Madison: University of Wisconsin Press, 1988], 222–23).

15. Howard Baker, "Wallace Stevens and Other Poets," *Southern Review* 1 (Autumn 1935): 373–96. Frank Doggett and Susan Weston have both called attention to the influence of Jung on Stevens. See Doggett, *Stevens' Poetry of Thought* (Baltimore: Johns Hopkins University Press, 1966), 38–45; and Susan B. Weston, *Wallace Stevens: An Introduction to the Poetry* (New York: Columbia University Press, 1977).

16. Although Lentricchia suggests that such disturbing dislocations are largely a modernist malaise (see in particular p. 168), Kelly describes a similar pattern in the poetry of Dante: "She [Beatrice] remains shadowy and remote, for the focus of his poetry has shifted entirely to the subjective pole of love. It is the inner life, *his* inner life, that Dante objectifies" (p. 37). It may well be that such division of masculine identity, in particular the "divestment" of that which is perceived as the feminine, forms part of a larger pattern of poetic experience throughout Western history.

17. The first edition of *Ideas of Order* opened with "Sailing After Lunch," a poem that makes the possible spiritual content and intent of the first edition much more obvious. Just as the first edition (1935) was being published, however, Stevens suffered several well-known critical attacks, most of which condemned his lack of social awareness. (The most famous of these is Stanley Burnshaw's review of *Ideas of Order* in *New Masses* 17 [October 1, 1935]: 41–42.) The second edition, which begins with a new poem written after these

reviews—that is, "Farewell to Florida"—might correctly be seen as Stevens' attempt to make his poetry more socially relevant.

18. Although some critics might suggest that the speaker of this poem is a female, I believe a male is much more consistent with the rest of Stevens' verse. As an interesting parallel, consider Lentricchia's (I think) faulty analysis of Stevens' early sketch in which a young man opens a picture of his sweetheart only to find it is an image of himself as an act in which the feminine image is "empathetically assumed," not "trivialized in macho perspective" (p. 222). Despite Lentricchia's dismissal of Sandra Gilbert and Susan Gubar, I do not think that these critics would interpret this sketch in such a sympathetic way. The replacement of the female with the male image would rightly, I believe, signal an instance of total phallocentric mastery. Similarly, if the speaker of "Two Figures" *were* a female, we would have a poem of extreme empathy rather than of male mastering. Nevertheless, the latter possibility, that the female presence is silenced by masculine ruminations, seems much more consistent with the poetry of Stevens discussed thus far.

19. Thomas Walsh, *Concordance to Wallace Stevens* (University Park, Pa.: Pennsylvania State University Press, 1963). It is also interesting that, combined, forms of speaking and forms of voice appear 285 times in Stevens' corpus. Conversely, and very curiously, words for Stevens are almost never "written"—this term appears a mere 20 times, in fact.

20. "All Over Minnesota" appeared as the first section of "Primordia," published in *Soil* 1, no. 2 (January 1917): 76–78.

21. As a point of comparison for the climate of the times, see *Others: The Spectric School*, a celebrated hoax that contains a number of poems by the actually male "poetess" Elizah Hay, including "Spectrum of Mrs. X," "Of Mrs. Y," "Of Mrs. Z," and "Of Mrs. & So Forth," which intentionally parody the kinds of poems by Stevens I am discussing here. *Others* 3, no. 5 (1917): 10–11.

22. While there are many critics who have discussed "The Idea of Order at Key West" in such positive terms, see in particular, Marie Borroff, "Wallace Stevens: The World and the Poet," in *Wallace Stevens: A Collection of Critical Essays*, ed. M. Borroff (Englewood Cliffs, N.J.: Prentice-Hall, 1963), 9; and Linda Mizejewski, "Images of Woman in Wallace Stevens," *Thoth* 14 (1973–1974): 13–21.

23. I have discussed this aspect of Stevens' poetry at length in "Wallace Stevens: Poems Against His Climate," *Wallace Stevens Journal* 11, no. 2 (1987): 75–92.

24. See Lentricchia, 217.

25. In this regard, see Mary Arensberg, "'Golden Vacancies': Wallace Stevens' Problematics of Place and Presence," *Wallace Stevens Journal* 10, no. 1 (1986): 36–41, in which she discusses the usual figuration of the female in Stevens as an *absence*.

26. I am indebted to Frank Doggett and Dorothy Emerson for this observation. See "A Primer for Possibility for 'The Auroras of Autumn,'" *Wallace Stevens Journal* 13, no. 1 (1989): 53–66.

27. See Bates's *Wallace Stevens*, 277–79.

28. "Though there are poets undeniably greater than Stevens, and poets whom I love as well, he is the poet whose poems I would have written had I been the poet he was" (Helen Vendler, *Wallace Stevens: Words Chosen Out of Desire* [Knoxville: University of Tennessee Press, 1984], 3).

2. "A Curable Separation": Stevens and the Mythology of Gender

1. Bela Grunberger, *Narcissism: Psychoanalytic Essays* (New York: International University Press, 1979), 13.

2. Ibid.

3. Jamake Highwater, *Myth and Sexuality* (Ontario: New American Library Books, 1990), 51.

4. Ibid.

5. Eric Gould, *Mythical Intention in Modern Literature* (Princeton: Princeton University Press, 1981), 55.

6. Kinereth Meyer and Sharon Baris, "Reading the Score of 'Peter Quince at the Clavier': Stevens, Music and the Visual Arts," *Wallace Stevens Journal* 12, no. 1 (Spring 1988), 56–67.

7. The protean possibilities of the interior paramour may be compared with some of Camile Paglia's sexual personae in *Sexual Personae: Art and Decadence from Nefertiti to Emily Dickinson* (New Haven: Yale University Press, 1990).

8. Meyer and Baris, "Reading 'Peter Quince at the Clavier,'" 61.

9. "Self-object" is used here in the sense of the late Heinz Kohut whose psychoanalytic school of "self psychology" uses the term to refer to an object outside the construct of self that mirrors and confirms the ego structure.

10. For a discussion of female genitalia and concealment, see Paglia's *Sexual Personae*.

3. A Woman with the Hair of a Pythoness

1. Michel Benamou, "Art, Music, Angels and Sex: A Note on the Shorter Poems of *Auroras of Autumn*," *Wallace Stevens Journal* 2 (Spring 1978): 3–9.

2. Edward Kessler, *Images of Wallace Stevens* (New Brunswick: Rutgers University Press, 1972), 16–17.

3. Ibid., 22.

4. A. Walton Litz, *Introspective Voyager: The Poetic Development of Wallace Stevens* (New York: Oxford University Press, 1972), 118.

5. See Holly Stevens' reference to her mother's hair in "Holidays in Reality" in *Wallace Stevens: A Celebration*, ed. Frank Doggett and Robert Buttel (Princeton: Princeton University Press, 1980), 105–6.

6. Harold Bloom, *Wallace Stevens: The Poems of Our Climate* (Ithaca: Cornell University Press, 1977), 45–46.

7. Stevens' figure of the "abstract, the archaic queen" as the embodiment of a cognitive principle has antecedents in the history of Western thought. To find the intellective principle in female form, however, one must travel by way of Christian Platonism to the *Noys* (Mind) of Bernard Silvestris in the 12th century, and to the Nous of Plotinus in the 3rd, noting Plotinus's exposition of the nature of Aphrodite Ouranos. In the classical period, one notes the continuity of Plato's Diotima in the *Symposium* with a pre-Socratic intellective principle: Parmenides's Goddess of Truth in the poem to "The Way of Truth." One should also consider the figure of the Divine Tetractys in this context, the holy triangle that formed the core of Pythagorean mystical mathematics. See George Economou, *The Goddess Natura in Medieval Literature* (Cambridge: Harvard University Press, 1972), 152; see also Ernst Robert Curtius, *European Literature and the Latin Middle Ages*, trans. Willard R. Trask (Princeton: Princeton University Press, 1953), 108–11; and Theodore Silverstein, "The Fabulous Cosmogony of Bernardus Silvestris," *Modern Philology* 66 (1948): 95–98.

8. C. G. Jung, "The Syzygy: Anima and Animus," in *Aion: Researches into the Phenomenology of the Self*, vol. 9, pt. 2 of *The Collected Works of C. G. Jung* (Princeton: Princeton University Press, 1968), 12–13.

9. Ibid., 14.

10. Jung, *Collected Works*, 17:198.

11. Mary Arensberg, "Wallace Stevens' Interior Paramour," *Wallace Stevens Journal* 3 (Spring 1979): 3–7.

12. Ibid. The reference is to Michael Beehler's "Meteoric Poetry: Wallace Stevens' 'Description without Place,'" *Criticism* 29 (1977): 241–59.

13. Ibid.

14. Bloom, *Wallace Stevens*, 110–11.

15. See John Hollander, *The Figure of Echo: A Mode of Allusion in Milton and After* (Berkeley and Los Angeles: University of California Press, 1981), 98. See also Angus Fletcher's discussion of the acoustical principle of echo in *The Transcendental Masque: An Essay on Milton's Comus* (Ithaca: Cornell University Press, 1971), 198–99.

4. Imaginary Politics: Emerson, Stevens, and the Resistance of Style

1. Richard Poirier, ed., *Ralph Waldo Emerson* (New York: Oxford University Press, 1991), 92.

2. Ibid., 90.

3. Ibid.

4. Ibid.

5. Joel Porte, ed., *Emerson: Essays and Lectures* (New York: Library of America, 1982), 310.

6. Although it is clear that Emerson derived much inspiration from the German romantic writers and thinkers, including Hegel, he seems to have derived even more from their English mediators, Coleridge and Carlyle. In Michael Lopez, "Transcendental Failure: 'The Palace of Spiritual Power,'" in Joel Porte, ed., *Emerson: Prospect and Retrospect, Harvard English Studies* (Cambridge: Harvard University Press, 1982), 121–54, Lopez makes some instructive comparisons especially between Emerson and Carlyle on the question of vocation and doing one's own work. Emerson, unlike Carlyle, never identifies the power with which one is to move along as anything other than this unique (yet plural) and publicly active self. Carlyle, however, identifies power with, for example, the age's increasingly secular form of Puritanism that "can steer ships, fell forests, remove mountains;—it is one of the strongest things under the sun at present" (p. 133). Stanley Cavell says in *Conditions Handsome and Unhandsome: An Essay on the Constitution of Emersonian Perfectionism* (Chicago: University of Chicago Press, 1990) that Emerson's interest is in the ultimate perfection of spontaneity and creative power in each entity of the whole. Car-

lyle's more immediately opportune interest is in the currently steering worldly power. In "Aversive Thinking: Emersonian Representations in Heidegger and Nietzsche" (pp. 33–63), Cavell characterizes the reading relation in Emerson as the uncanny transference relation of an attained to an unattained possibility of oneself on the traditional philosophic model of the pedagogic pair of friends. I would argue that this secularization and internalization of the ontological and empirical dimensions of the subject, when radically democratized by modern higher education and mass media culture, takes the postmodern form of the narcissistic personality structure of grandiose ego ideal and wounded ego. Where I differ with Cavell is on the question of "moral perfectionism" in Emerson. To speak exclusively in this fashion of Emerson is to harken back to the ascetic tradition of working on the self that, through the hedonic overtones of "the vocation of abandonment," I believe Emerson begins to leave behind. For a related sense of "abandonment" in Emerson, see Cavell's "Thinking of Emerson," in *The Senses of Walden* (San Francisco: North Point Press, 1980). For a different critical sense of Emerson, see Donald E. Pease, *Visionary Compacts: American Renaissance Writings in Cultural Context* (Madison: University of Wisconsin Press, 1987), 203–34.

7. See, for example, the still-excellent discussion of Emerson in his time in O. W. Firkins, *Ralph Waldo Emerson* (Boston and New York: Houghton Mifflin Co., 1915).

8. I have chosen "The Over-Soul," rather than "Self-Reliance," precisely because I think it partakes more immediately of its time with its transcendental religiosity. But even "Self-Reliance," an antithetical complement to "The Over-Soul" in *Essays: First Series*, ironically undoes the elaborate structure of self-trust it has erected in the climactic passage on "Aboriginal Power" that makes all mere talk of "self-reliance" nothing but prattle. This self-subverting irony thus prepares the ground for the later move to the major message of "The Over-Soul," that the self is plural, even if we wanted to question many of the terms in which its plurality is discussed.

9. Porte, *Emerson: Essays and Lectures*, 388.

10. Ralph Waldo Emerson, "Poetry and Imagination," in Richard Poirier, ed., *Ralph Waldo Emerson: Oxford Authors* (New York: Oxford University Press, 1990), 448.

11. Porte, *Emerson: Essays and Lectures*, 396.

12. Emerson, "Quotation and Originality," in Richard Poirier, ed., *Ralph Waldo Emerson*, 436.

13. Porte, *Emerson: Essays and Lectures*, 400.

14. Ibid., 155.

15. Ibid., 128.

16. Peter Collier and Helga Geyer-Ryan, eds., *Literary Theory Today* (Ithaca: Cornell University Press, 1990), 167–76.

17. Ibid., 168.

18. Ibid.

19. Ibid.

20. Eleanor Cook, *Poetry, Word-Play, and Word-War in Wallace Stevens* (Princeton: Princeton University Press, 1988), 99.

21. Barbara Fisher, *Wallace Stevens: The Intensest Rendezvous* (Charlottes-ville: University of Virginia Press, 1990), 152.

22. Julia Kristeva, *Black Sun: Depression and Melancholia*, trans. Leon S. Rondrey (New York: Columbia University Press, 1989), 14.

23. As cited and discussed in Daniel T. O'Hara, "Lava-Writing: A Status Report on Stevens and Feminism, 1988" in "Stevens and Women," *Wallace Stevens Journal*, special guest ed. Melita Schaum, 12, no. 2 (Fall 1988), 173–80.

5. The Fat Girl in Paradise:
Stevens, Wordsworth, Milton, and the Proper Name

1. For Stevens' understanding of "decreation," which he opposes to "destruc-tion," see *NA*, 174–75. For a suggestive reading of Stevens as the author of a "decreative" Genesis and a "recreated" Apocalypse, see Eleanor Cook, "The Decreations of Wallace Stevens," *Wallace Stevens Journal* 4, no. 3/4 (Fall 1980): 46–57.

2. Jacques Derrida, *De la grammatologie* (Paris: Minuit, 1967), 156–57.

3. Frank Lentricchia, *After the New Criticism* (Chicago: University of Chi-cago Press, 1980), 32.

4. Derrida, *De la grammatologie*, 165.

5. Jacques Derrida, *Of Grammatology*, trans. Gayatri Chakravorty Spivak (Baltimore: Johns Hopkins University Press, 1976), 112.

6. Jacques Derrida, "White Mythology," in *Margins of Philosophy*, trans. Alan Bass (Chicago: University of Chicago Press, 1982), 251.

7. William Wordsworth, *The Prelude* (1850), in *The Prelude: 1799, 1805, 1850*, ed. Jonathan Wordsworth et al. (New York: Norton, 1979), bk. II, lines 269, 316–19. Unless otherwise specified, all quotations in this chapter are from the poem of 1850.

8. On the traditional association of the feminine with the specular, see Luce Irigaray, *Speculum, de l'autre femme* (Paris: Minuit, 1974). On Eve as a figure for the dangers of figuration, see Patricia A. Parker, *Inescapable Romance: Studies in the Poetics of a Mode* (Princeton: Princeton University Press, 1979), 114–23; also, Christine Froula, "When Eve Reads Milton: Undoing the Canonical Economy," *Critical Inquiry* 10 (December 1983): 321–47. For a suggestive reading of the association of the feminine with the material or literal in nineteenth-century fiction, to which this chapter is much indebted, see Margaret Homans, *Bearing the Word: Language and Female Experience in Nineteenth-Century Women's Writing* (Chicago: University of Chicago Press, 1986).

9. Frank Lentricchia, *Ariel and the Police, Michel Foucault, William James, Wallace Stevens* (Madison: University of Wisconsin Press, 1988), 227.

10. "Pleasure," Roland Barthes notes: No sooner is the word said—somewhere, by someone—than two "policemen," the political and the psychoanalytic, are ready to jump. Roland Barthes, *The Pleasure of the Text*, trans. Richard Miller (New York: Hill and Wang, 1975), 57. For Stevens, the former went by the name of Stanley Burnshaw (before Lentricchia, whose argument he more or less anticipates), the author of an attack on the first edition of *Ideas of Order:* "But nobody stopped to ask if he had any ideas. It was tacitly assumed that one read him for pure poetic sensation; if he had 'a message' it was carefully buried and would take no end of labor to exhume" (Stanley Burnshaw, "Turmoil in the Middle Ground," *New Masses* 17 [October 1935], as quoted in *Wallace Stevens: A Critical Anthology*, ed. Irvin Ehrenpreis [Harmondsworth: Penguin Books, 1972], 100). Stevens responded to Burnshaw's review with "Owl's Clover," a poem he considered calling "Aphorisms on Society." Bloom aptly characterizes it as Stevens' "largest failure," which suggests that the political muse was something of siren for the poet of "It Must Give Pleasure." Bloom, no less aptly, argues that Stevens was incapable of forming any social vision less archaic than the one he inherited from his family and his class (Harold Bloom, *Wallace Stevens: The Poems of Our Climate* [Ithaca: Cornell University Press, 1977], 113, 118). Certainly lines such as "The employer and employee contend, / Combat, compose their droll affair" (*CP*, 182) betray virtually all there is to be had of Stevens' political ideas. But to belabor the point that Stevens is not a progressive political thinker is to shoot fish in a barrel and betrays one's own political irrelevance: "It is increasingly clear in today's world (if it had ever been in doubt) that a Left which cannot grasp the immense Utopian appeal of nationalism (any more than it can grasp that of religion or of fascism) can scarcely hope to 'reappropriate' such collective energies and must effectively doom itself

to political impotence" (Fredric Jameson, *The Political Unconscious: Narrative as a Socially Symbolic Act* [Ithaca: Cornell University Press, 1981], 298). Jameson's sense of the utopian appeal of religion and fascism, to which Eliot and Pound stand as testimony, might be extended to include pleasure. Not that pleasure can or should be "reappropriated" in the manner suggested above. Nor will the revolution come about through an improvement in sensual enjoyment. But the former will be accompanied by the latter—for Marx, the end of capitalist property relations will herald the advent of sensuous consciousness—and "Notes" is to be taken as Utopian figuration of the same.

11. Eugene Vance, "Chaucer's *House of Fame* and the Poetics of Inflation," *boundary 2* 7 (Winter 1979): 19. Vance is discussing a much earlier "economy" that (I would argue) culminates in romanticism.

12. Ralph Waldo Emerson, "Nature," in vol. 5 of *The Complete Works of Ralph Waldo Emerson* (Cambridge: Riverside Press, 1903), 3.

13. Emerson, "Self-Reliance," in vol. 2 of *The Complete Works*, 68.

14. John Milton, "Ad Patrem," in *John Milton: Complete Poems and Major Prose*, ed. Merritt Y. Hughes (New York: Odyssey Press, 1957), 64–66. In English: "Phoebus himself, wishing to part himself between us, gave some gifts to me and others to my father; and, father and son, we share the possession of the divided god."

15. William Wordsworth and Samuel Taylor Coleridge, *Lyrical Ballads*, 2nd ed., ed. W. J. B. Owen (Oxford: Oxford University Press, 1969), 162.

16. Friedrich Nietzsche, *On the Advantage and Disadvantage of History for Life*, trans. Peter Preuss (Indianapolis: Hackett Publishing, 1980), 11–12.

17. Sigmund Freud, *Moses and Monotheism*, trans. Katherine Jones (New York: Vintage Books, 1958), 156.

18. Luce Irigaray, *Le Corps-à-corps avec la mère* (Ottawa: Pleine Lune, 1981), 15–16.

19. Aeschylus, "The Eumenides," in *Oresteia*, trans. Richard Lattimore (Chicago: University of Chicago Press, 1953), 658–60.

20. Irigaray, *Le Corps-à-corps*, 17.

21. Strictly speaking, the immaculate conception refers to the virgin birth of Mary rather than Christ. I have, however, deliberately misused the term, or used in its popular rather than theological sense. My reason for doing so is perhaps obvious: the popular misuse of the term, which effaces Mary, replicates the effacement of the maternal (the body of Anne) that is the theological meaning of the term.

22. Aeschylus, "The Eumenides," 1–8.

23. Freud, *Moses and Monotheism*, 144–45.

24. Aeschylus, "The Eumenides," 278–79.

25. Biblical scholars disagree about both the strength of the etymological connection that binds *tehom* to Tiamat and the extent to which Genesis depends on the Mesopotamian text. E. A. Speiser, for example, places Genesis in an allusive and systematically critical relation to *Enūma eliš* (E. A. Speiser, *Genesis: The Anchor Bible* [Garden City: Doubleday, 1964]). Cassuto, on the other hand, minimizes the dependence of the former on the latter (Umberto Cassuto, *A Commentary on the Book of Genesis*, pt. 1, trans. Israel Abrahams [Jerusalem: Magnes Press, 1961]). For a helpful survey of the relevant scholarship and a suggestive reading of Milton's reading of Genesis, see Mary Nyquist, "Gynesis, Genesis, Exegesis, and Milton's Eve," in *Cannibals, Witches, and Divorce: Estranging the Renaissance*, ed. Marjorie Garber (Baltimore: Johns Hopkins University Press, 1987), 147–208. It seems to me that Nyquist is right in discussing the difference in scholarly opinion as an essentially ideological dispute: commentators such as Cassuto, for example, are anxious to avoid any suggestion that our most canonical myth of origins is in fact derivative or secondary. This is, however, precisely the suggestion of the opening movement of "Notes."

26. Derrida, *Of Grammatology*, 107.

27. Lentricchia, *Ariel and the Police*, 227.

28. Louis Althusser, *Pour Marx* (Paris: Maspero, 1965), 203–4; trans. Ben Brewster as *For Marx* (New York: Pantheon Books, 1969), 198–99.

29. Geoffrey Hartman, *Saving the Text: Literature, Derrida, Philosophy* (Baltimore: Johns Hopkins University Press, 1981), 16.

30. See Edward Said's distinction between beginning and origin: "I use the word *beginning* as having the more active meaning, and *origin* the more passive one: thus 'X *is the origin of* Y,' while 'The beginning A *leads to* B.' In due course I hope to show, however, how ideas about origins, because of their passivity, are put to uses I believe ought to be avoided." *Beginnings: Intention and Method* (Baltimore and London: Johns Hopkins University Press, 1975), 6. In Said's terms, my argument might be rephrased as follows: "It Must Be Abstract" implicitly argues that there never has been, never can be, an origin, although for ideological reasons, which include, of course, sexual politics, beginnings tend to be transformed into origins. Stevens' poem, I argue, reverses this process.

31. Lentricchia, *Ariel and the Police*, 225–26.

32. Karl Marx, "Private Property and Communism," in *Early Writings*, trans. T. B. Bottomore (New York: McGraw-Hill, 1963), 160, 30.

33. Milton, *Paradise Lost*, bk. IV, lines 467–73.

34. On the history and etymology of the name "Phoebus," see Marcel Detienne, "Apollo's Slaughterhouse," *Diacritics* 2 (Summer 1986): 46–53.

35. Plutarch, "De E apud Delphos," 20 393c, in vol. 5 of *Moralia*, trans. Frank Cole Babbit (Cambridge: William Heinemann, 1969).

36. Derrida, *Of Grammatology*, 71.

37. Plato, *Sophist*, in *The Collected Dialogues*, trans. Edith Hamilton and Huntington Cairns (Princeton: Princeton University Press, 1961), 1002.

38. I accept Bloom's contention that the "you" does not refer, or does not only refer, to Henry Church, to whom "Notes" is dedicated; Bloom, *Wallace Stevens*, 167.

39. On "differentiated from" as a possible translation of the phrase the King James Bible renders as "taken out from," see Phyllis Trible, *God and the Rhetoric of Sexuality* (Philadelphia: Fortress Press, 1978), 100–101.

40. Milton, *Paradise Lost*, bk. V, lines 483–95.

41. Wordsworth, *The Prelude* (1850), bk. XIV, lines 86–99.

42. Milton, *Paradise Lost*, bk. V, lines 510–12.

43. Wordsworth, *The Prelude* (1799) first part, lines 308–13.

44. Cynthia Chase, "The Accidents of Disfiguration: Limits to Literal and Rhetorical Reading in Book V of *The Prelude*," *Studies in Romanticism* (Winter 1979), 553–54. My reading of the gender determinants of this passage and their relation to Lacanian poetics is very much indebted to Homans, *Bearing the Word*, 45–48 et passim.

45. Wordsworth, *The Prelude* (1850), bk. XII, lines 238–45.

46. Ibid., bk. II, lines 238–44.

47. Ibid., lines 276–78.

48. Jacques Lacan, *Ecrits: A Selection*, trans. Alan Sheridan (New York: W. W. Norton, 1977), 851–54.

49. Jacques Lacan, *Le Seminaire Livre XX: Encore* (Paris: Seuil, 1975), 68.

50. Harold Bloom, "The Anxiety of Influence," in *New Perspectives on Coleridge and Wordsworth*, ed. Geoffrey Hartman (New York: Columbia University Press, 1972), 267.

51. Milton, *Paradise Lost*, bk. IV, lines 32–39.

52. See C. A. Patrides, "The Godhead in *Paradise Lost:* Dogma or Drama?" in *Bright Essence: Studies in Milton's Theology*, ed. W. B. Hunter et al. (Salt

Lake City: University of Utah Press, 1973), 74–75; also, John Guillory, *Poetic Authority: Spenser, Milton, and Literary History* (New York: Columbia University Press, 1983), 115–16.

53. Patrides, "The Godhead in *Paradise Lost,*" 75.

54. Milton, "The Christian Doctrine," bk. I, 5.

55. Milton, *Paradise Lost,* bk. VII, lines 1–5.

56. Guillory, *Poetic Authority,* 123.

57. Milton, "The Second Defense of the English People," 834.

58. Michel Foucault, *The Order of Things: An Archaeology of the Human Sciences* (New York: Random House, 1970), 117–18.

59. Walter Benjamin, *The Origin of German Tragic Drama,* trans. John Osborne (London: New Left Books, 1977), 224–25.

60. Milton, *Paradise Lost,* bk. IX, line 1067; bk. XI, lines 632–33.

61. Northrop Frye, *A Study of English Romanticism* (New York: Random House, 1968), 140.

6. **Wallace Stevens:** The Concealed Self

1. Helen Vendler, *Wallace Stevens: Words Chosen Out of Desire* (Cambridge: Harvard University Press, 1986), ch. 3.

2. See Milton J. Bates, *Wallace Stevens: A Mythology of Self* (Berkeley: University of California Press, 1985).

3. Both critics are fundamentally at odds with Joan Richardson's recent attempt at psycho-biography (see *Wallace Stevens: The Early Years, 1879–1923* [New York: William Morrow, 1986]). Vendler fiercely attacks it in the *New York Review of Books,* November 20, 1986, 42–47, while Bates keeps his distance, praising it where he can, but not really sympathizing with Richardson's approach (see the *Wallace Stevens Journal* 10 [Fall 1986]: 113–16). I found the biography a chore to work through because it is not well written and is overly long. Its insensitivities and heavy-handedness are bound to give applied psychoanalysis another black eye. But there is much gold in the forbidding landscape, much to learn about the unconscious dimension of Stevens' life and art. Yet one must work at it and be very selective. The recently published second volume of Richardson's biography is better written but less insightful than the first, and particularly inadequate in its over-all judgment of Stevens' life (see *Wallace Stevens: The Later Years, 1923–1955* [New York: William Mor-

row, 1988]). My own review of this volume may be found in *the Wallace Stevens Journal* 13 (Spring 1989): 74–76.

4. See Peter Brazeau, *Parts of a World: Wallace Stevens Remembered, an Oral Biography* (New York: Random House, 1983), 294–96.

5. For Bates's remarks on the conversion, see *Wallace Stevens*, 208, 296–97.

6. Vendler, *New York Review*, 43.

7. C. Roland Wagner, "A Central Poetry," in *Wallace Stevens: A Collection of Critical Essays*, ed. Marie Borroff (New Jersey: Prentice-Hall, 1963), 73.

8. See Harold Bloom, *Wallace Stevens: The Poems of Our Climate* (Ithaca: Cornell University Press, 1977), 28, 45–46.

9. Adelaide Kirby Morris's valuable study, *Wallace Stevens: Imagination and Faith* (Princeton: Princeton University Press, 1974), discusses the enormous number of Christian symbols in Stevens' work. She comes close to seeing Stevens as a latent Christian. She cites James Benzinger as explicitly affirming Stevens to be a believer (pp. 113–15).

10. See Morris, *Wallace Stevens*, 10–11.

11. A few days after Stevens married, he and his wife sent a picture postcard to his parents displaying the Chapel of the Good Shepherd at General Theological Seminary, Chelsea Square, which was near their apartment on West Twenty-first Street. Stevens' message was, "Our floor is next to the top. Therefore we face the chapel, which is only across the street. Chimes every evening. We are not a part of the chapel—but apart from it. Hence, the word apartment. Hope this is clear" (*SP*, 246). The poem "Less and Less Human" was written about thirty-five years later.

12. See Vendler, *Wallace Stevens: Words Chosen Out of Desire*, 32.

13. See Vendler, *New York Review*, 42.

14. Quoted in Richardson, *Early Years*, 289.

15. Brazeau, *Parts of a World*, 30 and n.

16. See Phyllis Greenacre, M.D., *The Quest for the Father* (New York: International Universities Press, 1963), 16. Although Greenacre judges that the "diminished firmness of the barrier between prrimary-process and secondary-process thinking" is part of the normal character structure of the artist, she sees a danger in this and in the strong element of orality and passivity in the artist's character (p. 22).

17. Brazeau, *Parts of a World*, 211.

18. Ibid., 167–68. Richardson, *Early Years*, aptly describes Stevens' avoidance of dialogue as "the impossibility of truly *speaking* his mind." She writes

that he "either yielded wholly to the one who 'always [had] reason on his side [his father]' . . . or he totally ignored that voice instead of attempting to engage it in open dialogue" (p. 355). But Richardson dissipates the force of these insights by failing to apply them to Stevens' work as a whole. For example, she naively writes of "the fluent ease Stevens developed in integrating even the most complex philosophical and scientific ideas into his poetry" (p. 43). The fact is that although Stevens shows a profound feeling for certain of the problems of epistemology ("our knowledge of the external world") and phenomenology, his philosophical, even his ordinary analytical abilities are quite limited. And this limitation is particularly evident in those areas that encroach on primal experience, the pursuit of the ultimate object.

19. See Bates, *Wallace Stevens*, 49–82.

20. Ibid., 75–77.

21. Ibid., 80–81.

22. Ibid., 65.

23. Ibid., 67.

24. See Richardson, *Early Years*, 450–51.

25. Ibid., 318–19.

26. Ibid., 71. See also Brazeau, *Parts of a World*, 10.

27. Richardson, *Early Years*, 441.

28. Ibid., 392.

29. Bloom, *Wallace Stevens*, 45–46. Bloom does not place any special emphasis on the pre-Oedipal as distinct from the Oedipal mother. But the imagery of the face and other oral images in Stevens' poetry, as well as his intense mystical yearnings, suggest the importance of the pre-Oedipal object in his unconscious.

30. Bates, *Wallace Stevens*, 82.

31. The English word "foyer" is derived from the French word for fireplace or hearth. It once referred to the room to which theater audiences went for warmth between the acts.

32. Cf. Vendler in her discussion about "Of Mere Being" says, "There is something in [the desired world of the higher or theoretical senses, eye and ear] for seeing and hearing alike, though not for those 'lower' senses, taste and touch" (*Wallace Stevens: Words Chosen Out of Desire*, 42).

33. See Otto Fenichel, *The Psychoanalytic Theory of Neurosis* (New York: Norton, 1945), 330. See also Géza Róheim, "Aphrodite, or the Woman With a Penis," in *The Panic of the Gods and Other Essays*, ed. W. Muensterberger (New York: Harper, 1972), 169–205. Róheim writes that the statue of Aphrodite "on Cyprus is bearded, but wears a woman's dress, holds a scepter, and has a

masculine build" (p. 169). Another form of the phallic mother in the Western tradition is the witch (p. 179) and "Serbian witches have a beard" (p. 180). In light of what has been said (and will be said below) about Stevens' relationship with his wife, it is interesting that Róheim states that, according to sixteenth century writers, "One natural function interfered with by the witch is coitus— but never eating" (p. 187).

34. Frank Doggett, in *Stevens' Poetry of Thought* (Baltimore: Johns Hopkins University Press, 1966), 42, does not separate the earth mother from the "bearded queen." Madame La Fleurie is not only *linked with* the bearded queen, for Doggett she *is* the queen. Although I think Doggett's analysis is incorrect—the grammar alone of the last two lines makes this reading un- likely—it does support my sense of the fluidity of Stevens' mother image and its two-sided character. Doggett argues that there is "an accentuation of the ani- mus, the male element, latent and hidden within the woman now emerging in the beard of Madame La Fleurie and in the innate 'animosity' of this image (the pun is from Jung)." What Doggett most loses is the initial distinction between bad (real) wife and good (mythical) mother.

35. See Brazeau, *Parts of a World*, 133, 187.

36. Ibid., 21, 250.

37. Ibid., 246.

38. Ibid., 238.

39. Ibid., 276.

40. Richardson writes that, on the eve of his marriage, apart from travel fantasies, books, and work, Stevens' "most important" concern was his stomach. "He repeated his culinary orders to Elsie so many times that she finally made him promise neither to speak of 'grub' again when they were together nor to mention it in his letters." He apologized but explained that "ever since he had been at college, the thought of being home had always been associated with food" (*Early Years*, 356). Richardson has much to report about Stevens' passion for desserts.

41. Bates, *Wallace Stevens*, 276.

42. Cf. William Pritchard, "Poet of the Academy," *Southern Review* (Autumn 1979), 851–76. See especially p. 865.

43. Lucy Beckett, in *Wallace Stevens* (Cambridge: Cambridge University Press, 1974), 193, argues that the sense of religious, not merely human other- ness, lies at the heart of the poem. I disagree, but it may be so.

44. See Doggett, *Stevens' Poetry of Thought*, 172 n.3.

45. See Beckett, *Wallace Stevens*, 199.

46. Brazeau, *Parts of a World*, 213.

47. Bates, *Wallace Stevens*, 292.

7. Getting Wisdom: The "Rabbi's" Devotion to *Weisheit* and its Implications for Feminists

1. In 1936, Stevens said, in a set of sentences that are surely "autobiographical in spite of [the] subterfuge" (*NA*, 121), "We have a sense of upheaval. We feel threatened. We look from an uncertain present toward a more uncertain future" (*OP*, 225). A. Walton Litz comments that Stevens' response to the critics of "Owl's Clover" reveals "a man off balance" (*Introspective Voyager: The Poetic Development of Wallace Stevens* [New York: Oxford University Press, 1972], 205–6). Joseph N. Riddel and Samuel French Morse see the poet exposed in what Riddel calls, "a crisis, not only of craft but of self" (*The Clairvoyant Eye* [Baton Rouge: Louisiana State University Press, 1965], 123; Samuel French Morse, *Poetry as Life* [New York: Pegasus, 1970], 149). Harold Bloom makes similar comments in *Wallace Stevens: The Poems of Our Climate* (Ithaca: Cornell University Press, 1977), 88–89, 113.

2. Stevens complained of "periods of moodiness" (*SP*, 146–47). "The Domination of Black," "The Region November" and "Madame La Fleurie" attest to the life-long recurrence of feeling states Stevens described as being "in the Black Hole again" (*SP*, 128).

3. Leonora Woodman's *Stanza My Stone: Wallace Stevens and the Hermetic Tradition* (West Lafayette, Ind.: Purdue University Press, 1983) is an important study of Stevens' indebtedness to spiritual alchemy. Woodman focuses on the determining influence of a belief system rather than on the role of the artist, or on the complex dynamic of Stevens' psychological attachments.

4. Stevens characterized the Zeller family of Tulpehocken, Pennsylvania, as "this family of religious refugees" amd dates their arrival in the New World as 1709 (*NA*, 99). He then ascribes to them the path historians say the Palatinate refugees followed from the Schoharie region in New York to Pennsylvania. He stressed that "on my mother's side, I am Pennsylvania Dutch," when explaining to Victor Hammer about the photo of George Zeller's gravestone from which he wanted a bookplate made (*L*, 541). To one of his genealogists he explained that the Zellers "were consecrated to the glory of God. These people, whatever else they were, were fanatics" (*L*, 534). His father's family did not seem to him "like a family of farmers," however. "While I knew of the Dutch names in the

background," Stevens explained, "the impression [his father's people] made was an English impression and not a Dutch impression" (*L,* 405). Stevens used the terms "Pennsylvania Dutch" and "Pennsylvania German" interchangeably. Stevens wrote that he "used to think [he] got [his] practical side from [his] father, and [his] imagination from [his] mother" (*SP,* 8).

5. A number of critics have pointed out the androgyneity of Stevens' creative self and of his approach to metaphor. Of the numerous "betrothals" and "marriages" some clearly refer to a figurative strategy. Others, as in "Artificial Populations" (*OP,* 112–13), refer to a psychic condition: "a healing-point in the sickness of the mind." I argue that Stevens' goddess is both maternal and bridal.

6. During the 1940s, Stevens steeped himself in regional histories. His letters suggest that he found Julius Frederick Sachse's two-volume study an important source (*The German Pietists of Provincial Pennsylvania: 1694–1748* [Philadelphia: Printed for the author, 1895 and 1900], and *The German Sectarians of Provincial Pennsylvania: 1708–1800* [Philadelphia: Printed for the author, 1895 and 1900]). References to these volumes are found in Stevens' bluebooks, the Wallace Stevens Collection, box 77(4), Huntington Library, California. Stevens was a regular reader of the *Pennsylvania Magazine.* One article that interested him particularly was Oswald Seidensticker's "The Hermits of the Wissahickon" (1887), 427–41. Woodman, *Stanza My Stone,* provides an introduction to the religious groups in Colonial Pennsylvania and to their uses of Hermetic doctrine (pp. 155–60). My reading of the Pennsylvania sources suggests a greater reliance on the work of Jacob Boehme than Woodman reports. Dennis Barone briefly describes the lifelong significance to Stevens of his mother's Pennsylvania German heritage in "Journey Home: Pennsylvania German Ethnicity in Wallace Stevens," *Pennsylvania Folklife* 36 (1986–87): 90–94.

7. Catherine F. Smith, "Jane Lead: The Feminist Mind and Art of a Seventeenth Century Protestant Mystic," in *Women of Spirit: Female Leadership in the Jewish and Christian Traditions,* ed. Rosemary Reuther and Eleanor McLaughlin (New York: Simon and Schuster, 1979), ch. 6, 187. This essay gives a concise summary of Behmenism.

8. I am presently reworking a book-length study of Stevens' use of his family past, tentatively titled "His Mother's House: Colonial German Pennsylvania in the Work of Wallace Stevens."

9. The universal creative process, according to Boehme, is a sexual one, involving an ongoing movement toward union and then separation, toward creation and then decreation. In one place in this dialectical process, the Sophia is Logos/Christ/God's utterance, an aspect of Him, and thus in a sense masculine

in Her attributes. In another, she is God's opposite—earthly, female, and of the body. With the phrase "androgynous process," I would like to suggest that at times the masculine principle that both Stevens and Boehme called the "No," dominates, and at other times the feminine principle that both called the "Yes," dominates. Woodman, *Stanza My Stone*, discusses Stevens' uses of the tradition of the hermetic dyad. See especially chapter 6, pp. 86–103.

10. Helen Vendler, *On Extended Wings: Wallace Stevens' Longer Poems* (Cambridge: Harvard University Press, 1969), 16–18, 32, and passim.

11. Helen Vendler, *Wallace Stevens: Words Chosen Out of Desire* (Cambridge: Harvard University Press, 1986), 6, 80. Vendler argues for the "tethering" of Stevens' poems to "human feeling," a position with which I agree. But Stevens' feelings did not, in my view, simply occur in response to "life occasions"; they were in him from the start. To be sure, the "real" was the "base of the design," but for Stevens, after age sixty, the "real" was a complex amalgam of worlds, not least of which was the one he was born with and into.

12. Hugh Kenner, *The Pound Era* (Berkeley: University of California Press, 1971), 507.

13. Stevens' quotation of a description of "the local Christian minority" by the pietist Justus Falkner of Germantown and his applause for their attitudes is recorded in his bluebook, the Wallace Stevens Collection, box 77(4), Huntington Library.

14. Smith, Ibid., 89.

15. John Joseph Stoudt, *Sunrise to Eternity* (Pittsburgh: Pennsylvania University Press, 1957), 140. This volume provides a readable account of the essential points of Behmenism. Stevens knew some of Stoudt's other work on Pennsylvania German folklore.

16. For a general introduction to Wisdom, see Virginia R. Mollenkott, *The Divine Feminine: The Biblical Imagery of God as Female* (New York: Crossroad, 1985), especially chapter 17: "God as Dame Wisdom," 97–105. Also useful is Northrop Frye, *The Great Code: The Bible and Literature* (New York: Harcourt Brace Jovanovich, 1981), 121–29. The Wisdom books of the Bible are Proverbs, Ecclesiastes, and Job, and to a lesser extent, Psalms and Canticles. In the Apocrypha the Wisdom books are Ecclesiasticus and the Wisdom of Solomon. These books are often referred to as the "poetical books" of the Bible.

17. Edwin M. Fogel, "Proverbs of the Pennsylvania German," *Pennsylvania German Society Proceedings* 36 (1929): 1–221.

18. In *Anne Bradstreet Revisited* (Boston: G. K. Hall, 1991), I argue that Bradstreet made extensive use of the Wisdom tradition, with a heavier reliance

on alchemy and other Renaissance sciences than has been reported heretofore. She, and a small group of friends and associates, differed in this regard from others in the Commonwealth.

8. Aesthetics and Politics: Marianne Moore's Reading of Stevens

1. See Celeste Goodridge, *Hints and Disguises: Marianne Moore and her Contemporaries* (Iowa City: University of Iowa Press, 1989).

2. Marianne Moore, *The Complete Prose of Marianne Moore*, ed. Patricia C. Willis (New York: Viking Press, 1986), 91.

3. Cf. Stevens' "Jacket Statement from *Ideas of Order*":

> We think of changes occurring today as economic changes, involving political and social changes. Such changes raise questions of political and social order.
> While it is inevitable that a poet should be concerned with such questions, this book, although it reflects them, is primarily concerned with ideas of order of a different nature, as, for example, the dependence of the individual, confronting the elimination of established ideas, on the general sense of order; the idea of order created by individual concepts, as of the poet, in "The Idea of Order at Key West"; the idea of order arising from the practice of any art, as of poetry in "Sailing after Lunch." (*OP89*, 222–23)

4. Moore, *Complete Prose*, 94.

5. Marianne Moore to Wallace Stevens, October 29, 1936, Rosenbach Museum and Library, Philadelphia, Pa., V:63:22, T.L.C.

6. This unpublished letter is cited in Alan Filreis, "Voicing the Desert of Silence: Stevens' letters to Alice Corbin Henderson," *Wallace Stevens Journal* 12 (Spring 1988): 17.

7. See *The Letters of Wallace Stevens*, ed. Holly Stevens (New York: Knopf, 1966), no. 804 to Herbert Weinstock, 732–33; and no. 806 to Herbert Weinstock, 733–34.

8. Marianne Moore to H.D., November 10, 1916, Rosenbach Museum and Library, V:23:32, T.L.C.

9. James Merrill, *Recitative: Prose by James Merrill*, ed. J. D. McClatchy (San Francisco: North Point Press, 1986), 26.

10. Moore, *Complete Prose*, 91.

11. See Helen Vendler, *Wallace Stevens: Words Chosen Out of Desire* (Cambridge: Harvard University Press, 1986), 10. Vendler points out that "we must ask what causes the imagination to be so painfully at odds with reality. The cause setting the two at odds is usually, in Stevens' case, passionate feeling, and not merely epistemological query."

12. Moore, *Complete Prose*, 93.

13. Ibid., 91.

14. Ibid., 92.

15. Bersani, *A Future For Astyanax: Character and Desire in Literature* (New York: Columbia University Press, 1984), 74.

16. Moore, *Complete Prose*, 91.

17. Ibid., 92.

18. Loose notes found in the back of Moore's copy of *Harmonium*, Rosenbach Museum and Library.

19. Moore, *Complete Prose*, 93.

20. Vendler, *Wallace Stevens: Words Chosen Out of Desire*, 19.

21. Ibid., 18.

22. I am indebted to William Watterson for pointing out the allusion to Mozart's *Don Giovanni* in Stevens' "Last Looks at the Lilacs."

23. Poetry Workbook 1923–30, Rosenbach Museum and Library, VII:04:04, 1251/7.

24. Moore, *Complete Prose*, 96.

25. Ibid., 97.

26. W. H. Hudson, *Far Away and Long Ago* (1918; reprint, London: J. M. Dent & Sons, 1940), 187.

27. Ibid., 190.

28. Ibid., 329.

29. Loose notes found in the back of Moore's copy of *Harmonium*, Rosenbach Museum and Library.

30. T. C. Wilson to Marianne Moore, June 26, 1935, Rosenbach Museum and Library, V:78:04, T.L.S.

31. Marianne Moore to T. C. Wilson, July 5, 1935, Rosenbach Museum and Library, V:78:04, T.L.C.

32. T. C. Wilson to Marianne Moore, October 27, 1935, Rosenbach Museum and Library, V:78:04, T.L.S.

33. Loose notes found in the back of Moore's copy of *Harmonium*, Rosenbach Museum and Library.

34. Marianne Moore to T. C. Wilson, November 29, 1935, Rosenbach Museum and Library, V:78:04, T.L.C.

35. Moore, "Unanimity and Fortitude," *Poetry* 49 (February 1937): 271. (I quote from the original rather than from the revised version of this essay that appears in *Complete Prose*.)

36. Ibid., 272.

9. Views of the Political in the Poetics of Wallace Stevens and H.D.

1. Marjorie Perloff, "Revolving in Crystal: The Supreme Fiction and the Impasse of Modernist Lyric," in *Wallace Stevens: The Poetics of Modernism*, ed. Albert Gelpi (Cambridge: Cambridge University Press, 1985), 42.

2. Ibid., 47.

3. Mikhail M. Bakhtin, *The Dialogic Imagination*, ed. Michael Holquist (Austin: University of Texas Press, 1981), 284.

4. Bakhtin, *Dialogic*, 285.

5. Alicia Ostriker, "No Rule of Procedure: The Open Poetics of H.D." (Paper delivered at the H.D. Centennial Conference, Orono, Maine, 25 June 1986; later published in *Signets: Reading H.D.*, ed. Rachel Blau du Plessis and Susan Stanford Friedman [Bloomington: Indiana University Press, 1991].)

6. Perloff, "Revolving in Crystal," 47. Emphases mine.

7. Marjorie Perloff, *The Dance of the Intellect: Studies in the Poetry of the Pound Tradition* (Cambridge: Cambridge University Press, 1985), 180.

8. Ibid., 181.

9. Quoted in Michael King, ed., *H.D. Woman and Poet* (Orono, Maine: National Poetry Foundation, 1986), 436.

10. Susan Stanford Friedman, " 'Modernism of the Scattered Remnant': Race and Politics in the Development of H.D.'s Modernist Vision," in King, *H.D. Woman and Poet*, 94.

11. Ibid.

12. Ibid.

13. Susan Stanford Friedman, "Palimpsests of Origins in H.D.'s Career," *Poesis* 6, 3/4 (Winter 1985): 65.

14. Rachel Blau du Plessis, "Family, Sexes, Psyche: An Essay on H.D. and the Muse of the Woman Writer," in King, *H.D. Woman and Poet*, 75, 84.

15. Ibid., 74.

16. Alicia Ostriker, "The Thieves of Language: Women Poets and Revisionist Mythmaking," *Signs: Journal of Women in Culture and Society* 8, no. 1 (Autumn 1982): 81.

17. Susan Stanford Friedman, " 'Remembering Shakespeare Always, But Remembering Him Differently': H.D.'s *By Avon River*," *Sagetrieb* 2, no. 2 (Summer/Fall 1983). Quoted in King, *H.D. Woman and Poet*, 486.

18. Friedman, "Palimpsests of Origins," 62.

19. Robert Duncan, "[From the H.D. Book] Part II, Chapter 5 [section two]," *Credences* 1, no. 1 (1975): 52.

20. Robert Duncan, "The H.D. Book: Part II, Nights and Days, Chapter 4," *Caterpillar* 2, no. 2 (April 1969): 46–47.

21. Robert Duncan, "From the H.D. Book, Part II, Chapter 5 [section one]," *Stony Brook* 3/4 (Fall 1969): 336.

22. Ibid., 343.

23. Ibid., 344.

24. Ibid., 337.

25. Ibid., 336.

26. Hilda Doolittle, *H.D. Collected Poems 1912–1944*, ed. Louis L. Martz (New York: New Directions, 1983), 519.

27. H.D., *Collected Poems*, 517.

28. Duncan, II:5/1, 341.

29. Ibid., 338.

10. The Houses of Fathers: Stevens and Emerson

1. See Harold Bloom, *Wallace Stevens: The Poems of Our Climate* (Ithaca: Cornell University Press, 1977). See also, for example, David Leverenz, "The Politics of Emerson's Man-Making Words," *PMLA* 101 (January 1986): 38–56; Barbara Packer's "The Fugitive Slave Law and *The Conduct of Life:* Emerson in the 1850s," given at the Modern Language Association meeting on "American History in American Literature" (December 1985); Peter Brazeau, *Parts of a World: Wallace Stevens Remembered, an Oral Biography* (New York: Random House, 1983); Joan Richardson, *Wallace Stevens: The Early Years, 1879–1923* (New York: William Morrow, 1986); Frank Lentricchia, *Ariel and the Police: Michel Foucault, William James, Wallace Stevens* (Madison: University of Wisconsin Press, 1988), or the exchange between Lentricchia, Sandra M.

Gilbert, and Susan Gubar in Lentricchia's "Andiamo!" and Gubar's "The Man on the Dump versus the United Dames of America; or, What Does Frank Lentricchia Want?" both in *Critical Inquiry* 14 (Winter 1988): 386–413.

2. Ralph Waldo Emerson, *The Collected Works of Ralph Waldo Emerson*, ed. Robert Spiller et al., vol. 2 (Cambridge: Belknap Press of Harvard University Press, 1971–), 93.

3. Ibid., 2:94–95.

4. Ibid., 2:89.

5. Ralph Waldo Emerson, *The Journals and Miscellaneous Notebooks of Ralph Waldo Emerson*, ed. William H. Gilman et al., vol. 13 (Cambridge: Belknap Press of Harvard University Press, 1960–), 236.

6. Emerson, *Collected Works*, 1:39.

7. Ibid., 2:95–96.

8. Ibid., 2:29.

9. Leverenz, "The Politics of Emerson's Man-Making Words," 39–53.

10. Quentin Anderson, "Practical and Visionary Americans," *American Scholar* 45 (1976): 408–11, 405.

11. Emerson, *Collected Works*, 3:3.

12. Ibid.

13. Ibid., 3:29.

14. Ibid., 3:35.

15. Ibid., 3:49.

16. Indeed, in a journal entry for February 1841, Emerson notes that literary men "ought to be released from every species of public or private responsibility. . . . If he [the writer] must marry, perhaps he should be regarded happiest who has a shrew for a wife, . . . who can & will assume the total economy of the house, and having some sense that her philosopher is best in his study suffers him not to intermeddle with her thrift" (Emerson, *Journals*, 7:420). More often Emerson suggests simply that writers "leave to others the costly honors . . . of housekeeping," and opt for a more Spartan, celibate life (Ibid., 7:351).

17. Emerson, *Collected Works*, 3:112.

18. Muriel Rukeyser, *The Collected Poems of Muriel Rukeyser* (New York: McGraw-Hill, 1978), 498.

19. See Lentricchia, *Ariel and the Police*, 140, 172.

20. Stevens' father also stressed the fact that young American men needed to find a profession (see *SP*, 71). Further light is shed on Stevens' relationship with his father by Milton J. Bates, *Wallace Stevens: A Mythology of Self*

228 / NOTES TO PAGES 196-98

(Berkeley: University of California Press, 1985), 16–18, 32–36, 42–43, 87; Richard Ellmann, "How Wallace Stevens Saw Himself," in *Wallace Stevens: A Celebration*, ed. Frank Doggett and Robert Buttel (Princeton: Princeton University Press, 1980), 154–58; as well as in Joan Richardson's biography.

21. The link between this journal entry and the genteel poets is mentioned in Lentricchia, *Ariel and the Police*, 161–67, although it is also discussed in Lisa M. Steinman, *Made In America: Science, Technology, and American Modernist Poets* (New Haven: Yale University Press, 1987).

22. William Carlos Williams, "Comment: Wallace Stevens," *Poetry* 87 (January 1956): 234–35. See Kurt Heinzelman, "Williams and Stevens: The Vanishing-Point of Resemblance," in *WCW & Others: Essays on William Carlos Williams and His Association with Ezra Pound, Hilda Doolittle, Marcel Duchamp, Marianne Moore, Emanuel Romano, Wallace Stevens, and Louis Zukofsky*, ed. Dave Oliphant and Thomas Zigal (University of Texas at Austin: Henry Ransom Humanities Research Center, 1985), 85–113, especially 109ff. Joan Richardson discusses what Stevens and Dickinson have in common, noting that Stevens probably did not know Dickinson's work well, but equally probably would not have found it "effeminate" (*Early Years*, 126, 436, 466). At the same time, I suspect Stevens would have resented the comparison, at least coming from Williams, precisely because he would have thought Williams was viewing him as "lady-like."

23. Lentricchia, "Andiamo!," 412.

24. *The Complete Poems of Marianne Moore* (New York: Macmillan, 1967), 67.

25. Ibid., 272.

26. Cited, Brazeau, *Parts of a World*, 244. Brazeau goes on to point out that Stevens' silence was due to health problems as well, although it is worth noting that Stevens, when he discussed the subject, emphasized the burden of his family responsibilities (p. 245). As I suggest at the end of this essay, the two may have been related.

27. Edmund Clarence Stedman, ed., *An American Anthology, 1789–1900* (Boston and New York: Houghton Mifflin Co., 1900), xxviii; Ann Douglas, *The Feminization of American Culture* (New York: Knopf, 1977).

28. April 6, 1909, letter to Edgar Williams, cited in Steinman, *Made In America*, 16.

29. Harold E. Stearns, ed., *Civilization in the United States: An Inquiry By Thirty Americans* (New York: Harcourt, Brace and Company, 1922), 192.

30. For Williams' expression of regret, see "The Art Of Poetry VI," *Paris Review* 8 (Summer–Fall 1964): 124.

31. See Lentricchia, *Ariel and the Police*, 213.

32. See, for example, Stevens' letter to Elsie on not existing from nine to six at the office, cited in Joan Richardson, "Wallace Stevens: Toward a Biography," *Raritan* 4 (Winter 1985): 42.

33. See *SP*, 81–82; and Richardson, *Early Years*, especially 414–23.

34. Richardson, *Early Years*, 417; Lentricchia, *Ariel and the Police*, 171–72.

35. See Richardson, *Early Years*, 239–40.

36. See Lentricchia, "Andiamo!" 408–9; and Gilbert and Gubar, "The Man on the Dump versus the United Dames of America," 393–94.

37. Richardson, *Early Years*, 421–23.

38. As Kurt Heinzelman points out in "Williams and Stevens," 111, Williams commented upon what having Elsie's image on the coin of the realm might have meant to Stevens.

39. See Brazeau, *Parts of a World*, 245; and Lentricchia, *Ariel and the Police*, 216.

Select Bibliography

Bakhtin, Mikhail. *The Dialogic Imagination*. Edited by Michael Holquist. Austin: University of Texas Press, 1981.

Bates, Milton J. *Wallace Stevens: A Mythology of Self*. Berkeley: University of California Press, 1985.

Beckett, Lucy. *Wallace Stevens*. Cambridge: Cambridge University Press, 1974.

Bloom, Harold. *Wallace Stevens: The Poems of Our Climate*. Ithaca: Cornell University Press, 1977.

Borroff, Marie, ed. *Wallace Stevens: A Collection of Critical Essays*. Englewood Cliffs, N.J.: Prentice-Hall, 1963.

Brazeau, Peter. *Parts of a World: Wallace Stevens Remembered, an Oral Biography*. New York: Random House, 1983.

Cook, Eleanor. *Poetry, Word-Play, and Word-War in Wallace Stevens*. Princeton: Princeton University Press, 1988.

Doggett, Frank. *Stevens' Poetry of Thought*. Baltimore: Johns Hopkins University Press, 1966.

————, and Robert Buttel, eds. *Wallace Stevens: A Celebration*. Princeton: Princeton University Press, 1980.

Douglas, Ann. *The Feminization of American Culture*. New York: Knopf, 1977.

Fisher, Barbara M. *Wallace Stevens: The Intensest Rendezvous*. Charlottesville: University Press of Virginia, 1990.

Gelpi, Albert, ed. *Wallace Stevens: The Poetics of Modernism*. Cambridge: Cambridge University Press, 1985.

Gilbert, Sandra, and Susan Gubar. *Madwoman in the Attic: The Woman Writer and the Nineteenth-Century Imagination.* New Haven: Yale University Press, 1979.

Gould, Eric. *Mythical Intention in Modern Literature.* Princeton: Princeton University Press, 1981.

Highwater, Jamake. *Myth and Sexuality.* Ontario: NAL Books, 1990.

Jung, Carl G. *Aion: Researches into the Phenomenology of the Self.* Princeton: Princeton University Press, 1968.

Kenner, Hugh. *The Pound Era.* Berkeley: University of California Press, 1971.

Kessler, Edward. *Images of Wallace Stevens.* New Brunswick: Rutgers University Press, 1972.

King, Michael, ed. *H.D. Woman and Poet.* Orono, Maine: National Poetry Foundation, 1986.

Kristeva, Julia. *Black Sun: Depression and Melancholia.* Translated by Leon S. Rondrey. New York: Columbia University Press, 1989.

Lentricchia, Frank. *Ariel and the Police: Michel Foucault, William James, Wallace Stevens.* Madison: University of Wisconsin Press, 1988.

Litz, A. Walton. *Introspective Voyager: The Poetic Development of Wallace Stevens.* New York: Oxford University Press, 1972.

Moore, Marianne. *The Complete Prose of Marianne Moore.* Edited by Patricia C. Willis. New York: Viking Press, 1986.

Morse, Samuel French. *Poetry as Life.* New York: Pegasus, 1970.

————, and Joseph N. Riddel, eds. *The Clairvoyant Eye.* Baton Rouge: Louisiana State University Press, 1965.

Paglia, Camile. *Sexual Personae: Art and Decadence from Nefertiti to Emily Dickinson.* New Haven: Yale University Press, 1990.

Pease, Donald E. *Visionary Compacts: American Renaissance Writings in Cultural Context.* Madison: University of Wisconsin Press, 1987.

Perloff, Marjorie. *The Dance of the Intellect: Studies in the Poetry of the Pound Tradition.* Cambridge: Cambridge University Press, 1985.

Poirier, Richard, ed. *Ralph Waldo Emerson.* New York: Oxford University Press, 1991.

Porte, Joel, ed. *Emerson: Essays and Lectures.* New York: Library of America, 1982.

Richardson, Joan. *Wallace Stevens: The Early Years, 1879–1923.* New York: William Morrow, 1986.

————. *Wallace Stevens: The Later Years, 1923–1955.* New York: William Morrow, 1988.

Stevens, Wallace. *The Collected Poems of Wallace Stevens*. New York: Knopf, 1954.

———. *Letters of Wallace Stevens*. Edited by Holly Stevens. New York: Knopf, 1966.

———. *The Necessary Angel*. New York: Knopf, 1951.

———. *Opus Posthumous*. Edited by Samuel French Morse. New York: Knopf, 1957.

———. *Opus Posthumous*. Revised, Enlarged, and Corrected Edition, edited by Milton J. Bates. New York: Knopf, 1989.

———. *Souvenirs and Prophecies: The Young Wallace Stevens*. Edited by Holly Stevens. New York: Knopf, 1977.

Vendler, Helen. *On Extended Wings: Wallace Stevens' Longer Poems*. Cambridge: Harvard University Press, 1969.

———. *Wallace Stevens: Words Chosen Out of Desire*. Cambridge: Harvard University Press, 1986.

Walsh, Thomas. *Concordance to Wallace Stevens*. University Park, Pa.: Pennsylvania State University Press, 1963.

Weston, Susan B. *Wallace Stevens: An Introduction to the Poetry*. New York: Columbia University Press, 1977.

Woodman, Leonora. *Stanza My Stone: Wallace Stevens and the Hermetic Tradition*. West Lafayette, Ind.: Purdue University Press, 1983.

Contributors

MARY B. ARENSBERG is a lecturer in the departments of English and Humanities at the State University of New York at Albany. She is editor of the 1986 collection *The American Sublime*, essays on the American poetic tradition, and has published numerous articles on Wallace Stevens and the feminine, William Faulkner, literary theory, and literature and psychoanalysis. At present, she is writing a book on literature, film, and feminism.

JACQUELINE VAUGHT BROGAN, associate professor of English at the University of Notre Dame, is the author of *Stevens and Simile: A Theory of Language* and a recent study on the innovative American poetry between the wars titled *Part of the Climate: American Cubist Poetry*. Brogan's essays on twentieth-century American poetry have appeared in such journals as *Diacritics, American Literature,* and *American Poetry,* and she is currently completing a third critical book, *Poet Against His Climate: Stevens and the Strategies of Resistance*.

BARBARA M. FISHER is associate professor of English at the City College of CUNY and author of *Wallace Stevens: The Intensest Rendezvous*. Her work has appeared in a number of journals, including *Bucknell Review,* the *Wallace Stevens Journal,* and *Journal of Dramatic Theory and Criti-*

cism, and her essays have also appeared in critical collections such as the Virginia annual *Review,* the *Shaw Review,* and the Chelsea House series of *Modern Critical Views.*

CELESTE GOODRIDGE, associate professor of English at Bowdoin College, is author of *Hints and Disguises: Marianne Moore and her Contemporaries,* a work which examines Marianne Moore's criticism of modernist poets such as Wallace Stevens, Ezra Pound, William Carlos Williams, and T. S. Eliot. Her essays on modern and contemporary American writers have appeared in such journals as *Sagetrieb,* the *Wallace Stevens Journal,* and *Twentieth Century Literature.*

PAUL MORRISON is assistant professor of English at Brandeis University. A wide-ranging critic of literature, culture, gender, and critical theory, he has written on topics ranging from Jane Austen to Paul de Man to Robert Mapplethorpe, along with articles on Wallace Stevens and the "ideology of origins" in postmodern critical thought, published in the *Wallace Stevens Journal.* His latest work, titled *Sexual Subjects,* is forthcoming from Oxford University Press.

DANIEL T. O'HARA is known for his numerous published works on Irish and American literature and his studies of literary theory and criticism. His books include *The Romance of Interpretation: Visionary Criticism from Pater to de Man, Tragic Knowledge: Yeats' Autobiography and Hermeneutics,* and *The Question of Textuality: Strategies of Reading in Contemporary American Criticism,* co-edited with William Spanos and Paul Bove. He is on the editorial staff of the journal *boundary 2* and has recently completed a book-length work on American Renaissance writers.

ROSAMOND ROSENMEIER is professor *emerita* at the University of Massachusetts in Boston. She is the author of *Anne Bradstreet Revisited* and a volume of poetry, *Lines Out.* She has published several essays on Anne Bradstreet, and her poetry has appeared in the *Nation, Epoch,* the *Virginia Quarterly Review,* and other reviews. She presently serves on the editorial board of *Early American Literature* and has completed a new study titled *His Mother's House: Colonial German Pennsylvania in the Work of Wallace Stevens*.

MELITA SCHAUM is associate professor of English at the University of Michigan-Dearborn. She is author of *Wallace Stevens and the Critical Schools*, which won the Elizabeth Agee Prize for American Literary Studies in 1987, and was guest editor of the 1988 special issue of the *Wallace Stevens Journal* on "Women and Stevens." Her work has appeared in such journals as *Genders*, the *Wallace Stevens Journal*, and the *Denver Quarterly*, and her most recent book is *Gender Images/Gender Issues*, an anthology of readings in men's and women's studies.

LISA M. STEINMAN, professor of English and Humanities at Reed College, is the author of a book on American modernism, *Made in America: Science, Technology, and American Modernist Poets* and of two books of poetry: *Lost Poems* and *All That Comes to Light*. Her poems and essays have appeared widely in journals such as *Chicago Review, ELH*, and *Twentieth-Century Literature*, as well as in anthologies such as *Beyond Two Cultures, Marianne Moore: Woman and Poet*, and *The New Shelley*.

C. ROLAND WAGNER, professor of Humanities and Philosophy at the New College of Hofstra University, is the author of a number of early essays and reviews of Wallace Stevens, some written during Stevens' lifetime and which Stevens himself read and responded to. He has also published work on Thoreau, Camus, Forster, Svevo, and Santayana, along with reviews and essays on modern culture. One might quote Wallace Stevens himself, who, after meeting Professor Wagner on a business trip in 1952 remarked, "I saw him only for a moment but what I saw of him I liked."

Index

Works by Wallace Stevens

Proper Names